Understanding Power and Leadership in Higher Education

Within higher education, power is often perceived negatively. Rather than avoiding the idea of power, this book explores the importance of embracing and effectively engaging power to affect positive change on campus. *Understanding Power and Leadership in Higher Education* gives college and university administrators the tools to understand the relationship between leadership, power, and influence within higher education. Highlighting real stories of effective college and university administrators, this book helps readers understand and analyze the use of power, preparing leaders for the realities of today's administrative environment.

Mark Kretovics is Associate Professor of Higher Education Administration and Student Affairs at Kent State University, USA.

Understanding Power and Leadership in Higher Education

Tools for Institutional Change

Mark Kretovics

Routledge
Taylor & Francis Group
NEW YORK AND LONDON

First published 2020
by Routledge
52 Vanderbilt Avenue, New York, NY 10017

and by Routledge
2 Park Square, Milton Park, Abingdon, Oxon, OX14 4RN

Routledge is an imprint of the Taylor & Francis Group, an informa business

© 2020 Taylor & Francis

The right of Mark Kretovics to be identified as author of this work has been asserted by him in accordance with Parts 77 and 78 of the Copyright, Designs and Patents Act 1988.

All rights reserved. No part of this book may be reprinted or reproduced or utilized in any form or by any electronic, mechanical, or other means, now known or hereafter invented, including photocopying and recording, or in any information storage or retrieval system, without
permission in writing from the publishers.

Trademark notice: Product or corporate names may be trademarks or registered trademarks, and are used only for identification and explanation without intent to infringe.

Library of Congress Cataloging-in-Publication Data
A catalog record for this title has been requested

ISBN: 978-1-138-34176-0 (hbk)
ISBN: 978-1-138-34179-1 (pbk)
ISBN: 978-0-429-43997-1 (ebk)

Typeset in Sabon
by Swales & Willis, Exeter, Devon, UK

Contents

Preface xi
Acknowledgements xvii

1 Introduction 1
    What Is Power? *2*
    Politics in Higher Education *6*
    The Downside to Power and Politics *8*
    The Upside to Power and Politics *10*
    Concluding Comments *11*
    Reflective Questions *12*

Part I: The Context of Power and Leadership in Higher Education   **13**

2 Types and Tactics of Power 15
    Formal Authority *17*
    Personality *21*
    Knowledge *23*
    Other Bases of Influence and Power *25*
    Concluding Comments *28*
    Reflective Questions *28*

3 Organizational Context 29
    Higher Education in the U.S. *30*
    Institutional Structure *30*
    Governing Boards *31*

CONTENTS

       Senior Administrative Positions/Functional Areas   *38*
       The For-Profit Sector   *46*
       Concluding Comments   *48*
       Reflective Questions   *50*
       Possible Reflection Question/Activity   *50*

Appendix   *51*

       Administrator Personalities   *51*
       The Athlete   *51*
       The Lap Dog   *52*
       The Pundit   *52*
       The Bureaucrat   *52*
       The Eeyore™   *53*
       The Collaborator   *53*
       The Decepticon™   *53*
       The Singer   *54*
       The Floater   *54*
       The Counter Balancer   *54*
       The Competitor   *55*
       The Source   *55*
       Two Types of Bosses   *55*
       Reflective Questions   *56*

Part II: Power in Higher Education   57

4   Symbols and Sources of Power   59

       Symbols of Power   *59*
       Sources of Power   *63*
       Concluding Comments   *73*
       Reflective Questions   *73*
       Group Activity   *74*

5   Personal Attributes and Traits of Successful Administrators   75

       Communicator   *76*
       Confident/Self-Assured   *77*
       Energy and Physical Stamina   *78*
       Flexibility   *79*
       Humility (Manage Administrative Ego)   *80*
       Narcissism   *83*
       Nice/Likeable   *85*

CONTENTS

Planning and Setting Clear Goals *86*
Tolerance for Ambiguity *88*
Tolerance of Conflict *89*
Transparency *90*
Can You Be Too Honest and Too Trusting? *91*
Understanding Others *93*
Ability to Empower Others *94*
Concluding Comments *95*
Reflective Questions *96*

6 Using Power to Accomplish Your Goals   97

Using Power *97*
Framing *98*
Gaining Power by Giving Away Power *110*
Perception Matters *112*
Concluding Comments *113*
Reflective Questions *114*
Case Scenario *114*

7 The Power of Internal and External Influencers   115

The Power of External Consultants *115*
The Power of Free Speech *118*
The Power of Social Media *120*
The Power of the Search Process *121*
The Power of Intercollegiate Athletics *130*
The Power of Policies *133*
The Power of Rankings *134*
The Power of Donors *136*
Power of the Paradox *137*
Concluding Comments *139*
Reflective Questions *140*

Part III: Politics and Decision-Making   **141**

8 Politics and Political Behaviors   143

Political Interactions *144*
Reflective Questions *151*
Case Scenario *152*

vii

CONTENTS

    Appendix   153

        Misunderstood Machiavelli   *153*
        Twenty-First Century Higher Education Applications   *154*
        Concluding Comments   *157*
        Reflective Questions   *158*

9   Falling from Grace   159

        Part 1: What Went Wrong   *160*
        Part 2: Ethics, Integrity, and Moral Decisions   *165*
        Concluding Comments   *172*
        Reflective Questions   *173*
        Case Scenario   *174*

10   Paths to Power of the Presidency   175

        State of the Presidency   *175*
        Four Paths   *177*
        Getting There   *180*
        Staying There   *184*
        Advice to Those with High Aspirations   *187*
        Decision-Making   *191*
        Always the President   *193*
        Concluding Comments   *195*
        Reflective Questions   *196*

Part IV: Practical Perspectives   **197**

11   Now What?   199

        Free Speech   *199*
        Managing Enrollments   *200*
        Resource Allocation   *201*
        Mission Creep   *202*
        Intercollegiate Athletics   *203*
        Sexual Harassment/Sexual Assault   *204*
        Shared Governance   *204*
        Tenure   *205*
        Technology   *206*
        External Forces   *207*
        Institutional Leadership   *208*
        Concluding Comments   *209*
        Reflective Questions   *210*

12 Wrap Up   211

  Maintaining Control   *211*
  Communicate Effectively and Often   *212*
  Finishing   *212*
  Resource Control   *213*
  Hire and Supervise Well   *213*
  Self-Assess   *214*
  Be the Leader You Want to Be   *215*
  Create an Institutional Culture   *215*
  Depart with Dignity   *215*
  Concluding Comments   *217*

References   *219*
Index   *229*

Preface

For decades, the popular press and news media have chronicled government officials and corporate icons who have risen to the highest levels in their respective fields only to be brought down by moral or ethical lapse in their behavior. For some it may have been a single incident; while for others it was a pattern of behavior. Oftentimes when reviewing scandals it becomes apparent that many of these individuals used their *power* to promote their individual interests rather than the interest of those they were serving.

One of the most dramatic political collapses in U.S. history was that of Richard Nixon who was forced to resign the Presidency of the United States because of the Watergate break-in and subsequent cover-up. Nixon wanted to ensure his victory in 1972 and authorized the criminal behavior that led to his downfall because he put his personal ambitions ahead of the interests of the country. Nixon believed that as President of the United States he was above the law. During his time in the presidency he was also noted for his war against the media and individuals' right to *freedom of expression*.

In the corporate world there are numerous examples from which to choose. Perhaps two of the more dramatic falls involved Bernard (Bernie) Madoff and Kenneth Lay. Bernie Madoff was considered to be one of the most respected investment consultants in the country and served as Chairperson of NASDAQ for three years. However, instead of being a savvy investor, Madoff actually orchestrated the largest Ponzi scheme in U.S. history, defrauding unwitting investors out of billions of dollars. He pleaded guilty to eleven felony charges and was sentenced to 150 years in prison.

Kenneth Lay and Jeffrey Skilling brought down Enron Corporation through their use of creative accounting measures designed to conceal significant corporate losses. Lay, as CEO, had led Enron to become the fifth largest corporation amongst the Fortune 500 and shortly thereafter into bankruptcy. Lay and Skilling were both convicted of conspiracy and fraud charges.

Currently we have high-profile leaders in the U.S. and around the world who choose to use their power and influence to be divisive rather than inclusive. Often this is accomplished through bullying behaviors or by berating one's foes rather than promoting unity. When their behaviors, views, or decisions are questioned, instead of engaging in civil discourse, they quickly resort to immature behavior such as retaliating with an insult via Twitter™ or calling the information *fake news*. These behaviors, rather than being looked upon as extremely poor leadership, are often equated with the use of power, when in fact they are an abuse of power.

It is unfortunate that we can find so many high-profile examples of bad leadership and inappropriate use of power in our society. These examples reinforce the negative impression of power in our workplaces. It is my intent in the pages that follow to offer an understanding of power within U.S. higher education institutions. This book is not meant to be a guidebook on how to become a powerful leader nor is it meant to promote the status quo of organizational operations; rather it describes the current status (reality) of administration, leadership, and power and their impact on decision-making within institutions of higher education. What you are about to read may not be what you would like to see in higher education. However, I believe it to be an accurate representation of the realities of today's administrative environment within most higher educational institutions in the United States.

If you currently are, or if you aspire to be a Director, Department Chair, School Director, Dean, Assistant or Associate Vice President, Vice President, or perhaps President/Chancellor, then many of your colleagues may consider you to be *power hungry*. Therefore, it is critical that you understand the relationship between leadership, management, power, and decision-making. People who use power to accomplish goals are not bad, nor are they essentially good administrators; they are just individuals working within the current system trying to have an impact on their respective institutions, communities, and, in many cases, the nation. Together, we will look at some successes and some failures to try and understand the *why* behind them. The chapters that follow will give you an understanding of the current state of affairs of power, influence, and decision-making; and examine why some very bright people make very poor decisions. My hope is that this book can help you avoid some missteps in your career path, and ensure you have a long and productive career, at whatever level you so choose.

ORGANIZATION OF THE BOOK

This book has been written to aid current administrators, faculty who have become administrators, or higher education administrator wannabes, in their understanding of the relationship between power, leadership, and influence; and how these factors are currently being used within institutions of higher education across the United States. The chapters in each of the four sections are described briefly below.

Part 1 is 'The Context of Power and Leadership in Higher Education'. The book begins by briefly describing the political nature of decision-making within today's higher education environment. I then define leadership, management, and power and discuss how these terms are viewed and used in higher education. I discuss the relationship between power and politics and wrap up Chapter 1 with a look at the downside and upside to power and politics in our institutions.

Chapter 2, 'Types and Tactics of Power', reviews the eight social powers, nine influence tactics, three modalities of power, and their relationship to leadership. The definitions of power and the motivations for using each power and the reaction to the use of power gives the reader a better understanding of the types of power currently employed in higher education and some of the potential outcomes to their usage.

Chapter 3 is 'Organizational Context'. To understand the power structure within any institution, comprehending the organizational structure and context is a must. Therefore, I examine the different organizational structures within higher education in the U.S. This chapter provides new administrators and newcomers to higher education a context within which to view their position and the power that accompanies it. The provided review of the functional areas within higher education institutions can assist administrators to recognize who they need to know and with whom they should establish relationships. As a compilation of interdependent systems (silos), institutions of higher education may be difficult to navigate. Consider this a *program* or *play bill* that helps you identify the key performers.

At the end of this chapter is a listing of Administrative Personalities that identifies some personalities that you may or may have already encountered during your career in higher education. Being able to identify these individuals on your respective campuses may help as you look to progress through the hierarchical structure of higher education.

Part 2 is 'Power in Higher Education'. Chapter 4 looks at 'Symbols and Sources of Power'. Knowing the titles and positions described in Chapter 3 is a good starting point, but there are other sources of power feeding into leadership. Every institution has unique symbols that indicate who on the campus has certain types of power. This chapter takes a look at some of the more commonly identifiable symbols and sources found today within higher education institutions. It also identifies a few that may have escaped your view.

PREFACE

Chapter 5 is on 'Personal Attributes and Traits of Successful Administrators' When in an administrative role people tend to focus their attention on their strengths, usually the qualities that helped them achieve their current status. This chapter reviews many of the personal attributes and personality traits that over time have been observed in effective leaders. In reflecting upon these traits it is important to recognize your strengths and limitations and to understand what is within your power to change and what is not. Recognizing that you cannot be all things to all people is an important first step to fully understand who you are as a leader.

When you are in a position of power you will want to utilize it to accomplish the goals and objectives of the institution. Chapter 6, 'Using Power to Accomplish Goals', describes several tactics and strategies that can influence the decision-making processes in units, divisions, or on campuses. If you are not in a position to be able to use these strategies and tactics, understanding them can help you identify when others implement them.

Chapter 7 is on 'The Power of Internal and External Influences'. Within higher education a variety of internal and external issues influence decision-making practices. This chapter looks at some contemporary issues that can create or redistribute power on a campus depending on its institutional priorities. Although one's position on the organizational chart may be a symbol of power, one must understand that position does not always define one's power or influence.

Part 3 is 'Politics and Decision-Making'. Chapter 8 focuses on 'Politics and Political Behaviors'. Political behavior is a given in any organization that has two or more employees. Recognizing that politics is ubiquitous is an important first step to becoming an administrator who can navigate the internal politics of an institution. I believe power and political behavior are inseparable and are a part of every *effective leader's* portfolio. Knowing when and how to use political skills to your advantage can be a powerful asset as you look to advance your career or to understand what is happening around you.

Chapter 9, 'Falling from Grace', reviews a few of the more egregious examples of power abuse within higher education in recent memory. I describe what happened in each case and try to give some guidance on how one can avoid these pitfalls. Each of these leaders had an exemplary career within the academy but at some point chose a path that ended in them leaving their position or institution under a cloud. Review these situations and learn from the mistakes of others.

In Chapter 10, 'Paths to Power of the Presidency', I highlight the information gathered through my conversations with several university presidents about their path to that position. These presidents candidly spoke about the skills and attributes they believed were helpful in forwarding their careers and which were helpful in keeping them at the top. As you will see, individuals with diverse academic and professional backgrounds can become successful college and university presidents.

Part 4 is on 'Practical Perspectives'. Chapter 11, 'Now What?', looks at several issues that this generation of higher education administrators and institutional leaders will need to address on their respective campuses. Whether you are in a mid-level or senior-level position you will have to confront controversial topics on your campus and how you respond to these controversies will impact not only your institution but will likely have a significant effect on your career. Understanding your power position and the political context of your institution will serve you well.

The business of higher education is constantly evolving and how future leaders respond to these changes will influence the success of individual institutions or systems of institutions. Chapter 12, 'Wrap Up', will provide you with a few key points that can help position you within your institution or perhaps the broader higher education environment, to be successful at motivating others to do things they would normally not do on their own. Recognizing that power and political behavior are not automatically bad, but rather are critical to being an effective leader within higher education, \is an important starting point.

REFLECTIVE QUESTIONS

At the end of each chapter there are a few reflective questions to help readers more fully engage with the material presented. A few chapters also have case scenarios or group activities that can also be helpful in integrating the material into one's current context. These reflective questions can be used to help stimulate one's individual professional development or for use with students or other colleagues for discussion purposes.

Acknowledgements

I want to thank the college and university presidents and corporate CEOs that graciously gave their time to talk with me about their career journeys. Their contributions greatly enhanced this book. Additionally, thank you Fabrizio Ricciardelli for lending your expertise. And to Deb Saito, this effort would not have been possible without your loving support.

While there will be times when national, international, or local politics are addressed, the intent of this book is to focus on the local, day-to-day, and micro level of institutional power and politics that impact our daily lives.

Chapter One

Introduction

The book begins by briefly describing the political nature of decision-making within today's higher education environment. Next, I define leadership, management, and power and discuss how these interrelated terms are viewed and used in higher education. I then discuss the relationship between power and politics and wrap up the chapter with a look at the downside and upside to power and politics in our institutions.

The higher education landscape across the United States is comprised of a wide variety of colleges and universities. According to the National Center for Educational Statistics (NCES), in the spring of 2016 there were 4,583 Title IV degree granting institutions in the United States. This included 1,579 two-year and 3,004 four-year institutions. These institutions can be differentiated by a variety of parameters including: institutional type, mission, size, and tax status, to name a few. These factors along with the fact that the U.S. has no national system of higher education and most states have multiple systems within their borders (two-year and four-year systems are most common), make higher education in the U.S. quite unique compared to the rest of the world. Add to this the host of independent and religiously affiliated private institutions and you have a very dynamic and incredibly rich non-system of higher education (see Chapter 3). All of these institutions, regardless of their size, location, or tax status, are complex organizations in an evolving industry that has been around for centuries, and is continually adapting to the ever-changing world.

Within this mosaic of higher educational institutions there are tens of thousands of administrators who make decisions and allocate institutional resources on a daily basis. Those decisions impact millions of students, staff, and faculty throughout the U.S. and are influenced by power and politics within the institutions and from each institution's external stakeholder groups. As in most relationships, there are power imbalances

INTRODUCTION

(Wolfe and McGinn, 2005) between the various stakeholder groups, which in turn influence the decision-making processes within higher education.

As we explore the issue of power within higher education, it is important to define the terms which we will be looking at: *power* and *politics*. Politics is involved in the decision-making process of every organization, and therefore the use of politics and power is in every organization; power and politics are ubiquitous. It seems that not a day goes by without a colleague referencing the *political nature* of a decision that was recently made. When discussing a decision, most of you have heard a colleague utter the phrase *that was pure politics* or something very similar. My question to you is, why does that matter? I submit that the vast majority, if not all, administrative decisions made on college and university campuses (or any complex organization) involve power and are political in nature. I also contend that there is nothing inherently wrong with political decisions or the use of power. Usually we invoke the *use of power or political* refrain when we disagree with the decision, not when we are in agreement. Simply put, political decisions are decisions! Whether the decision is made behind closed doors in an elusive process or made publicly in what appears to be a transparent process, it is a political decision.

Within higher education, power is perceived quite negatively. Most faculty, staff, and administrators in higher education view *power* as a dirty word that should not be discussed let alone be the subject of a class or administrative training. In higher education we prefer to talk about leadership or administrative/managerial abilities and skills when referring to institutional executive officers.

It is my intent to utilize this book to demonstrate that the concept of power should be embraced and not avoided. As Townley (1993) states, "power is the desire to know. Power is not negative; on the contrary, it is creative" (p. 521). If you aspire to be in a leadership role in any organization, it is important to understand how power can be used to help further an agenda or perhaps to undermine a competing agenda. If you see yourself as someone who believes that power is harmful, then this book can be useful in helping you understand what others are doing (perhaps doing to you) as they move within the institutional hierarchy. If you view power as helpful then this book can be useful in understanding how one can affect positive change within organizations through the use of power. Regardless of how you frame power, institutional change does not occur without the utilization of some form of power.

WHAT IS POWER?

Power, leadership, and management are interrelated concepts that unfortunately are treated separately and individually when defined in the literature. Therefore, before defining power, I believe it is important to first take a brief look at leadership and management and how they have been so defined. Numerous authors have stated that *management is doing things right and leadership is doing the right things*. As you will see in the following paragraphs, the crucial difference in the literature may be the focus of the individual; a focus on people is often equated with leadership, while a focus on the results or tasks is more often attributed to management (O'Leary, 2016).

Leadership

Briefly, looking at leadership, one finds a variety of definitions and as Yukl (1989) puts it, "they differ in many respects, including important differences in who exerts influence, the purpose of influence attempts, and the manner in which influence is exerted" (p. 252). The definition of leadership I believe fits best for the purposes of this book is – motivating or influencing people to do things they would not do on their own. A plethora of books on the topic of leadership spend a great deal of time discussing how to motivate employees to accomplish the organizational mission. If these employees would normally strive to accomplish the mission on their own, there would be no need for leadership to motivate them.

Several authors connect leaders and leadership with the use of power: According to Zaleznik (1998) "Leadership inevitably requires using power to influence the thoughts and actions of other people" (p. 63). Additionally, Sousa and van Dierenfonck (2017) state that "One's level of power will influence one's ability to lead and of course, effective leadership will increase one's power or potential to influence, in a positive and reinforcing feedback loop" (p. 18). Finally, Herdlein et al. (2011) suggest "that power is an essential tool of decision-making and is utilized through effective leaders, such as senior student affairs officers" (p. 41). Recognizing the link between leadership and power is the first step in understanding that power, like leadership, is not inherently a negative or a positive; rather, how power is used determines how it is perceived.

Maxwell (2013) believes that, to be effective, a leader must be a lifelong learner and a student of her or his profession. Additionally, he believes that, in order to reach the higher levels of leadership (levels 4 and 5), individuals must overcome their insecurities and realize that "good leaders forge ahead, break ground, and make mistakes" (p. 106).

Management

Management is often thought of in terms of four functions: planning, controlling, organizing, and leading (Nickels et al., 2008). One of the most

INTRODUCTION

important responsibilities of managers is to ensure that the employees they supervise are helping the organization accomplish its goals and objectives so it can fulfill its mission. This is more often than not achieved by motivating their employees to do things they would not do on their own.

Vecchio (2007) connects management and power when he states that "power is an essential feature of a manager's role. Without some degree of power, a manager would find it very difficult to direct the efforts of subordinates" (p. 69). Additionally, Hill and Lineback (2011) mention that "management is defined by responsibility but done by exerting influence. To influence others you must make a difference not only in what they do but also in the thoughts and feelings that drive their actions" (p. 127). Vecchio also contends that it is important for managers to realize "that the tendency to use power can lead to greater effectiveness, while failure to use power can have the opposite effect" (p. 73).

Based on the definitions of leadership and management posited above, one can see that, at least on one level, leadership and management are similar, if not one and the same. Going forward I believe that to be *effective*, managers must be leaders and leaders must be managers, and effective leaders and managers *do the right things the right way*. According to O'Leary (2016) whether one calls it leadership or management is not an issue because what the individuals are doing (tasks, duties, responsibilities, etc.) are essentially the same.

Power

If we can accept that a common definition of leadership and management is to *motivate individuals to do something they would not normally do*, then it is also appropriate to connect leadership and management with power. The effective use of power, according to David McClelland (1976) and Jeffrey Pfeffer (1992) is getting people to do things they would not normally do on their own. Therefore, power, leadership, and management are inextricably linked. Based on the definitions provided above, I would modify that, to read – strong leadership requires strong management and the *effective use of power*. To be an effective leader, one must be able to get others within the organization to do things they, for whatever reason, would not do on their own.

As mentioned earlier, far too many people, especially those in higher education, tend to view power as a negative behavior and view leadership and management as positive or at worst neutral behaviors (see Figure 1.1). When administrators are successful, we tend to laud them with accolades about their vision and leadership abilities. However, when individuals fail or make an inappropriate decisions, all too often that gets attributed to the

Figure 1.1 Power Continuum

quest for power. As you search through history you will find numerous examples of effective and ineffective leaders and managers who used power in an attempt to accomplish organizational and/or personal goals.

One of the major problems people have with the concept of power is their individual perception of what power means. Many people conflate power with a term with a similar definition – manipulation. This may help to explain why so many people perceive power negatively: they equate power with manipulation, which has a negative connotation, instead of leadership, which is viewed positively. After all, to a certain extent, good leaders and/or powerful people do manipulate others to accomplish their goals and objectives: they motivate or encourage people to do things they would not normally do on their own. In some instances this manipulation is done in a positive way through positive motivation or *reward power*, and in other cases it may happen with a negative spin or the use of *coercive power* (see Chapter 2). In higher education you will not see a job announcement for a senior administrator as seeking candidates with *strong manipulation skills* or a *power-hungry* individual; instead, we prefer to recruit *good or excellent leaders*, or at least that is our intent. In reality, good leaders are in fact good manipulators. The leaders we hold in high regard are able to convince *people to do something they would not normally do on their own.*

As you survey the higher education landscape and corporate world, you will be hard pressed to find a successful leader who does not embrace the use of power. A successful leader uses power to forward the goals of the institution. "[P]ower is part of leadership and is necessary to get things done – therefore, leaders are naturally preoccupied with power" (Pfeffer, 2010a, p. 7). On one hand, great leaders and managers typically use power in positive ways to accomplish goals, objectives, and mission of the organization. On the other hand, many bad leaders and managers use power in negative ways, mostly to accomplish their individual goals or for self-promotion. Nonetheless, leaders and managers use power and therefore, by extension, are powerful people. It is unfortunate that the use of power is perceived so negatively, primarily due to the numerous examples of individuals who have abused the power afforded them. In most instances, the individuals who abused power did not give any indication that they would behave so poorly; in other instances, colleagues and co-workers could have predicted such performance by looking at the individual's past performance. Sadly, there is little if anything that can be done to prevent such abuses by those who become enthralled with their newfound power. Therefore, it becomes critical that college and university administrators understand how to use their power in an appropriate and ethical manner so as to minimize the impact of errant leaders.

POLITICS IN HIGHER EDUCATION

No conversation about power within higher education would be complete without a discussion of organizational politics. As Hill (1978) stated, "the struggle for power, more commonly known as politics, pervades [all organizations]" (p. 21). Additionally, Pfeffer (1992) defines political activity as "those activities taken within organizations to acquire, develop, and use power and other resources to obtain one's preferred outcome in a situation in which there is uncertainty or disagreement about choices" (p. 74). One's ability to navigate the political dynamics of an organization is essential to one's ability to become a successful organizational leader. There are two types of politics that higher education administrators encounter on a regular basis – internal (micro) and external (macro) (Kretovics, 2011). At the state and national levels, as long as resources continue to be constrained, universities will need to compete with other politically powerful and meritorious sectors such as prisons, roads, and K-12 education among others. This competition for resources increases external political activity: the macro level. Simultaneously, individual colleges and universities (micro level) are interdependent organizations in which administrators need the assistance of others to accomplish their goals and objectives. This interdependence makes them political organizations (Pfeffer, 1992).

By their very nature, institutions of higher education operate as political systems. Additionally, because these institutions have multiple interdependent parts (departments and divisions) there is the presence of power within the administrative structure. Pfeffer (1992) points out that power is used more frequently under conditions of moderate interdependence. Where there is little or no interdependence there is little or no need to develop power or exercise influence because units do not need to rely on others for assistance in accomplishing their goals. In organizations where there is a high level of interdependence (perhaps dependence), units must work together and coordinate their activities. A failure to collaborate will result in an organizational failure, therefore, cooperation and collaboration are strong in these organizations and the exercise of power is minimal (Pfeffer).

INTRODUCTION

Whether public or private, not-for-profit or for-profit, two-year or four-year, colleges and universities are highly politicized organizations because there are so many different stakeholder groups, internal and external, with competing interests. Each group wishes to help direct the mission and vision of a particular institution with the hope of benefitting their respective cause. Political behaviors and the appropriate use of power provides leaders with tools necessary to move their institutions forward. Having spent over forty years in higher education, mostly in administrative roles, I firmly believe there is no organization more political than an institution of higher education.

Gary Yukl (1989), in his review of leadership theory and research, pointed out that not much had changed regarding leadership research, except that there was now a recognition of the political processes within organizations. Thirty years ago he encouraged managers and leaders that political activity in organizations needed to be brought to the fore and thought of as a skill to be honed not shunned.

Politics within higher education is unavoidable and, as Hill and Lineback (2011) state, it "arises from three features inherent in all organizations: *division of labor*, which creates disparate groups with disparate and even conflicting goals and priorities; *interdependence*, which means that none of those groups can do their work without the others; and *scarce resources*, for which groups necessarily compete" (p. 128). Connecting this with Pfeffer's comments about interdependence it becomes clearer that politics and power are inseparable: where you find one you will ultimately find the other. Herdlein et al. (2011) mentioned that in a survey of senior student affairs officers, "over 96% agreed that not employing politics in your everyday work, is to participate in student affairs without a full range of resources" (p. 46).

Within higher education all three features mentioned by Hill and Lineback (2011) are present. The divisions of labor can be quite obvious: faculty, academic administrators, student affairs, enrollment management, budget and finance, among others (see Chapter 3). Institutions of higher are structured with interdependent systems operating throughout. Without Enrollment Management, especially Admissions and Financial Aid, institutions would struggle to recruit the appropriate students for faculty to teach. Without maintenance, grounds, and housekeeping, the physical facilities wouldn't be prepared for students or visitors. And finally, without faculty, students would not have an appropriate academic experience. Regarding scarce resources, with few exceptions, departments within higher education institutions are constantly competing for scarce financial and physical resources.

Many academics will profess that they do not use power or political behavior and denounce their use as reprehensible in higher education. It is my belief that those with such views are simply deluding themselves. Power

INTRODUCTION

and political behavior are natural functions in any bureaucratic/hierarchical organization, particularly large ones such as colleges and universities (Herdlein et al., 2011; Hill and Lineback, 2011; Pfeffer, 1992). Power and political behavior are not inherently evil or unethical but rather must be viewed as tools that when used appropriately can aid administrators in accomplishing the goals and objectives of *the institution*. As a current or potential administrator you will need to understand how to maneuver through the ever-changing and evolving landscape of higher education politics by utilizing the power and influence you have at this particular point in your career. Throughout this book, it is my intent to provide you with an understanding of the current and potentially future environment of higher education and how to become a politically competent administrator by being able to identify the power plays that pervade our institutions and our industry. As Gilley (2006) notes, "the ability to navigate politics well is an essential ingredient to the success of any administrator" (p. 1).

Instead of pretending that power and politics do not belong in education, I challenge you to embrace these concepts and use them to become the most effective administrator possible. If administrators understand how to effectively utilize these tools for leading and motivating others, they can move their institution forward and simultaneously improve their individual career prospects. If, however, power and politics are used inappropriately or ineffectively, these tools can undermine the goals and objectives of the organization and create a culture of fear and distrust, leading to much lower levels of productivity. Preventing or minimizing these unproductive behaviors becomes the responsibility of all administrators within the institution and to do so one must be able to identify the behaviors and recognize them before it is too late and the damage is done. Julius (2009) comments that many administrators "encounter difficulty in comprehending the political dynamics of the decision-making environment" (p. 73). Political actions/behaviors are omnipresent in our institutions, from seemingly simple decisions as to who teaches what classes at what times to more complex processes like budgeting or hiring decisions.

I have already stressed the presence and importance of power and politics within higher education, so now in the next few paragraphs I will briefly introduce some of the positive and negative aspects of power and politics. These will be more fully articulated later in the book. Let's begin by taking a look at the downside.

THE DOWNSIDE TO POWER AND POLITICS

Hardly a week goes by without an article in *The Chronicle of Higher Education* or *Inside Higher Ed* in which you will find examples of individuals using their power inappropriately to accomplish personal or institutional goals, and as a result create problems for their respective institutions. Regardless of institutional type, size, or location, the abuse or misuse of power will be problematic. A sampling of headlines gives you an idea of some issues:

> "2 Embattled Presidents Resign"
> "U of Louisville Sues Former President Over Misuse of Foundation Funds"
> "Questions Swirl Amid Reports of Baylor President's Firing"
> "Nevada Higher-Education Chancellor Resigns After Email Scandal"
> "Acrimony at Akron"
> "The Mount St. Mary President was a Corporate Test Case. It Failed Miserably"

Oftentimes, these problems or failures are attributed to an individual believing, arrogantly, that she/he is smarter than anyone else at the institution or that the institution's policies and procedures do not apply to his or her position, not unlike former President Richard Nixon during the Watergate scandal. This overreach of authority is usually seen as leaders letting *power* get the better of them or that a decision was *politically* motivated rather than being evidence based. Other times it may simply be a bad *fit* between the leader and the institution. Regardless of the circumstances, these are situations in which individuals worked their way into positions of significant power and prestige only to lose it because of their arrogance and perhaps a major error in judgment or a series of mistakes. As Abraham Lincoln noted, "if you want to test a man's character, give him power" (www.keepinspiring.me/abraham-lincoln-quotes/).

> *Common reasons for administrative missteps*
> Arrogance
>   Rules don't apply to me
>   I am smarter than anyone at this institution
>   I alone was hired to make decisions and fix problems
>   Failure to recognize one's own poor decision(s)
> Surrounding oneself with *yes* people
> Refusing to listen to or dialogue with others
> Not properly delegating

INTRODUCTION

During your career you will most likely encounter some executives who exhibit narcissistic behavior which can be seen as a trait of powerful and successful leaders (more on this in Chapter 5), but it is also quite obvious that these behaviors can have negative effects on institutions. According to O'Reilly et al. (2013), narcissistic leaders are more likely to violate integrity standards, create destructive workplaces, have unhappy or disengaged workers, and restrict the free and open exchange of information (p. 226), all of which characterize a toxic work environment.

Additionally, according to Vigoda (2000, p. 326):

> Perception of organizational politics was found to have had a negative relationship with job attitudes (e.g., job satisfaction and organizational commitment), a positive relationship with intention to leave the organization (exit), and a stronger positive relationship with negligent behavior (neglect). It is suggested that public employees will tend to react to workplace politics with negligent behavior rather than by leaving.

Power and politics are not always used for the good of the organization and in some instances you may find that the power you exercise to benefit your unit may, in reality be damaging to the overall institution. For example, you may believe that it is important to increase the selectivity of your department and begin restricting entry by capping enrollment. However, where institutions are tuition driven, capping enrollment in one area may restrict the overall revenue to the institution. So, while your program now may be considered highly selective and looks more impressive to your colleagues across the country, as a result, your institution might experience some financial pain.

THE UPSIDE TO POWER AND POLITICS

Individual institutions of higher education are designed to operate as interdependent systems. In order to effectively carry out their respective missions, each institution must develop processes in which the various internal and external stakeholder groups can have input into the strategic planning processes. Helping to decide in what direction an institution is headed is viewed as one of the most important decisions an institution makes. Institutional budgets are financial representations of institutional priorities (Kretovics, 2011) and those priorities should be stated in the institution's strategic plan. Throughout the planning process, the effective use of politics and power is critical to ensure that as many stakeholder groups as possible have an opportunity to influence administrative decision-making.

Power is seen as an essential feature of an administrator's role because without the use of some degree of power, an administrator will find it very difficult to direct the efforts of subordinates (Vecchio, 2007). As an administrator, you will supervise others. If they perceive you as having no power you will struggle in accomplishing the goals for your unit. Effective administrators understand that their ability to use power can help determine their personal or departmental success, while failure to use power can have the opposite effect (Vecchio, 2007).

CONCLUDING COMMENTS

Kotter (1998) pointed out that "strong leadership with weak management is no better, and is sometimes actually worse than the reverse" (p. 38). What Kotter didn't address was the use of *power* as a leader or manager. As discussed above, leadership, management, and power are inseparable within organizational settings such as institutions of higher education. Pfeffer (1992) and Kruse and Prettyman (2008) view power as an important social process, which is often required to accomplish one's goal when working in an organization with interdependent systems. Every institution of higher education, by its very nature of being bureaucratic and hierarchical, is comprised of interdependent systems. While power and politics are constantly in use and sometimes used inappropriately, it is important to point out that the vast majority of leaders in higher education end their careers as *successful* leaders. You may not always agree with what they did (or are doing) or the processes in which they engaged with you and other stakeholders, but that does not mean they were wrong or that their decisions were mistakes.

We live in a country that tends to value independence and recognizes that there are discrepancies in the balance of power between individuals (Hofstede, n.d.). To some, these power differentials are seen as inherent (Wolfe and McGinn, 2005), as part of the *just world phenomenon*, which Merelman (1986) describes as "people having a need to believe they live in a world where people get what they deserve" (p. 285). Therefore, people who acquire power and advance into leadership positions are deserving of their status. To others, these power differentials are seen as part of our social fabric and those who acquire power and prestige did so by navigating the political aspects inherent in hierarchical and bureaucratic structures, thereby earning the power obtained. Hill (1978) posits that power is embedded in human nature and will persist within higher educational institutions. Higher education has been described by various authors as anarchies (Birnbaum, 1988; Hill, 1978; March and Cohen, 1974) which by definition require the use of power and politics to accomplish their goals.

INTRODUCTION

In order to be successful in an administrative or leadership role within higher education one needs to develop and effectively utilize a certain amount of power and political savvy. To do so, one must first understand the types and uses of power and the process of a political interaction. It is also helpful to understand the complex environment of higher education.

REFLECTIVE QUESTIONS

1. Who are the internal and external stakeholders for your institution?
2. From your position within the institution, describe a scenario in which you witnessed the effective (good or bad) use of power?
3. What do you need and/or need to do to gain power at your institution?

Part I
The Context of Power and Leadership in Higher Education

Chapter Two

Types and Tactics of Power

If *power* is defined as a social process that enables one to persuade others to do things they would not ordinarily do, this then begs the question, just how do you get people to do things they would not normally do? Is it through motivation? Influence? If so, how do you motivate others? In this chapter we will explore the types of power that enable administrators to motivate or influence others to accomplish the goals of the unit or institution.

French and Raven (1968) defined five different types of *social power*: **reward, coercive, referent, expert,** and **legitimate** (see Figure 2.1). Since the publication of these social powers, others have added to them. For example, Hersey et al. (1979) added **connectional** and **information**, and Yukl and Falbe (1991) added **persuasive** as types of power. Additionally, Yukl and Falbe posited that **charisma** was a type of power but did not find enough differentiation with referent power so they decided to consider it as part of referent power.

Another possible type of power, **knowledge power** has been found in the literature, but the evidence to support it as a stand-alone is not compelling. For example, with *knowledge power*, more often than not the individual is an *expert* in a particular area, whether that be the maintenance worker who completely understands the HVAC system or the computer programmer who understands how to make the new Customer Relation Management system work with the existing information systems on campus. Rather than a type of power, I agree with Gilley (2006) in using knowledge as one of the overarching categories of power that includes *expert, informational,* and *connectional* powers.

Figure 2.1 shows the eight types of power supported by the research literature and the two types of power that are mentioned in the literature but found to be too similar to one of the other types. During your administrative career you will witness each type of power in use within colleges and universities at which you work.

THE CONTEXT OF POWER AND LEADERSHIP IN HIGHER EDUCATION

Formal Authority (Control of Resources)

> ***Legitimate*** *– stems from the belief that someone has the right to influence one's behavior. The most common example would be supervisors and/or individuals above you in the hierarchy*

> ***Reward*** *– when one has the ability (or perceived ability) to mediate some type of reward for someone, typically based on behavior or performance*

> ***Coercive*** *– when one has the ability (or perceived ability) to mediate punishment for someone typically based on behavior or performance or the lack-there-of*

Personality

> ***Referent*** *– when someone looks up to another or admires the other individual, wanting to be like that person or at least associated with that person; then the other has referent power over the admiring individual*

> ***Persuasive*** *– has the ability to use data and logic to present a persuasive case*

Knowledge

> ***Expert*** *– when one is perceived to have special knowledge or ability in a specific area*

> ***Information*** *– someone has the ability to control the availability and accuracy of information you need to work effectively*

> ***Connectional*** *– reflects the influence that leaders possess as a result of whom they know and the support they engender from others as a result (i.e., the bandwagon effect)*

(Adapted from French and Raven, 1968, and Yukl and Falbe, 1989)

Figure 2.1 Types of Power
Adapted from French and Raven (1968) and Yukl and Falbe (1990)

As we explore these *social powers* a brief description and a few examples are provided to demonstrate how they may work within your institution. The examples provided are for illustrative purposes and not meant as a recipe for how to use the power being described. In reviewing these powers it will be helpful for you to think about your particular circumstances and when you may have encountered each of these powers. Also, remember that exercising these *social powers* typically relies on some degree of an interdependent relationship. Gilley (2006) believes that the use of power is interpersonal not personal.

The eight social powers described (Figure 2.1) are based in interdependent hierarchical organizations, which of course describes colleges and universities. However, like Henry Ford noted, *you don't have to hold a position in order to be a leader* (Andersen, 2013), so you will see that not all of these powers are linked to a position title within the institutional hierarchy. The social powers are anchored in three contexts: Formal Authority and/or control of resources (legitimate, coercive, and reward), Personality (referent and persuasive), and Knowledge (expert, information, connectional) (Gilley, 2006). Power is employed in interdependent systems and it is used with the intent of having the employees comply with the request or commit to the action or goals. If used inappropriately, power can also encourage resistance from within the organization. Let's begin our review by looking at the powers anchored in formal authority.

After each of the *social powers* listed below I provide a box describing the motivation for using the power and the potential reaction from subordinates. There are three potential reactions to the use of power – compliance, commitment, or resistance.

FORMAL AUTHORITY

There are three types of power related to one's formal authority within an institution – legitimate, reward, and coercive. These three powers tend to be connected to one's position within the institution's hierarchy. These powers tend to be the most readily identifiable within the institution and are the ones used most often by immature or inexperienced leaders.

Legitimate Power

This type of power is the easiest type of power to see and describe within any organization. This power is based on the formal authority associated with one's position within the hierarchy of the institution. When you look at your institution's organizational chart you will see direct reporting lines indicating a position's authority (power) over the positions to which it is connected, beneath it in the structure. Oftentimes you can make a similar assessment based on positional title within a particular institution (note that titles are not consistent throughout higher education). For example, a director typically will supervise coordinators, deans will supervise department chairs or school directors, vice presidents supervise deans and directors among others. Therefore, the very nature of your job as a college or university administrator affords you certain types and levels of power. Additionally, the higher you sit on the organizational chart of your institution the more access you will have to additional power. Administrators with supervisory responsibilities generally have legitimate power over their subordinate staff members. The administrator typically will help the employees determine their daily priorities, evaluate the employees, and in many instances help determine compensation (possibly raises or bonuses).

Legitimate power can have an impact on communication within an organization. Dr. Albert Green, Physicist and former CEO of Kent Displays, mentions that for him "the dynamics of the room change when the president or CEO walks in, and what people say changes, so you have to rely on other people to tell you what is going on." This is a situation in which, almost always, having legitimate power somewhat hinders organizational communication.

One downside to *legitimate power* is that some administrators simply want more. In most institutions the hiring of additional staff is seen as increasing one's power and prestige within the organization. The belief is the more people and resources you control the more important you must be. As Maxwell (2013) asserts:

> Positional leaders feed on organizational politics – they do what they can to get the largest staff and the biggest budget they can; not for the sake of the organization's mission but for the sake of expanding and defending their turf
>
> (p. 32)

It is interesting to note that not all of the powerful individuals in an organization are quite as obvious from their location on the organizational chart. There are many individuals who have power far greater than their position within the hierarchy would dictate. Those types of power are discussed in the Personality and Knowledge sections.

> **Motivation for using Legitimate Power** – comes from being the boss or being above someone in the hierarchy – you use the power because you can.
>
> **Reaction to the use of Legitimate Power** – Subordinates typically comply with legitimate power because of the authority that comes with the position; they are not likely to commit to the task at hand, but do it because it is their job.

Reward Power

Coming from an individual's ability to provide an incentive or other type of reward, *reward power* is utilized to influence another's behavior to accomplish the desired behavior or result in return for the promised incentive. Pfeffer

(2013) believes "the most effective way to control others' behavior is to control when and how they receive reinforcement" or rewards (p. 74). Within higher education, rewards can be as simple as a faculty member being given the desired teaching time or course load and as complex as a merit pay structure. Providing incentives to encourage specified behaviors is not new in any industry. On the faculty side of a university the tenure process is a great example of reward power in use. Many large universities publicly tout teaching, service, and research as the three legs of the tenure process. Pre-tenured faculty are expected to deliver high-quality instruction, participate in the committee structure and shared governance, and publish scholarly articles in peer-reviewed journals and/or bring in significant amounts of money from research grants. The reality in most research or aspiring research institutions is that what enables a faculty member to receive tenure is a solid record of publications or grant activities. While good teaching and a commitment to service are acknowledged, it is the scholarly record that permits one to receive tenure, hence the old adage of *publish or perish*. Simply put, what gets done is what gets rewarded, in this case it is research.

For those administrators and managers outside the classroom there are a variety of ways in which supervisors can reward their subordinates. For example, in residence life a hall director can be rewarded by receiving a preferred residence hall assignment or a favorable on-call assignment/schedule. In other areas supervisors may let staff members leave early, provide individuals with flexible schedules, permit some members to take *comp time* for working longer or weekend hours, or give preference for professional development opportunities. It is often when particular staff members receive a benefit not available to all that others within the institution begin to see the reward power in action.

Former Kent Displays CEO, Al Green, preferred to use reward power to motivate others and, as he states: "I am more of a carrot person than a stick person. I believe that people tend to respond to encouragement and praise rather than threats."

Motivation for using Reward Power – comes from wanting to encourage people to work harder or to accomplish specific tasks and having the resources necessary to provide an incentive.

Reaction to the use of Reward Power – most likely individuals will comply with the request because there is the potential of a reward/incentive for completing the task(s). They are not necessarily committed to the task or project.

Coercive Power

The opposite of *reward power*, *coercive power* is a threat of a negative outcome if the employee does not comply with the request or directive. The senior administrator has the ability to punish employees for inappropriate behaviors or failure to complete the desired tasks or comply with requests. This is not the same as withholding a reward. The threat of job termination or a demotion is a use of coercive power. When employees do something out of fear they are being coerced. In an ideal organization the use of this power would not exist, however, institutions of higher education are not necessarily ideal organizations. We have our share of bullies in the academy. Here is an example of a dean using a bit of coercive power:

> During my pre-tenured time on faculty, the new dean of the college scheduled two meeting times for all of the tenure-track faculty members who were not tenured so he could discuss his views of the tenure process. At the appointed time for the first gathering, nine of the 15 junior faculty members were in attendance, the dean however, was nowhere to be found and no word as to how long he might be. After 15 minutes I left. Slightly over 20 minutes late the dean arrived and began his conversation. Later that day when the dean saw me talking with the associate dean, he reminded me that there was another meeting scheduled the next day. I responded that I would check my calendar to see if I could make it. He immediately stepped between the associate dean and me, stuck his finger in my face and stated "you don't understand, you will be there" and not waiting for my response, he walked away. The associate dean then quipped "I guess I know where to find you tomorrow at 1:00." By the way, the dean showed up 20 minutes late for that meeting as well and again with no apology or explanation.

The unstated threat is that if you do not attend this meeting you may not be successful in your bid for tenure. While this type of coercion may not be commonplace in higher education it does occur. And for this dean he was able to impart his wisdom to all of the pre-tenured faculty within the college.

On the staff or administrative side of an institution or department, employees may be disciplined for arriving late to work or not completing an assignment in a timely fashion or for simply not obeying their supervisor. Pusser and Marginson (2012) believe that power is ultimately embedded in elite and coercive structures, the institutionalization of authority and leadership. The structural model of authority is essential to thinking about power in higher education because it turns attention to the distinction between normative understandings of authority relations, such as shared governance, and the formally codified exercise of authority by rules, legal authority, and legislative action.

(p. 93)

According to Jeffrey Pfeffer (2010a), "Condoleezza Rice's credo, was that people may oppose you, but when they realize you can hurt them, they'll join your side" (p. 87). This suggests that using coercion is a viable approach and is similar to Machiavelli's statement extolling the benefits of people fearing you rather than loving you.

Perhaps the most recent and most public display of coercive power has been the sexual abuse cases from the entertainment and governmental sectors. This abuse of power has spawned the *me too movement* bringing attention on how coercion is used to induce compliance.

> **Motivation for using Coercive Power** – leaders use this approach when they believe they cannot control their subordinates. They believe it is best to have their employees fear them.
>
> **Reaction to the use of Coercive Power** – Use of this power will most often garner compliance from subordinates – born out of fear of punishment. There is also a high risk of individuals actively resisting the requests or potentially sabotaging the task(s).

PERSONALITY

Power related to one's personality can be associated with two of the social powers identified in the literature – *referent power* and *persuasive power*. These powers are not directly connected to one's position within the institution but rather based on the individual's personality traits (see Chapter 4).

Referent Power

A person has *referent power* when others, internal or external to the organization, admire that individual and like to be seen or associated with her. Have you ever worked at an institution where there was someone in the organization that you respected or admired so much that you would do anything asked (within reason)? Serve on committees, work a weekend event, volunteer for extra assignments? That is referent power, doing something based on this admiration and not because the person is in a supervisory role or a higher level administrator. In some instances you will notice others may change their behaviors to mimic those of the admired individual (Tiedens and Fragale, 2003), which may include dressing like and perhaps even talking like the admired individual. You see this with celebrities such as entertainers or professional athletes and their followers.

Referent power is often attributed to charismatic leadership (Yukl, 1989) and while not exactly the same there is enough overlap to warrant a mention. Also, Bass points out that "attaining charisma in the eyes of one's employees is central to succeeding as a transformational leader. Charismatic leaders have great power and influence" (p. 304). People like to be associated with these leaders and many "employees want to identify with them, and they have a high degree of trust and confidence in them" (p. 304). In general, charismatic leaders are seen as inspiring and in some cases as cheerleaders encouraging followers to put in the extra effort or double down.

> **Motivation for using Referent Power** – comes from knowing that people want to please the individual asking in hopes of continuing or developing a relationship – they like being with powerful people because it makes them feel more powerful.
>
> **Reaction to the use of Referent Power** – Individuals most likely will be committed to the tasks or project because of the relationship with the person asking. They want to please the person asking and hope to receive some recognition.

Persuasive Power

Individuals using *persuasive power* are usually quite good at making evidence-based presentations (formal and informal) to large or small groups. They speak with confidence and often in a more forceful tone. Their utilization of data makes it more difficult to challenge their positions.

These are the administrators who, through their presentation skills, can convince fellow administrators and other staff members to buy into the idea(s) being put forward. They are often considered dynamic, charismatic, and polished. As Clayton Spencer (2018) stated in an essay for the *Chronicle* "effective leadership depends less on positional authority than on persuasion."

> **Motivation for using Persuasive Power** – comes from knowing that you have the ability to energize the group or individual: you can convince them to do what you want them to accomplish.
>
> **Reaction to the use of Persuasive Power** – Followers are excited by the skillful and articulate presentation of information and are more likely to commit to the tasks because they believe in the administrator asking.

KNOWLEDGE

Knowledge is the basis or anchor on which three types of power are developed. Townley (1993) contends that knowledge "is integral in the operation of power" (p. 521).

Expert Power

Being an expert is not based on the person's position within the hierarchy but rather on what the person knows or on some special skill the person possesses. For example, there may be a faculty or staff member at the institution who is an expert in an area of need within the institution. This person may be called upon to share this expertise and will be able to influence others because of this specific knowledge. These are often the faculty members called by reporters for their keen insights or area of expertise (meteorologists, economists, political scientists, etc.).

Similarly, there may be a staff member with special skills or talent required to help resolve a vexing problem on the campus. When that special skill or talent is in demand that individual has the ability to influence others, thus possessing expert power. This could be someone with a background in enrollment management, assessment, technology, sustainability, food insecurity, etc.

> **Motivation for using Knowledge Power** – comes from a belief in the expert's knowledge of the situation and knowing that others will listen to you because they believe you know what you are talking about.
>
> **Reaction to the use of Knowledge Power** – Individuals most likely will be committed to the tasks because of the belief in the person asking.

Information Power

The premise that an individual has information or access to information which you need for your work to be effective gives that individual *information power*. This could be in the form of policies or procedures that must be followed to ensure something. For example, in most departments on a university campus there are key personnel such as administrative assistants who know how to navigate the overly cumbersome and bureaucratic systems of the institution and also know which forms need to be filed and to whom they will go. This information may be needed for you to complete the process of paying vendors on grants or processing the reimbursement of travel expenses.

> **Motivation for using Information Power** – comes from wanting demonstrate to others that you have or have access to the information necessary to complete the task.
>
> **Reaction to the use of Information Power** – Individuals will comply with requests because they believe you have the information necessary to complete the task.

Connectional Power

Individuals with a connection to someone else with power and influence have power based on that relationship and not their position within the institution. These *power brokers* leverage their relationships to advance their agenda or the agenda of others. For example, if you have a personal relationship with a more senior-level administrator in another department and your supervisor was interested in developing a partnership with that department, you could use your connection to introduce your supervisor to your *friend*, enhancing your profile in the eyes of your supervisor.

This *connectional power* can also potentially lead to negative behaviors such as when a mid-level administrator has a personal relationship with a senior-level administrator and she decides to circumvent the traditional reporting lines and goes around her supervisor to the senior-level administrator with a concern or issue that should have been handled at a lower level. This behavior erodes the authority/power of the supervisor, creating future difficulties and mistrust between all those involved.

> **Motivation for using Connectional Power** – comes from wanting access to others in positions of power and influence.
>
> **Reaction to the use of Connectional Power** – Individuals will comply with requests in an effort to gain favor or avoid falling out of favor.

As you review these eight types of power you should be able to identify individuals within your institution who utilize each. Some individuals may be quite effective and may be utilizing their *power* for the greater good while others may be using it for their own self-aggrandizement. You should also notice that there will be individuals who have power that is well beyond their position within the institutional hierarchy. They do not need to be in a position of authority (legitimate power) to influence administrators. What types of power do you have?

Figure 2.2 summarizes the motivation to use these social powers and the likely reaction from one's subordinates when each is used in the workplace.

OTHER BASES OF INFLUENCE AND POWER

There are two other bases of influence and power that have a presence in the literature that are worth mentioning here. Yukl and Tracy's nine Influence Tactics and Elizabeth Allen's Three Modalities of Power. Each takes a slightly different approach to power and influence than did French and Raven and there is enough overlap to make a connection with the social powers described above.

Yukl and Tracey (1992) define nine *influence tactics* (Figure 2.3) that can also be construed as aspects of or types of power. There is overlap between those listed below and the types of social power described above.

Elizabeth Allen (2001) in her article, *Rethinking Power*, discusses three modalities of power from a feminist empowerment perspective. Her

Power	Motivation	Reaction
Legitimate	being the boss or being above someone in the hierarchy – you use the power because you can	Subordinates comply with legitimate power because of the authority that comes with the position, but oftentimes, they are not necessarily committed to the tasks at hand.
Reward	wanting to encourage people to work harder or to accomplish specific tasks.	Individuals most likely will comply with the request for potential reward/incentive for completing the task(s). They are not likely to commit.
Coercive	leaders use this approach when they believe they cannot control their subordinates. They prefer to have their employees fear them.	Use of this power will most often garner compliance from subordinates-born out of fear of punishment. However, there is also the risk of individuals resisting the requests or potentially sabotaging the task(s).
Referent	wanting to please the individual asking in hopes of continuing or developing a relationship – being with powerful people makes you powerful.	Individuals most likely will be committed to the tasks because of the relationship with the person asking.
Persuasive	excited by the skillful and articulate presentation of information.	Followers are more likely to commit to the tasks because they believe in the administrator asking.
Knowledge	belief in the expert's knowledge of the situation	Individuals most likely will be committed to the tasks because of the belief in the person asking.
Connectional	wanting access to others in positions of power and influence.	Individuals will comply with requests in an effort to gain favor and avoid falling out of favor.

Figure 2.2 Power Motivations and Reactions

modalities are related to the social powers listed above and give one a slightly different view on how to approach power within organizations. The three modalities are *Power-over*, *Power-to*, and *Power-with*.

Power-over is the ability of an actor or set of actors to constrain the choices available to another actor or set of actors in a nontrivial way (Allen, 2001, p. 33). With this modality leaders are typically operating within a more vertical or hierarchical frame of reference where power is seen as finite and possessed and it is often exercised over others (Allen et al., 2006). This is most closely related to the **Formal Authority** *social powers* of *legitimate, coercive,* and *reward* described by French and Raven. This *power-over* others is often exhibited by individuals who, when new to

> **Rational Persuasion** – The person uses logical arguments and factual evidence to persuade you that a proposal of request is viable and likely to result in the attainment of task objectives.
>
> **Inspirational Appeal** – The person makes a request or proposal that arouses enthusiasm by appealing to your values, ideals, and aspirations or by increasing your confidence that you can do it.
>
> **Consultation** – The person seeks your participation in planning a strategy, activity, or change for which your support and assistance are desired, or the person is willing to modify a proposal to deal with your concerns and suggestions.
>
> **Ingratiation** – The person seeks to get you in a good mood or to think favorably of him or her before asking you to do something.
>
> **Exchange** – The person offers an exchange of favors, indicates willingness to reciprocate at a later time, or promises you a share of the benefits if you help accomplish a task.
>
> **Personal Appeal** – The person appeals to your feelings of loyalty and friendship toward him or her before asking you to do something.
>
> **Coalition** – The person seeks the aid of others to persuade you to do something or uses the support of others as a reason for you to also agree.
>
> **Legitimating** – The person seeks to establish the legitimacy of a request by claiming the authority or right to make it or by verifying that it is consistent with organizational, policies, rules, practices, or traditions.
>
> **Pressure** – The person uses demands, threats, or persistent reminders to influence you to do what he or she wants.
>
> (Yukl and Tracey 1992, p. 526)

Figure 2.3 Definition of Influence Tactics

an institution, believe they were brought in to accomplish an agenda or some specific goals. In using this power their subordinates will usually comply with the directives but rarely commit to the goals of the individual leaders. In many instances this *power-over* is met with resistance from the faculty, staff, and other administrators.

Power-to is the ability of an individual actor to attain an end or series of ends. According to this definition, the terms "empowerment" and "*power-to*" are roughly synonymous (Allen, 2001, p. 34). Using this modality leaders typically exercise power to effect change by working with others as a strategy to achieve a particular goal.

The use of *power-to* is most closely related to the use of **Knowledge** powers such as *expert*, *knowledge*, and *connectional* powers. Subordinates will most likely comply with requests and seldom resist the leader's agenda.

Power-with is the ability of a collectivity to act together for the attainment of a common or shared end or series of ends (Allen, 2001, p. 35). Allen views this power being "based on the receptivity and reciprocity that characterize relations among members of the collective" (p. 35). These leaders are often viewed as facilitative and being willing to work alongside and in collaboration with others.

Power-with is most closely related to **Personality** powers such as *persuasive* and *referent*. These leaders are sometimes referred to as servant leaders or charismatic leaders and are more likely than the others to development commitment among their subordinates.

CONCLUDING COMMENTS

When considering the many different types of power, I believe it prudent to consider the comment of Maxwell (2013): "Just because you have the right to do something as a leader does not mean that it is the right thing to do" (p. 33). Power by itself is not good or bad, it is how, and for what purpose(s) it is used that *makes it so*. As you will see in Chapter 2, there are numerous leaders and managers in institutions of higher education with legitimate power that is vested in their respective positions. Their ability to use this power effectively can be dependent on where they reside within the structure (Pfeffer, 1992) and what other types of power they can harness during decision-making processes.

If you recall, effective leadership was equated with the effective use of power and the effective use of power is doing the right things for the right reasons. Therefore, I submit to you, to be a successful leader or administrator you must use power effectively and it becomes incumbent upon you to *do the right things, the right way, for the right reasons*.

REFLECTIVE QUESTIONS

1. Based on your current position, describe the types of power you have and over whom (general terms or positions not individual names)?
2. How have you used this power to influence the behavior of these individuals?
3. Give an example of how you have seen at least two of the types of power used at your institution.

Chapter Three

Organizational Context

The political nature of organizations in general, and the hyper-political nature of higher education specifically, makes it increasingly important to understand the system, or lack-there-of, of higher education in the United States. Knowing how higher education in the U.S. operates and how some individual institutions are structured can be of value as you navigate the bureaucratic systems in place. This chapter examines the macro picture of higher education in the United States to give you a better understanding of how institutions are generally organized and where there may be pockets of power. The organizational charts that follow are meant to provide an example of what currently exists based on institutional type. These charts are not meant to be ideal models for institutional structure. They are simply examples of structures and descriptions of functions that currently exist to give you a basic understanding of most higher education institutions within the United States.

Within each of the organizational structures provided, you will see position titles and reporting structures that are somewhat generic across the U.S. Additionally, with these titles and their respective hierarchical positioning, it is hoped that you will gain a better understanding of positional or legitimate power within many institutions. The structures provided should also give you a better idea as to with whom you will need to work across functional lines and with whom you should consider networking as you progress along your career journey.

Before examining the organizational structures, you need to understand that the reporting lines represented in each depicts the supervisory relationship and does not necessarily indicate the flow of information. Information will flow through formal and informal channels. Formal channels follow the reporting lines, while informal channels are determined by personal connections between the parties.

HIGHER EDUCATION IN THE U.S.

Most countries in the developed world have a single system of higher education controlled at the national level. In some instances, the president of the country has final say in determining the leadership of individual institutions. However, in the United States, constitutionally, the education of its citizens has been decentralized and has been established as a state's right, not the responsibility of the federal government. Every state in the U.S. has developed its individual approach to providing higher education opportunities for its residents. Within each state, one will find a variety of individually chartered postsecondary options, be it public or private, two-year or four-year institutions, and for-profit or not-for-profit types of institutions. Essentially, each state, through its version of a coordinating board or legislative body, determines which institutions can operate within its borders and what degrees those institutions can offer. This autonomy has proven to be the one of the greatest strengths of higher education in the United States and is what permits and perhaps even fosters the development of such a diverse offering of postsecondary opportunities. As such, it is precisely this diverse set of institutional offerings that became the envy of the world in the early twentieth century.

INSTITUTIONAL STRUCTURE

The governance and coordination of higher education institutions differs depending on whether it is under public or private control (Zusman, 2005); however, there is not as much of a difference in the actual institutional structure as one might think. The general organizational structure of individual institutions of higher education is bureaucratic and hierarchical in nature. Regardless of tax status (not-for-profit and profit), ownership structure, or whether they are public or private, there are several common elements across institutions and institutional type. Almost all institutions of higher education in the U.S. have some sort of governing board (trustees, regents, directors), a chief operating officer (chancellor or president), a chief academic officer (provost or dean), and a layer of vice-presidents or directors. Figures 3.1 through 3.4 provide a sample of what these organizational structures may look like.

When you look at the organizational chart of an institution you are looking at a bureaucracy that is anchored to a hierarchical structure, which by its very nature is where power and power-struggles reside. Within each structure you will see representations of a governing board, administrators, and faculty. In most institutions, the faculty are typically responsible for the curriculum including the curricular development process; the administrators manage the day-to-day activities and are responsible for implementing the organizational mission and vision; and the governing board, as the ultimate authority, has the final say in the institutional decision-making process. Typically though, the institution's board focuses on fiscal and personnel matters and delegates the responsibility of the operation to the administration. Regardless of institutional type, tax status, or state of origin, virtually every institution has one thing in common – they are all bureaucratic and hierarchical.

The Carnegie Classification of Institutions of Higher Education has over 30 different groups in its "Basic Classification" link into which it sorts U.S. colleges and universities. For the purpose of showing organizational structures I have compressed them into three basic categories – Research Oriented (includes doctoral and masters universities), Baccalaureate Colleges, and Associate's Colleges. You will also see an additional organizational model (Executive VP) trending in some of today's larger institutions. Additionally, a few of the more common functional areas within higher education are briefly described to provide you with a better understanding of their potential power within institutions. These organizational charts give you a basic idea as to the hierarchical structure and positional (legitimate) power that exists within many of our institutions. As you look at the charts, notice where the positions sit within the institutional hierarchy as that may help you understand their relative power within the institution. Where you sit in the institution's hierarchy shapes how you view the rest of the institution.

GOVERNING BOARDS

Before looking at specific institutions, it may be relevant to look at how these institutions are governed. Much like large corporations with boards of directors, colleges and universities have governing boards as mentioned above. In the public sector, board members may be appointed (usually by the governor) or elected, or a combination of the two. Whereas in the private, not-for-profit sector, the board is typically self-perpetuating, meaning new members are appointed and approved by the current board members. The size of a board can vary depending on institutional type, with public institutions usually having fewer than 15 members and private institutions having significantly more, some having more than 50 members.

Mitchell and King (2018) indicate that institutional boards "are the fiduciary stewards who approve policy, and hire, nurture, and replace the president" (p. 12). In most institutions, boards and their individual members stay out of the day-to-day operation of the institution, delegating that to the president and central administration, and focus mainly on the *big picture* and the long-term future of the institution.

According to a 2016 report by the Association of Governing Boards (AGB), 74% of institutions require an orientation for new board members and another 16% have an orientation but do not require it for new members. I find it alarming that 26% of institutions surveyed do not require an orientation for newly appointed board members. Individuals moving into positions with this much authority and responsibility should be required to attend an orientation where they learn about the complexity of the institution, its mission, its history, direction, and their duties as fiscal stewards for the institution. The AGB study also indicates that only 30% of presidents believe board members understand the work of faculty, which by itself indicates a need for an orientation. After all, if we require first-year students to attend an orientation to learn about life on campus, shouldn't we require board members, who are the fiscal stewards of the institution, to have an understanding of that campus?

Transparency in higher education begins at the top, with the governing board. If the communication between the board and the institution's internal stakeholders is not clear it becomes difficult to have an effective *shared governance* system. According to the AGB report, the vast majority of board members believe *shared governance* is important to their respective institutions. And it is interesting to note that the preferred definition of shared governance – "a system of open communication aimed at aligning priorities, creating a culture of shared responsibility for the welfare of the institution, and creating a system of checks and balances to ensure the institution stays mission-centered" (p. 3), emphasizes communication. Also, keep in mind that within most institutions the term *shared governance* refers to the relationship between the board and administration and the institution's faculty and, unfortunately, not the staff. As Mitchell and King (2018) note, "[m]anagement is the glue that links governance to strategy. Management requires a clear line of authority with rules that engage and bind. It is the one area of campus where college and corporate life intersect" (p. 23).

The remainder of this chapter will provide the organizational overview of several institutional types and their respective organizational charts (senior levels). Also, you will find a listing of some administrative personalities that may be found on our campuses.

Research Oriented Universities

Larger universities are usually classified as research oriented or comprehensive universities and they can be public or private. Typically, these institutions are the largest universities within each state and include what is commonly called the *flagship institution*. While there may be some large, non-research institutions present, their institutional structures tend to closely approximate those of the research institutions. As shown in

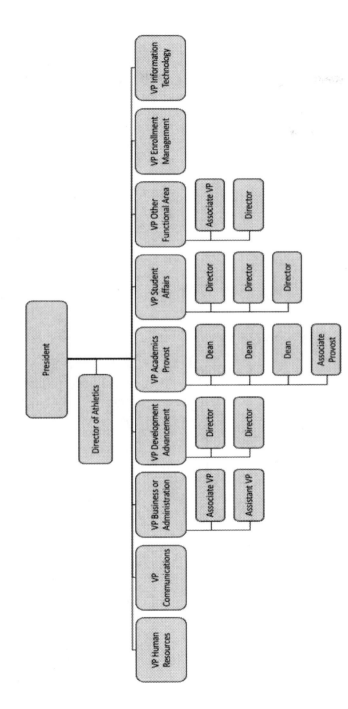

Figure 3.1 Large Research University

THE CONTEXT OF POWER AND LEADERSHIP IN HIGHER EDUCATION

Figure 3.1, research oriented institutions are hierarchical with several layers of administrative positions. This figure has only a portion of the top of the organizational chart and is meant to provide a framework for you to understand their complexity. Many of the larger research oriented universities will have 10 to 15 vice-presidential level positions that can include: Academic Affairs (Provost), Administration (Facilities and Grounds), Advancement (Development), Athletics, Business and Finance, Chief of Staff, Communications, Diversity and Inclusion, Enrollment Management, General Counsel, Global Initiatives, Human Resources, Information Systems, Marketing, Research, Strategic Initiatives, Student Affairs, or Systems Integration, among others. Additionally, for each vice-president, there are support staff, numerous assistant and associate vice-presidents, and directors and department heads. Later in this chapter some of these vice-presidential units or functional areas will be described in more detail.

Baccalaureate Colleges

Baccalaureate colleges encompass institutions formerly known as four-year liberal arts colleges and four-year institutions with more comprehensive offerings such as professional degrees. While still bureaucratic in nature, these institutions differ from the larger research universities with the primary differences being the size of the bureaucracy and some of the position titles. These institutions will have fewer vice-presidents and oftentimes fewer layers within the organizational structure. There are still a few institutions in this category that choose not to use the vice-presidential title at all, referring to their senior administrative positions as deans (Figure 3.2). Because of the reduced layers and more streamlined structure, many senior and mid-level administrators wear multiple hats. For example, it is not uncommon for the dean of students to also serve as the director of housing and residential life and/or perhaps director of auxiliary services. With this

Figure 3.2 Liberal Arts College

leaner structure, however, there is a greater consolidation of power and the likelihood of administrative error may also increase.

There are many four-year institutions that call themselves liberal arts colleges when in fact they look and operate more like comprehensive institutions. Many of these former liberal arts colleges now call themselves universities offering professional and graduate degree programs. This mission creep began in the 1960s and has continued, reducing the number of true liberal arts institutions. Between the closures due to financial difficulties and the mission creep there are now fewer than 300 liberal arts colleges remaining. These closures and changes of mission have also shifted the power dynamics with these institutions. Where you sit academically and/or administratively may impact your power or the power of your position, but the changes mentioned will also impact that power dynamic as well (see Chapter 4).

Associate's Colleges

There are several types of associate's colleges (Carnegie classification title) whose educational offerings and functions differ based on their respective mission. There are junior colleges, technical and vocational colleges, city colleges, and community colleges. According to Cohen and Brawer (2008) the term junior college was applied to the private two-year colleges while community college was used to describe the publicly supported colleges. Additionally, the for-profit schools have typically been called vocational or technical colleges. Today all of these institutions are commonly grouped together and referred to as community or associate's colleges.

These colleges may take on one of many organizational structures. As these institutions continue to grow in size and complexity their organizational structures begin to resemble those of large research universities. Historically, these colleges offered associate degrees and certificates only. However, recently several states have granted these institutions the authority to offer baccalaureate degrees, dramatically influencing the organizational structures and power dynamics. This mission creep continues to blur the lines between institutional types and complicates making comparisons between institutions and even classifying them, i.e. the organizational structures (Figure 3.3) of these institutions are becoming similar to those of the research oriented institutions.

There are two important differences between two-year and four-year colleges. First is the degree offerings, certificates and associate degrees vs. bachelor's and advanced degrees. Associate's college will also have many certificate and career oriented programs, such as dental hygienist, accounting, emergency medical technology, welding, automotive technology,

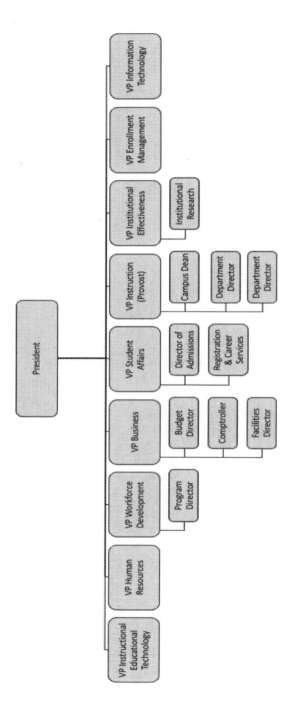

Figure 3.3 Community College Model

ORGANIZATIONAL CONTEXT

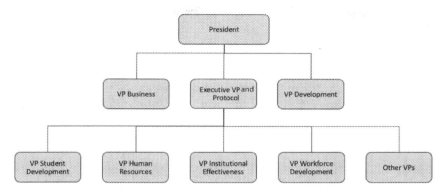

Figure 3.4 Executive VP Model

etc. Second is the connection to the community through its workforce development programs.

Executive Vice-President Model

In recent years many larger institutions, regardless of type (Research, Baccalaureate, or Associate's), have adopted a slightly different model by inserting a senior or executive vice-president into the hierarchical structure (Figure 3.4). In this model, the executive vice-president typically has expanded powers and quite often supervises one or more of the other vice-presidents. In most cases this executive vice-president also serves either as the provost or the vice-president for business and administration.

The executive vice-president has expanded authority (power) and is involved to a greater degree than the other VPs in the day-to-day decision-making and is often viewed as the internal president, thus freeing up the president to spend more time on fundraising and lobbying activities.

As you review the organizational structures above, recognize that they are being provided to give you a general idea as to how the organization functions, and who may have positional or legitimate power over others within the institution. Remember, these charts do not necessarily represent the institution's communication structure. Lines of communication do not always follow lines of supervision. As an employee, understanding your institution's actual communication structure may be even more important. Every organization has formal and informal communication channels. The informal lines of communication are where power can play an important role as to whose message gets heard and by whom. Equally or perhaps more important is who is the receiver of the information being shared; the more people sharing information with you the greater your power can be (Battilana and Casciaro, 2010). It is not uncommon for individuals to develop relationships with individuals throughout an institution and at varying levels within the hierarchy. Perhaps you served as an outside member on a search committee and were able to establish a relationship with a director or vice-president of a different functional area. Or you may have been asked to serve on a university-wide committee, such as the budget committee, where you now have access to a few vice-presidents and several deans and directors. These opportunities give people access to others in an institution they would not typically have and this level of access can become a source of power (Chapter 4). As Gilley (2006) states, "quite simply, organizational understanding is evident when you demonstrate an awareness of how things get done and who is essential in the execution of critical job functions" (p. 13), which is important to your success.

Institutions of higher education appear to be structured hierarchies with a position for every task. However, March and Cohen (1974) place these institutions in "a class of organizations that can be called organized anarchies" (p. 2). They go on to describe them as "characterized by problematic goals, unclear technology (it does not understand its own processes), and fluid participation [participants vary in the amount of time and effort they devote to the organization]" (p. 3). This class of organizations may help explain why there is such an assortment of organizational missions and structures within higher education. And perhaps it can shed some light on the power dynamics within these interdependent institutions.

SENIOR ADMINISTRATIVE POSITIONS/FUNCTIONAL AREAS

Within higher education institutions there are some titles that are often used interchangeably but may have slightly different functions depending on the state or campus structure. For example, the terms chancellor and president can refer to either the Chief Executive Officer (CEO) of a system or of an individual institution. Similarly, the titles of senior academic officer on university campuses are typically either the academic vice-president or provost. On most smaller liberal arts campuses, the senior academic officer may be called the academic vice-president or dean of the college. To date, there is not a common lexicon for titles within educational institutions so, when examining the figures presented in this chapter, remember that titles will vary depending on the individual institution's preference.

Academic Affairs

> The great constant across American campuses is that the faculty are the heart of the institution ... They are the nexus of innovation, tradition and creativity where education comes alive on a campus ... the daily watchdogs and commentators who shape college policy
>
> (Mitchell and King, 2018, pp. 144, 145)

The faculty and the curriculum are the backbone of every college and university and it is the senior academic officer (SAO) who is responsible for leading this division. The SAO will typically have one of two position titles, Provost or Vice-President. The size and complexity of the institution dictate the overall structure of this area. SAO offices at larger institutions with multiple colleges will have several subordinate staff, such as associate, assistant, or vice-provosts (see Figure 3.5) as well as various college deans. With the exception of college deans, these subordinate staff do not have direct authority over faculty but rather oversee support functions such as curricular processes, collective bargaining, or assessment and accreditation among others. At some institutions, the senior academic affairs officer may also oversee the division of student affairs.

While the subordinate staff may not have line authority, that does not necessarily limit their influence in academic matters. SAOs will usually surround themselves with trusted advisors and will oftentimes rely more on their counsel than that of the academic deans.

Historically, the SAO position was considered the stepping stone to the presidency. However, over the last decade or so higher education institutions have been recruiting college deans and others from outside of the academy to serve as presidents. Unlike assistant/associate/vice-provosts, deans are

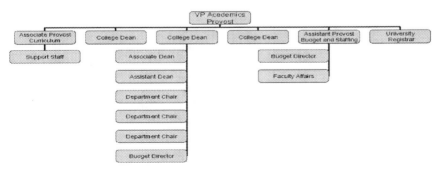

Figure 3.5 Academic Affairs

being recruited because of their budget and fundraising responsibilities in addition to their ability to develop relationships with faculty. Many of the non-academic higher education leaders are coming from the corporate world or from state or federal government positions. These individuals may be brought in for their demonstrated leadership abilities, political connections, business acumen, or fundraising abilities depending on institutional need.

In some institutions, primarily those with de-centralized budget models, the provost's role and subsequently power, has been weakened. Deans have more control over their colleges' resources and while the provost supervises the deans, it will be the deans who allocate the resources across their respective colleges. This decentralization has also moved the dean into the role of fundraiser for the college, giving deans this experience while provosts continue to focus internally, again weakening the actual power and influence of the provost in some institutions.

Administrative Affairs/Business and Finance

These divisions of institutions are generally headed by a vice-president and encompass non-academic units such as campus operations (maintenance, building and grounds, custodial services, and utilities), parking services, bursar (student billing), payroll, university budget office, procurement, institutional investments, and campus safety. At many institutions, these divisions will have the largest staff, but not necessarily the largest budget. It is of utmost importance to note here that while the vice-president in the business or finance area supervises the administration of the college or university budget, this office is not responsible for *determining* that budget. Every institution has its own budgeting process that usually includes input from a wide variety of institutional stakeholders such as faculty, staff, and in some instances, students, for whom the institution exists.

Human Resources

At many institutions, this division may be housed within the Administrative Affairs division, but at larger institutions it will have its own vice-president and supporting staff (Figure 3.6). Within this unit, you will find the institution's offices of compensation and benefits, training and development, affirmative action, staffing (albeit not faculty), employee orientation, employee wellness, and employee assistance program. Additionally, this is the office that usually is responsible for performing due diligence/background checks. It is unusual for this office to have the hiring authority, but it does hold quite a bit of influence in the hiring process.

ORGANIZATIONAL CONTEXT

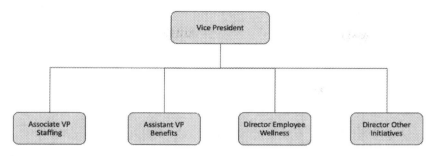

Figure 3.6 Human Resources

Institutional Research (IR)

Typically, this is subordinated in another division on the campus and will oftentimes have an assistant or associate vice-president as its leader. In larger institutions, however, Institutional Research may be a stand-alone unit, while in smaller and mid-sized institutions, this unit may be housed in academic affairs or within the administrative services area. This is an important unit when you are in need of data to support your point or to refute others'. This is the unit on campus responsible for providing data about the institution, its students, faculty, and staff to its internal and external stakeholders. While other units may collect data for their specific needs, the IR office is responsible for reporting institutional data to governmental agencies (U.S. Department of Education, State finance office), regional and professional accrediting bodies, and in most cases rankings organizations.

University presidents and corporate leaders agree on the importance of good data. Dr. Al Green, former CEO of Kent Displays, said, "The toughest thing is getting accurate information." And Mr. Jim Tressel President of Youngstown State University said, "If you don't have good IR you can't be successful [as] there will be no analytical thinking only anecdotal. You don't make good decisions without good IR. You need strong verifiable data, then you can make good decisions."

Advancement/Development

This is the fundraising arm of the institution and in today's world an institution without a fundraising arm is destined for very difficult financial times, if not outright financial failure. This area (see Figure 3.7) may include annual giving, major gifts, planned giving, and alumni affairs. The funds raised through these offices help institutions award scholarships,

41

THE CONTEXT OF POWER AND LEADERSHIP IN HIGHER EDUCATION

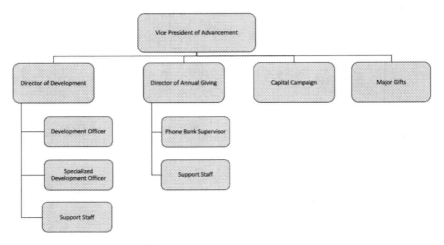

Figure 3.7 Advancement/Development

renovate or build new facilities, supplement faculty salaries (endowed chairs/professorships), provide travel funding, and supplement operational expenditures. In many large institutions this area has been slightly decentralized with development officers/directors housed in individual colleges and other units like athletics and student affairs.

Communications and Marketing

Institutions of higher education have realized that a coordinated marketing effort is needed to establish *brand awareness* and to communicate its mission externally and internally. This is the unit responsible for developing the institution's tag line such as *Excellence in Action* or *Preparing Tomorrow's Leaders Today*. It also promotes the institution through local and national press releases. Messages might be as simple as notices to students' hometown newspapers about who made the Dean's List or as complicated as damage control for some kind of scandal on your campus. In many institutions, this unit must give its approval for any type of publication or announcement that reaches outside the institution. This becomes more challenging as social media becomes omnipresent. With students, faculty, and administrators Tweeting and SnapChatting, it is difficult for the marketing and communications staff to keep an eye on all communication efforts, so they may oftentimes have to rely on college or departmental level communication or marketing personnel to keep them informed.

ORGANIZATIONAL CONTEXT

Enrollment Management

While the function has been around as long as institutions have been in existence, the division of enrollment management is relatively new, arriving on campuses beginning in earnest during the 1980s. Figure 3.8 shows a structure that includes admissions, financial aid, and the registrar. You may find these functional areas housed within the student affairs division as was the case at most institutions prior to this movement. Most institutions have realized the importance of coordinating admissions and financial aid decisions to maximize the yield rate of each incoming class. Within some organizational structures the registrar's office may be housed within enrollment management as opposed to academic affairs. The premise behind enrollment management is to coordinate admissions decisions and financial aid offers to maximize the number of first-time students enrolling in the institution. You may also find this area taking the lead on retention efforts on some campuses.

Student Affairs

This is the division that works directly with students, when and even before they arrive on campus. Student Affairs (SA) exists primarily to ensure the out-of-class experiences complement students' academic pursuits. As

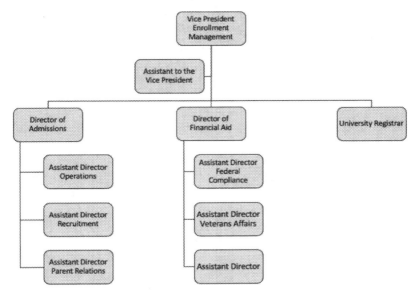

Figure 3.8 Enrollment Management

43

THE CONTEXT OF POWER AND LEADERSHIP IN HIGHER EDUCATION

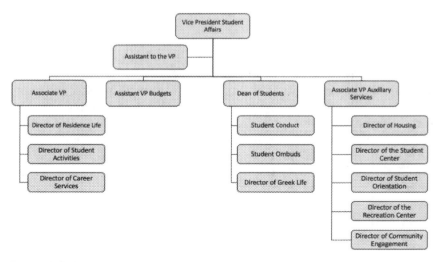

Figure 3.9 Student Affairs

shown in Figure 3.9, the more common functional areas in the division include student activities and organizations, residence life, recreational services (including intramurals), Greek life (social fraternities and sororities), student orientation, career services, non-traditional student services, veterans affairs, student government, judicial affairs, counseling and health services. Additionally, the student affairs division is sought to provide leadership in the retention of currently enrolled students. Mitchell and King (2018) point out that "the climate created by student life carries with it powerful impressions of what the college or university values, and what a college values translates into who self-selects into its applicant pool" (p. 85).

Many of the services provided within this division are supported through student fees collected simultaneously with each student's tuition. However, some of the functional areas within this division will also attach a user fee that is collected at the time the service is provided (e.g. admission to events such as concerts). Typically, the fees collected are not intended to cover the entire cost of the activity or event but rather serve as a partial user fee that helps the unit defray the costs of the production.

Student affairs is an integral part of every college or university in the U.S. and unfortunately it is not always understood by other campus administrators or board members. From a politics and power perspective it is very important for SA staff to work with colleagues across campus to network and to demonstrate their value and contribution to the mission of the institution. The more SA professionals can interact with their academic and business affairs colleagues, the greater influence they can have in the decision-making processes of the institution. While it is important to have a vice-president level position and a voice at the cabinet level, it is equally important for mid-level administrators to be active contributors across the campus. As student activism increases and students demonstrate or protest on our campuses, whether it is free speech advocates or gun rights activists pushing for conceal and carry laws, it will be the student affairs professionals who are there to help ensure the experience is safe and educational.

Auxiliary Services

This is perhaps the most misunderstood set of departments on our campuses. Hopefully, this brief section will give non-auxiliary professionals a better understanding of how these departments operate. Auxiliary services typically, do not have a separate vice-president but rather are generally found within the divisions of student affairs or administrative/business affairs depending on the university's mission or operating philosophy. An auxiliary service is a unit (department) on the campus that is supposed to be self-sufficient, i.e. it must generate enough revenue through fees to cover its operating expenses. The most common auxiliary units on a campus are student housing and food service, the student center (union), and recreational services. Three other areas that may operate in this manner are parking services, student health services, and at some large institutions, intercollegiate athletics.

Auxiliary units are responsible for generating their operating revenues through user fees which can be built into the student fee structure that all students pay as part of their tuition and fees. Housing and food service are the exception in that they charge the students residing in the residence halls and using the dining facilities only. For other auxiliary units, many institutions charge students a fee whether the student uses that facility/service or not. So, a student may never use the recreation center, participate in a student activity, or use the student health center; but the student still pays the fee.

The financial independence of auxiliary units can create confusion on campuses among internal and external stakeholders, especially when money is tight and these areas seem to have excess financial resources in their coffers. Because they are auxiliary units, they will more often than not run a surplus and put the excess money into a reserve or rainy-day account. This money is not supposed to be distributed to other units but rather is there in case of unexpected costs such as a roof leak in a residence hall; the need for new equipment in the food service kitchen, or needing to replace the heating and cooling units in the recreation center or student union. The self-generated funds allow these units to keep on top of routine maintenance and avoid the deferred maintenance problems on the rest of the campus.

However, because of the resources these units control, they can have certain power and potential influence over some other units on a campus. Oftentimes, the level of power is determined by the leadership of the units or the division under which they fall. I have seen instances of auxiliary units expanding their physical facilities while the institution as a whole is experiencing significant fiscal constraints. Likewise, I have witnessed auxiliary units being used like a bank by the central administration when financial problems arose. In some instances, the administrators responsible for auxiliary services were unable to protect their reserve accounts or they were required to pay a larger overhead/shared services fee (tax) to the institution's general fund to help defray the institution's overhead costs.

THE FOR-PROFIT SECTOR

Two of the key distinctions between for-profit and not-for-profit institutions are their tax status and what they are permitted to do with excess revenues. For-profit institutions must pay corporate income tax on their excess revenues (profit) whereas not-for-profit institutions do not. In the for-profit sector, institutional profits are distributed amongst its owners while at not-for-profit institutions, the profit remains with the institution and must be reinvested in the institution.

During the past several years, for-profit colleges and universities have experienced numerous closures and mergers. Several closures came about because of fraudulent activities, while others were simply decisions made by owners based on lack of profitability. According to the National Center for Educational Statistics, in Spring 2016, there were over 4,100 degree granting institutions in the U.S. Of those institutions, 617 were for-profit. This represents slightly less than 15% of all degree granting institutions. This sector is down slightly from 2014 (710 institutions) but still significantly higher than in 2000 (207). The recent decline is due in part to the closure of some of these institutions (e.g. Corinthian Colleges and Education Corporation of America, among others), while a few others changed their tax status to not-for-profit (e.g. Grand Canyon University).

These proprietary institutions are typically privately owned by an individual or family or they are owned by a corporation and, in some instances, their stock may be publicly traded. The organizational structures can vary widely depending on ownership type. Many of the positions commonly found within the not-for-profit institutions are not necessarily present within the for-profit sector. However, many of the functions, such as marketing, recruitment and admissions, financial aid, and academic

ORGANIZATIONAL CONTEXT

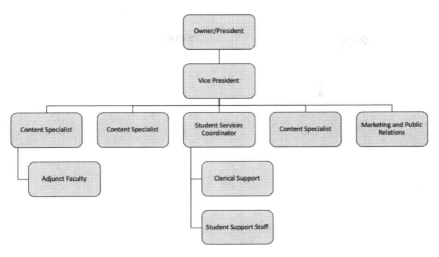

Figure 3.10 Privately Owned University

affairs are present. Two structures are shown below. Figure 3.10 represents a structure for a privately owned (individual or family) institution. Figure 3.11 represents a structure for the larger national (perhaps international) universities owned by corporations.

As you look at the organization charts, you will notice that for-profit institutions do not have as many vice-presidents nor do they have some of the student support services found at most not-for-profit institutions. These

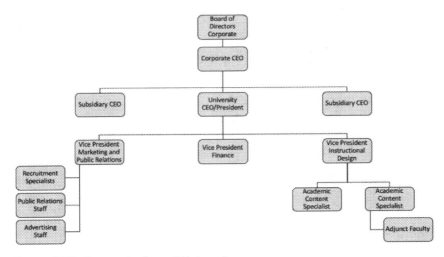

Figure 3.11 Corporate Owned University

institutions run lean operations because the motivation is to make money and provide a return on the investment of their respective owners. It is not about students but rather about profits – the business just happens to be educating students. Additionally, in the for-profit sector, corporate owned institutions' governing boards are called boards of directors, not trustees or regents. In this sector, board members are appointed by the board chair and like other corporate boards, they are often paid a yearly stipend. In the privately owned institutions, you will notice that there is no governing board, rather the owner/president sits atop the chart and is in complete control of the institution and its operations.

CONCLUDING COMMENTS

Understanding the organizational structure of an institution permits new administrators (or applicants) to view the institution's hierarchical structure and positional (legitimate) power. Knowing where you sit on the organizational chart may help you better understand and perhaps appreciate your position. This chapter has been about the hierarchy of the institution and the potential power that comes with the position. Understanding the organizational structure and at least a little about the varying functional areas may be helpful in navigating the political and power dynamics of your institution. Every decision you make within an institution impacts a variety of individuals depending on their position within the division of labor outlined in the organizational structure. "A central feature of modern organizations is interdependence, where no one has complete autonomy, where most employees are tied to many others by their work, technology, management systems, and hierarchy" (Kotter, 1998, p. 44), therefore, as an administrator, to accomplish your goals, you will oftentimes need to rely on people throughout the institution over whom you have no direct authority. For example, academic deans are responsible for the finances of their colleges, but they have little to no control over the recruitment of their students. That is done by the admissions office, which recruits for the entire university, not specific colleges or programs. Recognizing this interdependence will encourage you to develop relationships with colleagues before they are necessary. It becomes easier to work with individuals with whom you have a positive relationship than with those you have not met.

In reviewing organizational charts many individuals may aspire to climb towards the top or perhaps covet a specific position or title. Maxwell (2013) cautions individuals who are enamored of position titles – "people who rely on rules, regulations, policies, and organizational charts to control their people may be bosses but they are never leaders" (p. 7). Later he warns that some leaders thrive in political environments, doing what they can to maximize their staff and their budgets, ultimately trying to increase their own power and influence.

I strongly encourage you to heed Maxwell's warnings. If you are looking for advancement, understand why moving up may not be the best move for you, depending where you are in your career and what you hope to accomplish. Al Green and Dan Mahony weigh in on aspiring to a position for the sake of the position or title. As Al Green (former CEO Kent Displays) states:

> If your singular goal is to be on top in the corner office, I've never seen that work ... those people get found out and it's not going to work ... you have to be motivated by other things ... you have to take passion of each of the steps along the way.

Similarly, Dan Mahony, President of Winthrop University said, "make sure you want the job you are applying for. Sometimes people move up a level beyond where they are happy simply because they think they should move to the next level." Oftentimes, this results in the Peter Principle – people are promoted to their level of incompetence (Peter, 1969).

Finally, you need to recognize that your view of your organization depends on in which chair you are sitting. Much like climbing a tree, the higher you climb, the further you can see; the further you see, the better your perspective of your institution and the better you will understand your surroundings. The higher you climb within your institution's hierarchy the more of the institution you see, and hopefully, the better you understand its inner workings. So, regardless of which path you are on within higher education, it becomes important to familiarize yourself with as much of the institution as possible; as President Deeb (Trocaire College) said, "when you move up within the institution you are expected to have a broader view of the institution." Several university presidents I interviewed mentioned that, at the cabinet or executive level, it is important for individuals to put the institution ahead of their respective areas of responsibility. Figure 3.12 offers some suggested questions for you to

> *Who gets things accomplished?*
> *Who do other administrators listen to?*
> *What are the symbols of power at this institution?*
> *Who controls the resources you need to be successful?*
> *Who controls the agendas?*

Figure 3.12 Identifying Power Players on Your Campus

answer that will assist you in identifying some of the powerful individuals on your campuses. These questions are also addressed later in this text.

REFLECTIVE QUESTIONS

1. In looking at your current division or unit, diagram the communication network and compare that with your current organizational chart.
2. What types of power does your position have?
3. What types of power does your supervisor have?
4. Are there benefits to a shared governance system? Where does the power lie in such a system?

POSSIBLE REFLECTION QUESTION/ACTIVITY

Identify your organizational structure. Imagine that you are preparing for a position at a university with an organizational structure that is very different than yours (e.g. Large Research to Privately Owned). In terms of organizational power, what powers can you expect to be transferred and what powers can you expect to be lost in your transition into the new organization? Alternatively, which powers will be gained? How might you prepare to showcase your abilities to fit the new organizational structure and remain competitive with those who have already experienced success in the target organization – and how can you prepare to win over those in the target organization who might be opposed to your university structure?

POSSIBLE REFLECTION QUESTION/ACTIVITY

Identify your institution's organizational structure. Outline your personal five-year plan to advance within this organization. What positions/individuals on your road to advancement are currently not within your professional or communications network? Will those individuals likely be in the same positions within your five-year plan? Identify practical steps and opportunities to network with these individuals as you enact your personal five-year plan.

Appendix

ADMINISTRATOR PERSONALITIES

I thought that after discussing the hierarchical structures of higher education institutions this would be an appropriate time to take a closer look at some *administrative personalities* that inhabit these bureaucracies. The listing of *administrative personalities* in this chapter should reflect individuals whom you will encounter or may have already encountered in your administrative career. This is not meant to be an exhaustive list, but rather is a list of the more common individuals whom I have experienced during my 40+-year career in higher education. Within every organization, individuals play multiple roles based on their respective positions within the hierarchical structure. In these roles, administrators often adopt different personalities depending on which role they are playing. As I describe these personalities, it may be very easy for you to place your colleagues into one or more of the personalities depending on the institutional context and the situation at hand. Similarly, your colleagues may see you in several of these descriptions. How you view your colleagues and how your colleagues view you is partially dependent on where you and they sit within the hierarchy of the institution.

THE ATHLETE

These are the individuals who seem to succeed regardless of the task at hand. They are intelligent, incredibly flexible in how they handle situations, entrepreneurial in nature, are results focused, and get things done. They have stamina, energy, focus, and self-control among other traits. These individuals rarely seem stressed and practice routines that keep themselves organized and energized throughout the day.

The Athlete is more likely to tell you what you *need* to hear rather than tell you what you *want* to hear. These individuals can be excellent sounding boards for new ideas and are good colleagues to have at your side, especially during tough times.

THE LAP DOG

These are the administrators who can also be considered *yes* people, but I believe they take *yes* to a new level. These individuals will typically sing the praises of the institutional leaders (anyone above them in the hierarchy) regardless of the decisions being made, and will often publicly admonish those who do not agree with the decision or direction the institution is headed. They *gush* over every decision made or new marketing materials developed, making it seem like the institution would be in such trouble if it weren't for the current leadership team (oftentimes including themselves on that team). *The Lap Dogs* believe that by complimenting those above them in the hierarchy and helping them to feel good about themselves, they in turn will garner more power and enhance their relationship with their superiors.

These individuals are not concerned about the institution's success, but rather are focused on whether the senior leaders *like* them. They are most often recognized for their *loyalty* rather than their *abilities*. They tend to have aspirations for higher level positions and believe that connections, not competence will help them advance.

THE PUNDIT

There are two distinct characteristics of these administrators. First, they refuse to admit they are incorrect or that they do not know the answer or have a solution. They have the need to be right all of the time, or at least have an answer, and they want everyone to know just how smart they (think they) are. Second, they always have a very strong opinion about every topic being discussed, regardless of their level of knowledge of the subject at hand. They will speak with confidence and in a forceful tone, giving the impression that they have sufficient knowledge.

THE BUREAUCRAT

These are the rule-bound by-the-book individuals who ensure that everyone follows *their interpretation* of the institution's policies, practices, or collective bargaining agreement (in union shops). There is no room for other interpretations and they will make sure that those beneath them in the hierarchy do as they are told without deviation. They have a difficult time delegating authority because they believe tasks need to be performed their way. They work best when people do what they are told and show blind faith in the bureaucrat's decisions.

Bureaucrats are uncomfortable in entrepreneurial settings or where innovation and creativity abound. They prefer consistency and stability and are most effective when the status quo is desired.

THE EEYORE™

Named for the beloved donkey in the children's story, Winnie the Pooh™, these are the individuals who always look at the negative side of the issue.

Eeyores are not naysayers who try to undermine decisions or derail projects, but rather these administrators are always looking for the catch. If you offer to provide additional resources for their department or unit they will complain about not being involved in the decision to do so and will continually look for the *strings attached*. If you suggest that they should hire additional staff, they will take it as a criticism of their ability to accomplish the organizational goals or a critique of the contributions of their current staff. You get the picture: nothing is ever as it seems regardless of the benefit. *Tut tut looks like rain.*

THE COLLABORATOR

Always willing to team up on a project, wants to help, and is willing to recruit others to join the team. This is not Pollyanna-ish behavior, rather it is genuine enthusiasm for getting others involved. They believe that you need to involve as many stakeholders as possible so you can ensure the decision will be well received by all. A bit idealistic perhaps, but also very optimistic.

These individuals can help boost team morale and are very useful when implementing new programs or policies that others may view as controversial. They are quite good at helping gain the support or buy-in from others in the institution.

THE DECEPTICON™

Based on the villains in the Transformer movies, these are individuals who publicly appear to be one type of person but in reality are quite different. They can come across as very trusting and trustworthy and you would swear they are engaging in good faith – but in fact they are doing just the opposite behind your back, doing all they can to undermine you and your authority. They will plant doubt and whisper mistrust, all while appearing to support and encourage you. They are great at hiding their true intentions and enjoy setting people up for failure.

These individuals see everyone as a threat to their success. They do not like to see others succeed so they actively attempt to sabotage others' projects or programs.

THE SINGER

Me, me, me, me! It is all about me. They are convinced that self-promotion is the key to their success. These are the individuals who have the need to *make an entrance* into the event, even if it is simply a meeting, they like to have everyone's attention. What they lack in administrative talent, they make up for in egocentric behavior.

Blaming of others is a given for *The Singer*. If a project fails, regardless of their level of involvement, it is never their fault. Similar to the pundit, it is extremely difficult (borderline impossible) for them to admit a mistake. They are always looking for the proverbial scapegoat to whom they can affix the blame. *Singers* will also do what they can to discredit others in the organization by belittling their credentials or accomplishments and, in some instances, through personal attacks. They can be masters at *damning with faint praise*. Many times they work behind the scenes to undermine the ideas of others while promoting their own agenda.

THE FLOATER

Always seeming to drift along or go with the flow. *Floaters* are not yes people because they do not pretend to champion the projects, instead they follow along quietly, going with the flow of the leadership team. They do not seek attention and rarely, if ever, will they publicly disagree with a decision. They do not like to deviate from the status quo and prefer not to make any waves.

Oftentimes, others will see these individuals as good team players simply because they don't ask questions or make suggestions. Unfortunately, their unwillingness to contribute ideas or challenge assumptions can create problems instead of helping move towards solutions.

THE COUNTER BALANCER

Likes to slow the process down by exposing problems or limitations to ideas being presented. These administrators are not necessarily trying to stop the idea from moving forward, rather they are trying to ensure that it is well thought out and realistic, based on the institutional mission and available resources. Their motto is *question everything*.

These individuals make very good team members because they help prevent the group from making an incorrect or inappropriate decision based on a perceived need to hurry. When making presentations they are well organized and prepared to answer questions. They believe it is far better to put their energies into the decision-making process than to spend time correcting mistakes later.

THE COMPETITOR

These are individuals who view everything as a competition or a fight they must win. They do not know how to separate personal competition from institutional goals/objectives. They are too focused on winning, calling the shots, and not wanting others to be seen as contributing positively to the institution. They lose sight of what is important for the institution and more importantly, for the individual stakeholder groups for which they are responsible. Every situation is viewed in *win–lose* terms – *if someone else looks good, I must look bad*. Ultimately, they see everyone as a threat to their success.

By taking competition to the extreme, *Competitors* can do damage to an organization by creating a difficult, perhaps toxic, work environment. They have difficulty trusting others and when they do delegate tasks they make it clear that the final decision is theirs. Regardless of how well done, they will review the work and *correct* it so they can claim the end result as theirs.

THE SOURCE

Individuals who are *The Source* are the people at your institution or in your profession who are very well connected and seem to know everyone and perhaps more importantly, everyone knows them. They may act as lynchpins on the campus, holding things together based on the relationships they have developed or they may be the go-to person for connecting you to colleagues in your field. These individuals also tend to be very good at remembering names and faces, once you meet them, they will remember you.

TWO TYPES OF BOSSES

Peter Drucker said that there are two kinds of bosses; those who like stories and those who like data. I prefer to label them as the Reference Librarian and the Data Analyst. Which of these is more descriptive of your preferences for receiving information?

The Data Analyst

These supervisors want to see the data: not just a snapshot, but the verifiable data. They will ask tough questions and are concerned about the sources of data and methods used to collect the data. When you prepare reports for these individuals, do not spare the details. Your executive summary will have some highlights and the key points you want to get across, but the body, or at least appendices, will need to go much deeper into the data and any identifiable trends.

With budgets, save the interpretations and stick to the numbers. For most analytics, the numbers are the story, or at least tell the story. They will create their own narrative around the numbers and they tend to prefer their interpretation, not yours.

The Reference Librarian

These bosses like the story, the narrative that is developed from the data. Don't confuse them with too much data, they tend to *zone out* when confronting the numbers on pages of spreadsheets.

With budget information, make sure you include a narrative piece to explain the numbers and trends being presented. The reference librarian likes to have data interpreted, so providing brief snippets or visuals such as charts or concept maps will be greatly appreciated. Oftentimes a success story or two can help evoke emotions that can lead to discussions necessary for strategic planning.

REFLECTIVE QUESTIONS

1. Which "administrator personality" do you see yourself relating to the most?
2. In terms of your organization, how do you see administrator personalities in action?
3. Can you identify these personalities in your institution?
4. How would your co-workers classify you?

Part II

Power in Higher Education

Chapter Four
Symbols and Sources of Power

Within any institution there are a variety of symbols and sources of power that can help one identify who the *power players* are and which units may be held in high regard. There is no formula that provides a way to calculate the level of influence, instead there are multiple indicators that help an observer or participant contextualize each institution and the power dynamics within. Throughout your career you will realize that the importance of the symbols and sources described below will be valued differently depending on a variety of factors including, size and complexity of the institution, type of institution, location of the institution, and the financial health of the institution.

SYMBOLS OF POWER

In any organization there are symbols of power, and many are remnants of bygone days, i.e. the corner office or office with a window (especially for faculty), number of subordinates, size of budget, and impressive job title. There are other symbols of power not quite as obvious, such as clothing or committee membership, that can be equally or perhaps even more important as a symbol of power. Institutions of higher education are no exception as we have numerous symbols of power that exist today. In this section I will look at some of the more obvious symbols of power in higher education.

Position Title

One of the first symbols of power that comes to mind is an individual's position title. Titles can say quite a lot about the individual with whom you are meeting or discussing. A person's title conveys a certain amount of cachet, which is why in some private sector companies you will find more Sales Managers or VPs of Sales than actual sales associates. In higher education we may not be as liberal with Vice-Presidential titles, but the majority of our position titles carry some specific connotations (see Chapter 3). For example, at most institutions, the title of *director* is viewed as a mid-management position and implies the individual is responsible for a unit/department/division or portion thereof. It also implies supervisory responsibility and budget oversight. Similarly, the title of "coordinator" is viewed as an entry or lower level managerial or administrative position that has limited supervisory responsibilities and rarely carries meaningful budget responsibilities. When looking specifically at the academic affairs units you will find *department chairs* and *school directors* to be entry-level managerial roles. However, unlike most other entry-level positions, these academic administrative roles can have significant supervisory and budget responsibilities. The more senior administrative positions on the academic side that maintain significant budget and supervisory responsibilities are *deans* and *provosts* or other *vice-presidents*. At larger institutions you will find a host of assistant and associate, and director titles that provide support for deans, provosts, and other vice presidents.

Physical Facilities – Office Size, Windows, and Location

An individual's office can say a lot about how much that person is valued at the institution and a bit about her or his status within the institution. How large is the office, what type(s) of furnishings are provided, is there a seating area with a table and chairs, does the office have a window? Additionally, where your office is located might matter, as proximity to those with influence or to those you hope to influence comes into play. As you examine your institution and you look at office placement, what offices are closest to the president? Which VPs have informal access to the president and which VPs are located on different floors or perhaps a different building?

The building in which you and your unit are housed also signals your status within the institution to those inside and outside the academy. If the building in which you are housed has been recently renovated, it sends a very different message than being in a building that looks like a poster for deferred maintenance on your campus. When your physical facilities look rundown or poorly maintained, it can be challenging for others to take you seriously. This then becomes, in part, the rationale for senior administrators to have their offices painted or redecorated, especially when they are new to the institution or position.

For institutional presidents there is an additional aspect of location that comes into play, that of the location of the president's residence. Some institutions believe it is important for the president to be located on or near the campus in a university-owned house, while other institutions prefer to provide a housing allowance or stipend letting the president choose the location of her/his residence.

Location in the Hierarchy

Your position's location on the organizational chart is usually correlated with your position title. At the divisional level you typically find a vice-president at the top of the chart. The closer your position is to the top or the organizational chart the more powerful (legitimate power) the position and the more responsibility and authority you will have. As you look at your institution's organizational chart you will see which positions have authority and responsibility for other individuals and units/departments. Remember, one of the first rules of management is *you are responsible for everything beneath you in the hierarchy* (Kretovics, 2011).

Access to Those Above You in the Hierarchy

You may be in a position that is not located very high on the organizational chart or perhaps it is not listed at all. This does not mean you do not have power. Your power may come based on your access to those above you in the hierarchy. You may have a personal relationship with someone in a senior leadership position affording you access to that individual that would not ordinarily come with the level of your current position (connectional power). Or as mentioned in Chapter 3, you may have served on a search or other committee with more senior administrators. You may be in a fitness class with one or more senior leaders or your social circles may overlap. This type of *informal* power can be seen by others as a symbol of power attributed to you.

Professional Business Attire

Yes, business suits still indicate, or at least give the perception of, a certain level of power. Look around at your president, vice-presidents, and deans: how many are wearing professional business attire? Crafting and presenting an image is important and if you desire to move up it never hurts to dress like those above you in the hierarchy. When the Board of Trustees is on campus, or during orientation or commencement, you will most likely see administrators dressed in their "Sunday best" to convey a level of professionalism and, yes, power. As Pfeffer (2010a) suggests, how you look can help how you are perceived – "if you dress and act the part of a powerful person you begin to look like a person who fits the position to which you aspire" (p. 136).

Committee Membership

Shared governance and institutional citizenship are highly valued within higher education and Bolino (1999) points out that being recognized as a "good citizen" within an organization is part of an individual's impression management, which in turn can help the individual develop additional power within the institution. Volunteering for college or institutional committees is viewed by most as institutional citizenship. Therefore, volunteering for the *right* committees can help you be seen as a good institutional citizen and may also provide access to the powers-that-be within your institution. Which committees are the *right* committees to secure membership will depend on the institutional (and administrative) priorities of each campus. In most shared governance models there are specific committees making decisions which impact the institution as a whole and these committees are viewed as important by most in positions of power. For example, the budget committee or the strategic planning committee will oftentimes have senior administrative leaders such as the VP for Business and the Provost. Other committees on the academic side, such as the university curriculum committee and the promotion and tenure review committees, provide regular access to deans, department chairs, and the Provost. Attending these meetings and making useful contributions can make a positive impression upon the other committee members. If nothing else, at least you will have the opportunity to talk personally with individuals who may be able to help advance your career. As a new administrator, sitting on search committees can also play an important role in elevating oneself within the institution. Plus, you can see first hand how others perceive the mission of the institution. Being on a search committee for a senior administrator or dean can provide you with access to some of the more influential people on the campus and the higher the position profile the more recognition the committee normally receives. This also gives you *first access* to the new administrator and most new administrators remember who was on their search committee and may actually feel a sense of commitment to those members.

Your Digital Footprint

With everchanging technologies and the increasing use of these technologies in almost every aspect of running an institution of higher education, your digital footprint has never been more important. This is a newer symbol of power in higher education and it appears to be becoming increasingly more important with each generation. You and your unit are being evaluated by internal and external stakeholders based on ease of finding you on the institutional website. How many clicks does it take to locate your unit's page? How quickly can someone find you and how much information about you is available?

No single symbol of power determines an individual's level of power. These symbols of power provide you with more data, enabling you to begin forming an impression as to who on the campus has the power to make or influence decisions. As you review your institution to identify the influencers on campus you will also need to consider how those individuals are able to develop or harness the sources of power listed below.

SOURCES OF POWER

In addition to the symbols of power listed above, Jeffrey Pfeffer (1992) identifies several sources of power that seem to transcend organizational structure or industry segment. The following (Figure 4.1) will be discussed as they relate to various functional areas within higher education institutions:

> Develop and Enhance Relationships
>
> Location in the Communication Network
>
> Craft an Individual Reputation
>
> Be in the Right Unit
>
> Control Resources
>
> Surround Yourself with Competence

(Adapted from Pfeffer, 1992)

Figure 4.1 Sources of Power

Enhancing Relationships

Building relationships with the *right* people and in the *right way* can be the key to developing power and political influence within your organization.

Done properly, the relationships you develop and nurture can result in the creation of allies within your institution. These allies can be a significant resource for you in helping forward your administrative agenda while minimizing dissension among the ranks (Pfeffer, 1992). Similarly, Balderston (1995) suggests that "coalition building and bargaining have emerged as important features of the internal workings of universities, and the distribution of power" (p. 8).

Developing relationships knows no boundaries and it is not restricted by one's position title or to higher level administrators. Abbott (2009) suggests that building alliances is useful and as an administrator it is your responsibility to develop a strong relationship with the decision-makers throughout the institution. Additionally, the relationship between leaders and followers is critical, in that people do not like to follow individuals whom they do not know or do not trust.

For lower and mid-level administrators it is important for you to understand how to develop relationships that will create opportunities for you to enhance your power and/or political influence within the institution. Pfeffer (1992) suggests two essential tasks to help develop and nurture relationships within your institution. First, be a nice person, do favors for colleagues throughout the organization, not just those above you in the hierarchy. Secondly, when given the opportunity, hire or promote individuals that you believe to be supportive of you, your department, and who will do good for the institution (see Figure 4.2).

Doing favors can be as simple as volunteering to represent your department/unit by serving on a college- or university-wide committee or representing your institution at a community activity or event. The idea behind doing favors is for you to be remembered as someone who will step up and help out when needed (psychologically creating a *sense of*

Do favors
 The favors are not necessarily requested
 No obligation is specified
 The favor creates a generalized obligation

Hire or promote staff
 Reward based on one's productivity
 Reward individuals loyal to you

(Adapted from Pfeffer, 1992)

Figure 4.2 Developing Relationships

obligation). So when you need something the other party is capable of providing, such as access to resources or influence over a decision, it will be easier to obtain. Vecchio (2007) comments that ingratiation – giving compliments or doing favors – does create a notion of social responsibility or sense of obligation (p. 78). However, there are no guarantees that doing favors will necessarily invoke the reciprocity rule (Bolton and Ockenfels, 2000; Ouchi, 1980).

Similarly, you can also develop relationships by asking others to help you, especially if you are in a lower or mid-level administrative position. Asking someone above you in the hierarchy to mentor you or asking them for guidance can help get you in front of them in a positive light. Plus, most people consider it flattering when someone asks them for guidance or assistance. You must be careful not to abuse the relationship by asking too often, being mindful of their time.

When the time comes to fill a vacancy in your department/unit, seize this as an opportunity to build a team by surrounding yourself with individuals who are willing and able to help you accomplish the goals and objectives you have developed. This is not the time to hire *Lap Dogs* but rather look for the *Athlete* (see Chapter 3 Appendix) committed to your agenda who is also willing to challenge you when needed. *Lap Dogs* tend to diminish your reputation because others will see that you do not hire bright competent staff but prefer to surround yourself with people who tell you what you *want* to hear instead of what you *need* to hear. As you move higher in the organizational chart it becomes more important to hire loyal supporters who share your vision and direction. This may help explain why you tend to see significant turnover at the vice-president level when a new president is hired or at the dean level when a new provost arrives. As Jim Collins (2001) notes, people are not your most important resource – the *right* people are (p. 13).

Finally, when considering the development of relationships, you will realize that there are times in your career where you need to make critical relationships work to further your department's or unit's agenda. Pfeffer (2010a) believes for one to be successful, "you have to get over resentment, jealousies, anger, or anything else that might get in the way of building a relationship where you can get the resources necessary for you to get the job done" (p. 171). You will find, at some point in your career, you may become dependent upon others whom you do not like and in some instances individuals whom you do not respect. As a leader, you cannot let your personal tiffs derail important work. Al Green (former CEO, Kent Displays) mentions "you have to be tolerant of different personalities and skill sets, especially those that don't necessarily meld with yours. And you have to be okay working with people you don't necessarily blend with."

Communication Networks

With whom you communicate and how you communicate has a significant impact on your power and political well-being within your institution. Do you recall when your parents told you that others will judge you based on who your friends are? Turns out they were right. Within any organization and especially within the academy, individuals are oftentimes judged by the colleagues with whom they choose to associate – guilt by association or on the positive side connectional power. Your formal position within the institution affords you with access to certain power and privileges, but your informal position within the institution's communication network is more often a more accurate measure of your power or at least your potential access to power (Pfeffer, 1992). Your power is reflective of who communicates with you rather than with whom you initiate the communication (Battilana and Casciaro, 2010).

There are two key communication networks in every organization, the formal and the informal. The formal network encompasses the individuals and groups that you have regular contact with based on your formal position within the institution. This would include your supervisor, subordinates, and other administrators at similar levels throughout the organization. Informal networks (*Connectional Power*) might also include representation on standing committee meetings. When at those meetings, glance around the table and make note of who is in attendance and who is *represented* by a staff member. Pfeffer (1992) and Battilana and Casciaro (2010) suggest that your informal network is the more important of the two because it is not structured by the hierarchy, giving you access to others outside of the direct reporting lines of the college or university organizational chart.

Your communication network is not restricted to your work environment. The individuals with whom you associate outside of work, or at least outside of the structured work environment, indicate who you have access to and potentially who you may be able to influence. To determine who is in your network, and to a certain extent, in whose network are you in, ask yourself several questions. With whom do you meet on a regular basis? With whom do you socialize outside of the work environment? The higher you are in the institutional structure the more you need to be careful about with whom you associate. As several presidents shared with me, you are the institution's president 24/7 and someone is always watching what you do, with whom you meet, and how you respond to current events.

Most senior administrators have an individual who serves as a gatekeeper. This person has far greater power than the individual's position title would indicate. Controlling access to the administrator's calendar is almost as important as access to the individual. Have you ever tried to schedule an appointment with someone only to be told by the gate-keeper it would be at least a week but, when you go directly to the individual, miraculously you get an appointment for later that same day? If the gate-keeper does not like you or value your position, access to the administrator can be made more difficult. This individual helps the administrator by prioritizing appointments and meetings but this person can also be extremely useful in screening out particular individuals.

As mentioned earlier in this chapter, the location of your office can have an impact on your role in the communication network. The closer you are to the decision-makers the more likely you are to interact with them on a regular basis. Most administrators prefer to have those with whom they most commonly work to be nearby. On a college or university campus you will generally find the president's cabinet members located in the same building as the president because presidents like to have their confidants close or in physical proximity. Usually, there is one notable exception and this is the vice-president of student affairs. Quite often this VP is located in the student center. From a student affairs perspective it shows that the VP is closer and more accessible to the students. From an institutional power perspective it may signal that this position is not valued as much as the other VPs, or this may also indicate that the student affairs division might have less influence with the president than do other vice-presidents. According to Pfeffer (1992) "where one sits has an important effect on the number and content of one's interactions" (p. 121) with the key influencers of the institution.

Establishing a Reputation

You start the process of developing a reputation during your job interview. You are typically asked to highlight your strengths and describe your areas for improvement (weaknesses). If you follow the career coaching approach you will overemphasize your strengths and "turn your weaknesses into strengths", thereby avoiding a discussion of your limitations. This approach is a good way to help cultivate power once in the organization. As Pfeffer (2010a) notes "one of the best ways to acquire and maintain power is to construct a positive image and reputation, in part by coopting others to present you as successful and effective" (p. 12).

As an administrator it is helpful to understand how you are perceived by others, and the only way to do this is by asking those around you. You will need to ask colleagues for feedback on your performance as well as how others perceive you as an administrator and as a person. To ensure the most accurate feedback, you must develop an environment of openness and trust among your colleagues and subordinates. This requires you to be transparent in your decision-making processes. It may take a year or two to develop a reputation as someone who is competent and trustworthy so you must begin immediately. Establishing a record of success in planning and implementing projects or activities, writing grants, publishing research, or high-quality teaching helps to build a positive reputation across campus. According to John Kotter (1998) a key is to establish credibility so that people will believe in you and your message. To do so, realize that people will look at "the track record of the person delivering the message, the content of the message itself, the communicator's reputation for integrity and trustworthiness, and the consistency between words and deeds" (p. 46). The more they know about you and the more they believe in you and your message the more likely they are to trust you.

Recognize, too, that a reputation can be damaged very quickly by a single mistake (see Chapter 9). Picture yourself climbing a rock wall: one misstep and very quickly you are back at the bottom. You do not fall and remain unscathed, as it is more difficult to reestablish a good reputation after it has been damaged than it is to lose it in the first place.

For good or for bad, a reputation is not created overnight, instead it takes a bit of a history with the institution or in the profession to create your persona. Your reputation will be based on what you stand for and your record of successes and/or failures. Gordon A. Eadie believed that *if you don't stand for something you will fall for anything* (https://quoteinvestigator.com), encouraging leaders to make decisions based on values and beliefs. These value-based decisions become part of your reputation. Similarly, your work record, whether one of successes and accomplishments or one of controversy, takes time to develop. Early in your career, when beginning at an institution new to you or if you are in a new position at your current institution, you typically start with a *blank slate* that gets filled in as people observe your performance. If you start early with developing positive relationships and completing tasks, your reputation among your new colleagues will follow suit. As you progress in your career and you switch institutions or move into a new position within your current institution your reputation will follow along (Kretovics, 2011). The more positive the reputation the easier it is to make those moves.

Over five centuries ago, humankind recognized that appearance was important and how others perceived you made a difference in obtaining and maintaining power. According to Skinner (1981), Machiavelli noted that "men in general judge more from appearances than from reality. All men have eyes, but few have the gift of penetration."

Being in the Right Unit

Pfeffer (1992) believes that being in the *right* unit affords individuals greater power than their colleagues in different units. I believe that in higher education this also runs true, however, power is also associated with institutional type. There tends to be a pecking order of institutional type and that may vary depending on one's academic discipline or functional area (Chapter 3). In general, individuals from top-tier research universities tend to wield more power in their professional areas than do colleagues from other institutions. While there are always exceptions, there is a greater likelihood that individuals from highly regarded research universities will be selected for offices within professional associations or perhaps they will be higher on the list of experts to be interviewed on the national news. The remainder of this section will focus on individual institutions.

The individual units or divisions that will be viewed as more powerful than others is somewhat dependent upon institutional mission and structure, meaning every institution may have different powerful units depending on its mission and institutional leadership. Salancik and Pfeffer (1974) found that "subunit power accrues to those departments instrumental in bringing in or providing resources which are highly valued by the total organization" (p. 470). Those resources could be research grants, other external funding, and in some tuition-driven institutions, programs with larger enrollments.

When trying to assess which unit(s) is the *right unit* on your campus it is important to understand the structural and political communication networks of the campus (see Chapter 3). At most institutions there may be preferred units within each major division on the campus and there may also be a preferred division at the institution as a whole. Perhaps it is academic affairs that wields the greatest political clout on the campus and it may be that the college of natural sciences or arts and sciences may be the preferred unit within academic affairs. Within the division of student affairs the preferred unit may be housing or perhaps it is the student union/center. Another tip is to follow the money. During the last round of budget cuts, which unit seemed to have received the least in cuts, or perhaps during strong financial times, which unit seemed to receive a disproportionate share of the funding? Additionally, administrator bias may be based on the academic unit from which the senior administrator came. For example, on the academic side of your institution, if you have a provost and/or president with terminal degrees in the traditional liberal arts disciplines there will be a greater likelihood the college housing those degrees will be shown some preferential treatment, perhaps not overtly, but preference nonetheless. Likewise, if the vice-president for student affairs has a background in campus activities, preference may be shown towards that unit.

In large research universities, the colleges generating the most external funding, usually arts and sciences, engineering, or the medical school, are typically in a more powerful position than those with fewer external dollars. According to Brass (2002), "power was found to be related to a department's ability to secure outside grants and contracts, the national prestige of the department, and the relative size of the department's graduate program" (p. 148). In these research institutions, professional schools such as colleges of business, nursing, or education tend to receive less respect from senior leaders and faculty. Professional programs in business, nursing, or education are more likely to receive funding for training grants or consultations rather than the *pure* research associated with the sciences, yet it is the professional programs that oftentimes attract more undergraduate students.

At the departmental level, Bozeman et al. (2013) found power differentials between department chairs based on their ability to control resources and their autonomy to make decisions. For example, when negotiating with a potential new hire, chairs with access to resources can offer better *start-up* packages, research support, or load releases among others. More often than not, one will find the more powerful chairs located in the STEM fields indicating that being in the right academic unit gives one access to resources other units do not have.

For non-academic units on your campus there most likely is one or more unit(s) that appears to be shown favoritism, especially in the budgeting process and whether it be the business and finance, physical plant, enrollment management, or other unit will depend on institutional priorities at the time. For example, you will often find that during economic downturns, when more people are applying to colleges and universities, the enrollment management offices will not receive as much attention because you have more applicants than spaces available. However, when fewer people are applying and enrollment numbers are trending down, more attention is paid to enrollment management with the hope of reversing the downward trend. In general, on college and university campuses you will find that the academic side tends to be the preferred unit(s) when it comes to resource allocation. However, when looking at the student affairs division or student support services you will find that "[a]mong the professional staff working with students, student life administrators often receive the least respect" (Mitchell, and King, 2018, p. 88) and the auxiliary units tend to garner greater power.

Controlling Resources

The ability to control resources or to control others' access to resources (financial, physical, or human) is an extremely important and valuable source of power in higher education. At most institutions, departments and divisions are resource constrained and new resources are extremely difficult to come by. Jeffrey Pfeffer (1992) refers to this source of power as the "New Golden Rule: the person with the gold makes the rules" (p. 83). Brass (2002) mentions that

> Employees in central network positions have greater access to, and potential control over, critical resources than peripheral employees. Most empirical studies have found that a person's centrality in an intraorganisational network is related to power .... Control of critical resources is best captured by the betweenness measure of centrality '... act as brokers or go-betweeners, bridging the "structural holes" between otherwise disconnected others. They control the flow of critical resources between these disconnected others
>
> (p. 144)

Individuals and units on campus that have excess resources, especially financial, are considered more powerful. Most people have a tendency to equate larger staffs, larger budgets, and more physical space (or nicer/newer facilities) with greater power. This is reinforced by Bozeman et al. (2013) when they suggest that within the academy resources are simply proxies for power, and also by Jaques (1994), who contends that an administrator's "strength in an organization frequently lies in the number of subordinates that one controls ... As a general rule, the larger the team, the greater the political clout" (p. 17). While not always the case there is some merit to this perception.

Within higher education, budgets are seen as a financial representation of the institution's values (Kretovics, 2011). Therefore, the departments or units with larger per student or per faculty budget allocations are perceived by that institution to be more valued at that point in time. If the unit is more valued then it makes perfect sense it will be more powerful. Over the past few decades the financial resources available to higher education have fluctuated and during resource constrained times, the battle for limited financial resources intensified. Because higher education is a very labor-intensive industry, the vast majority of an institution's budget is tied up in its people, i.e. faculty, staff, and administrators, leaving little discretionary money available. That is why, historically, college and university administrators have tended to spar over small amounts of money, perhaps the reallocation of a single position, or the assignment of a single classroom, because sometimes that is all they have to fight for. It is definitely true that in higher education, "the politics are so fierce because the stakes are so small" (Wallace S. Sayre).

Another resource that is available and oftentimes overlooked is information or knowledge. Knowing who within your institution has specialized knowledge or is an expert in a specific field can be a great asset when trying to solve problems on the campus. Having access to the necessary information can be helpful in developing power. As Dixon (1998) pointed out several decades ago, "when the source of knowledge shifts so does the power. Where knowledge is, power is" (p. 161). While knowledge itself may not be a type of power, recall that in Chapter 2, knowledge was the base for three types of power – expert, information, and connectional, so access to it can be quite powerful.

Higher education institutions are bureaucratic in nature and, as Collins (2001) points out, "the purpose of a bureaucracy is to compensate for incompetence and lack of discipline." However, if you manage your resources properly and do a good job of hiring competent and trustworthy people for your positions, incompetence and lack of discipline should be minimized if not eliminated. Incompetence or unproductive personnel will be a problem that largely disappears if you have the right people in the right positions in the first place (Collins, 2001, p. 121). Using your resources wisely will help you acquire and maintain power within your institution.

Surrounding Yourself with Competence

As Machiavelli suggests, the true measure of a leader can be gauged by assessing those with whom she surrounds herself. If the leader believes she is the smartest person around and chooses to hire *Lap Dogs*, she most likely will not earn the respect of her followers. She will not garner Referent or Persuasive Power and will most likely have to rely on forms of Legitimate and possibly Coercive Power, resulting in people *complying* with her vision rather than embracing and supporting her vision. If the leader believes she needs to hire the best and brightest and chooses to surround herself with people willing to challenge and support her (*Athletes*), she will be more likely to develop a following based on Referent Power, who will be more engaged and willing to *commit* to her vision.

Mitchell and King (2018) espouse that "presidents [senior administrators] have the right to choose and fire the members of the senior staff, who owe both wise counsel and loyalty" (p. 141). Additionally, Pfeffer (2010a) cautions against hiring or surrounding yourself with people who make you feel good. While most people enjoy a bit of flattery, honesty is the all-important trait one must seek. Machiavelli (*The Prince*) warns "there is no other way to guard yourself against flattery than by making men understand that telling you the truth will not offend you." No leader should be offended by the truth, even when it is not what you wanted to hear. Leaders who are confident in their decisions and to open to constructive feedback are less likely to be taken in by a bit of flattery.

When you are in a position to hire professional staff or fulltime faculty members, it makes the most sense to hire the best and brightest you can find – surround yourself with high-caliber talent. As an administrator I thought it best to hire individuals who aspired to higher levels within the institution or the profession. These were the individuals willing to challenge me with thought-provoking questions and who were willing to tell me what I needed to hear and not necessarily what I wanted to hear. Surround yourself with people who can make you look good because of the high quality of work they perform. They will in turn excel in their positions which also demonstrates that you know how to evaluate talent and hire quality staff. I would much rather hire a superstar and retain that person for a year than hire a dud and be stuck with that person for a lifetime.

CONCLUDING COMMENTS

Symbols and sources of power will differ from institution to institution depending on mission, values, organizational structure, tax status, etc. For example, when looking at centralized and decentralized budget models, mid-level administrators in decentralized institutions can wield far greater influence/power than administrators at the same level in centralized institutions. Decentralization pushes decision-making and budget responsibility to lower levels of the institution such as deans, directors, and department chairs, while in centralized institutions those decisions continue to be made at a president's cabinet level. And as Pfeffer (2010a) contends, to acquire and wield power requires you to have control over the resources necessary for you to reward your allies. Therefore, the more discretion you have over resources the more power you will have to influence the behaviors of others within your institution (Bozeman et al., 2013).

Additionally, Herdlein et al., clearly outline the importance of knowing how to identify the power brokers on your respective campuses "Identifying decision-makers, formal and informal power structures, sources of power, and using power to influence decisions was seen by senior leaders as being of vital importance to successful practice" (2011, p. 55).

REFLECTIVE QUESTIONS

1. Look at your institution and identify which departments you believe have the most power.
2. Can you identify the units with control over the most resources?
3. Which departments/units have the most staff? Have the better physical facilities? Have the larger budgets?
4. Is there a *right unit* in your division or on your campus?

5. Who is in your communication network?
6. In whose communication networks are you located?

GROUP ACTIVITY

You are leading a new central support unit on campus, and you have the choice of residing in a beloved, historic building at the center of campus with charming, yet mostly outdated facilities, or you can renovate and modernize a building on the edge of campus, away from the daily flow of students, faculty, and staff. Which space symbolizes the most powerful choice? Why? In terms of politics and power discussed in this and previous chapters, what would be gained and lost in each location?

GROUP ACTIVITY

Your supervisor offers you a windowed, corner office on the highest floor of the building, alongside other team leaders in your unit. Your previous, windowless office was located alongside your staff offices on a lower floor. Which office do you take? In terms of power, what would be gained and lost with each decision?

Chapter Five
Personal Attributes and Traits of Successful Administrators

Social and behavioral science literature is replete with lists of attributes and characteristics of successful leaders and powerful individuals. Jim Collins in *Good to Great* states, "[g]ood-to-great companies placed greater weight on character attributes than on specific educational background, practical skills, specialized knowledge or work experience." (2001, p. 49). Additionally, Brass (2002) mentions that because of the *fundamental attribution error* people tend to attribute cause to individuals and their characteristics rather than to situational factors external to those individuals (p. 145). It is noted that the *fundamental attribution error* is so pervasive that even when people are informed about it they still have the tendency to overestimate the role of personality in leadership (Merelman, 1986, p. 286). There are also many who refute this trait approach, suggesting that there is not a strong nor consistent relationship between leadership behaviors/traits and organizational effectiveness (Howell et al., 2007, p. 363).

Regardless of which side of the fence you reside, there is plenty of evidence that supports the notion that some combination of attributes or characteristics *may be helpful* in one's quest for power and/or leadership within an organization. In the pages that follow, I have assembled a list of the more common attributes that appear in the social and behavioral science literature and several I have personally observed over the years. I believe it is important to emphasize, maintaining any or all of these attributes *will not* assure you a leadership position. Rather, the literature on leadership, management, and power points to these attributes as most common amongst powerful leaders in successful organizations throughout the United States.

Some of the characteristics or attributes that are valued may be in conflict with or contrast to others on the list. This occurs because there is no single definitive list for all organization types or organizational leaders. You will find throughout your career, and throughout history for that matter, different groups/organizations will need different types of leaders with different skills and attributes during different times in an organization's life-cycle. As President Bassam Deeb (Trocaire College) mentions, "I truly believe we all [college and university presidents] have seasons and the positive side is that there are 4000 institutions and so we are bound to find another one that matches our abilities" (personal communication). This connects with Pfeffer's (1992) contention that personal attributes become more or less important depending on the situation and context at the time. Additionally, Howell et al., (2007) noted that "no strong consistent relationship between particular leader behaviors and organizational effectiveness ha[s] ever been found" in the literature.

Therefore, the following attributes/traits are simply listed alphabetically and *not* in any hierarchical or prioritized order.

COMMUNICATOR

It should be obvious to everyone reading this book that the overwhelming number of successful leaders are good communicators. They must be able to make speeches (state of the college), give presentations (at training sessions), address large audiences (orientation), talk with individuals (one-on-one supervision), write correspondence (letters to parents, students, donors, among others), etc. However, the most important communication skill is that of *listening*. Being an effective and assertive communicator begins with being a good listener (Kretovics, 2011). Gilley (2006) stresses that communication skills enable you to develop a favorable rapport, which in turn aids in developing positive political interactions.

Gilley (2006), Pfeffer (1992), and others agree that listening is a powerful and important skill for administrative success. President Tressel of Youngstown State University suggests that "if you want to influence others you need to be influenceable and you do this by showing others you can listen." He goes on to state that "when you start a new position you need to meet everyone. It is important for your success to develop relationships, to do so you must listen, listen, listen." Tost et al. (2013), found that when leaders dominate a conversation they are seen as asserting their power and are not viewed as open to other ideas, which in turn reduces team performance. Maxwell (2013) noted that communication needs to be open, honest, and ongoing. When faculty and staff are not kept informed they will make assumptions, usually incorrect, which can inadvertently undermine the plans or priorities of the institution (p. 92).

Being an effective communicator also means being able to read people, whether that be one solitary individual or in a larger group setting such as a class or large meeting. Their reactions to what you are saying and how you are saying it are important in determining the receptivity to and effectiveness of your message. Many faculty members can attest to the importance of this based on their experiences in a classroom. As faculty, they notice the eye rolls, frowns, closed eyes, fidgeting in their seats, and sidebar conversations of their audience, i.e. students. Recognizing whether your audience (stakeholders) is engaged is critical in getting your point(s) across.

Finally, good communicators know how to ask good questions, i.e. those questions that elicit a more descriptive response and ones that do not put an individual on the defensive. For example, instead of asking *why did you make that decision*? you could ask – *what factors lead you to that conclusion*?

Overall, there are two basic types of questions – closed-ended questions and open-ended questions. Closed-ended questions elicit brief responses, often yes or no answers. Open-ended questions require a little more thought and allow the individual to respond with a fuller, more descriptive answer, providing a context for the response. When possible, it is better to ask an open-ended question. This can also help with a feeling of engagement in the decision-making process.

CONFIDENT/SELF-ASSURED

By definition leaders are (or are perceived as) confident individuals: they believe they can be successful and they believe they can be good leaders. Confident leaders engender trust and are also seen as trusting others, whereas "insecure leaders don't place their trust in others, nor do they engender trust from others" (Maxwell, 2013, p. 108). Self-confidence is an important aspect of strong leadership and acquiring power. According to Kay and Shipman (2014), confidence is as important as competence for individuals to be successful in their chosen pursuits. After all, confidence helps people put thoughts into action and it very well may be these actions that enable individuals to gain power and become successful.

Confidence is often attributed to how people present themselves or carry themselves in a variety of social settings such as meetings and presentation among other political interactions. Carney et al. (2010) found that open postures project high power and closed postures convey low power (p. 1364). Additionally, they suggest that, even if one is not confident or does not have power, the ability to pretend to be confident or to carry oneself in a confident manner, such as using open postures, can increase one's perceived power (p. 1367). Finally, they indicate that those in low power positions or individuals in marginalized groups may benefit from exhibiting behaviors that demonstrate confidence in one's abilities. If you do not show confidence in yourself why would others demonstrate confidence in you?

To be a successful leader it is important that you be self-confident and assured. Norman Vincent Peale stated you must "[b]elieve in yourself! Have faith in your abilities! Without a humble but reasonable confidence in your own powers you cannot be successful or happy" (www.brainyquote. com). I do want to add a word of caution. One must be careful here because there is a fine line between self-confidence and arrogance. Exhibit too much confidence and others may perceive you as arrogant and, remember, it is the viewers' perception that is important. Confidence inspires followers while arrogance creates disdain.

ENERGY AND PHYSICAL STAMINA

If you can't stay awake you will garner little, if any respect. If you aspire to be in a senior leadership role you must recognize the physical demands of these positions and the levels of energy and stamina needed to be successful. I have worked at several different types of institutions and worked for multiple presidents. While they did not work 24/7, all of them worked long hours and had to be as alert and attentive at 9:00 pm as they were at 7:00 am. In higher education, college, and university leaders are expected to be available for breakfast meetings as well as evening activities. Students, faculty, and staff take notice when members of the institution's leadership are not present at an event.

As McLemore states, "[I]t takes commitment, stamina, and resilience to run an organization ... successful leaders work hard, and the faint of heart need not apply for these leadership positions" (p. 1). Two examples of successful university leaders who exhibited a high level of energy and physical stamina are: former Kent State University President Carol Cartwright and University of West Virginia President Gordon Gee. President Cartwright had gatherings at her home that would last late into the evening and she would be responding to emails the next day by 5:00 am. She was renowned for walking to meetings anywhere on campus and, upon arrival, always seemed to have energy to spare. Gordon Gee, while president at the Ohio State University, was well known for showing up at off-campus student gatherings such as fraternity and sorority parties to connect with students. He would do so after putting in a full day in his office and would be prompt the next morning, ready for any presidential duties. These are just two examples of senior leaders who routinely put in long hours, all the time appearing to be enjoying every minute. The image they created on their respective campuses is one of the Energizer bunny – ready for anything, anytime night or day.

As an administrator, mid- or senior-level, you will be expected to attend numerous meetings throughout your day. Additionally, it will be expected that you attend, and participate in evening and weekend activities such as orientation sessions, student organization meetings and activities, athletic events, fundraising events, etc. James Gaudino, president of Central Washington University mentioned – "you always have to be seen or heard or present when the university is doing its thing, that kind of behavior is important." If you desire to increase your potential for upward mobility you will need to be seen and this means you must show up and engage with each group as if it were the first meeting of the day. Also, at some point in your career, it will be expected of you to be in your office when your boss is in the office even on weekends. I recall during my doctoral work I was on campus one Sunday, running some of my data, and when leaving the building I ran into the VP for Student Affairs. I asked why he was on campus and his reply was – "the president is in today so I need to be here as well."

Loehr and Schwartz (2001) suggest that a corporate athlete has endurance, strength, and flexibility. These tie directly to this trait of energy and physical stamina, implying that if you want to be successful in a leadership (administrative) role you need to start thinking of yourself as or begin training to become an organizational athlete. Additionally, Brass (2002) suggests that influencing others takes significant levels of energy; therefore, high levels of energy and physical stamina may be requisite characteristics of upwardly mobile administrators or others seeking powerful positions.

FLEXIBILITY

While being focused on the all-important end goal is valued, as an administrator you need to recognize that there are multiple paths to achieving departmental or institutional goals. It is in your best interest to be prepared to take a few detours along the way if necessary, especially when too many barriers are put in front of you. In higher education it is typically best to go around barriers rather than trying to bulldoze through them. Being *headstrong* and trying to break through barriers most likely will simply give you a headache. Flexibility is key and valuable not only in career planning but also in your administrative roles.

From a career perspective, I believe Dr. Beverly Warren, former President of Kent State University stated the need for flexibility best – "be open to opportunities that may present themselves and take advantage of them. You won't know where they lead, but they do open doors." Because there is not a single path to senior leadership or the presidency, you will need to be flexible with your career opportunities and your time line.

With regard to your administrative roles, you must understand that with every new position you take on or with each new supervisor you inherit, most likely you will be exposed to different communication and leadership styles and differing supervisory approaches. As Bassam Deeb, current president of Trocaire College stated, it is best to "allow yourself to be exposed to every aspect of the institution, because it can be frustrating when you are dealing with people who have only been exposed to one aspect of a university."

Flexibility is often interpreted as being indecisive. In actuality, it is anything but indecisive. Flexibility shows a willingness to look at the evidence and to consider different viewpoints on how to interpret what is being presented and from there how best to proceed and what course of action to take.

HUMILITY (MANAGE ADMINISTRATIVE EGO)

Leaders in institutions of higher education, regardless of level within the hierarchy, must uphold a semblance of humility in order to maintain respect from their subordinates. This can be challenging because the higher one climbs in the institution the more frequently others publicly tout one's successes. Good leaders need to be cognizant of how they are perceived and strive to maintain a measure of humility regardless of how successful they become. Sousa and van Dierenfonck (2017) mention "three essential aspects of humility (1) the ability to put one's accomplishments and talents in perspective, (2) admitting one's fallibility and mistakes, and (3) understanding of one's strong and weak points" (p. 13). Administrators who are mindful of these aspects and demonstrate humility will be more likely to be seen in a positive light. These aspects are also commonly attributed to *servant leadership*. Administrators who fail in one or more of these aspects are more inclined to let their *administrative ego* (Kretovics, 2011) influence decision-making practices.

When executive leaders in higher education let *administrative ego* dominate, their judgment becomes impaired and their decision-making loses its focus. It is this administrative ego that has presidents, vice presidents, deans, and other executive leaders concerned about the legacy they will leave behind – *for what will I be remembered?* – rather than focusing on what is in the best interest of the institution. Oftentimes presidents want their names on buildings or some other form of recognition for their years of service, and all too often they focus on big-splash items in the short term rather than looking at the long-term success of the institution. This is reinforced by a recent survey indicating that fewer than 20% of presidents view strategic planning as an area important for the future (Gagliardi et al., 2017). Building a new athletic facility, performing arts center, or classroom building may seem like a good idea in the short term, but leaders must also consider the long-term financial obligations of such investments because with every new building comes increased debt service, custodial, and maintenance costs. Additionally, a study by Selingo et al. (2017) for Deloitte's Center for Higher Education Excellence, concludes there is an "[e]mphasis on short-term wins at the cost of long-term planning" (p. 3). Sacrificing long-term planning does not help an institution develop its competitive advantage.

An example of a failure to manage the administrative ego happened at the University of Akron. During the late 1990s and early 2000s, the university borrowed over $500 million to expand and renovate its campus physical facilities. It was clear that the university needed to make some physical improvements and an aggressive expansion may have seemed like a good idea at the time. However, the financial obligation that resulted required the institution to grow its enrollment for a prolonged period of time, which ended up being unsustainable as there was a significant decline in its targeted demographics – namely, new high school graduates. The president who incurred the debt stepped aside just as the downward trend began to accelerate and the new president stepped into a financial quagmire. Enrollment declines due to lower high school graduation rates are relatively easy to forecast, but when one's ego supersedes the evidence it becomes difficult to control (perhaps an example of the Abilene Paradox). This significant decision, made with short-term thinking and administrative ego, increased long-term debt for the institution and continues to compromise its financial health. In 2018, the University announced staffing reductions and a 20% cut in its academic programs (www.ohio.com/akron/news/scarborough-says-he-has-learned-from-mistakes-but-blames-communication-as-the-key-mistake).

Pfeffer (2010a) notes that, with power,

> you become overconfident and less observant … It is easier to lose your patience when you are in power – power leads to disinhibition, to not watching what you say and do, to being more concerned about yourself than about the feelings of others (p. 207) … it can be hard to keep your ego in check (p. 208) … leave gracefully, with dignity and thereby influence your legacy.
>
> (p. 212)

In order to keep your ego in check it is likely that one will need to be seen, by Maxwell's definition, as a mature individual – having "the ability to think beyond yourself ... If your focus is always yourself and what you want, then people become an obstacle to your goals ... get over your selfishness, get outside of yourself, and help others get what they want" (p. 105).

As a leader, your focus needs to be on accomplishing goals and objectives that forward the mission of the institution not on making yourself look as good as possible. Remember, if the organization or unit does well, it then follows that the administrators responsible for the organization or unit are seen as successful as well. The converse is not always true. This is the classic conundrum – self-interest versus the collective good. For public institutions this takes on a larger context, as President Warren (Kent State University) said (in a personal communication),

> you need to ask yourself if you are focused on the collective good ... there are times when you have to do what is in the best interest of the state ... we have to balance our goals and needs with the collective good of the community and the state.

In short, keep your ego in check.

A leader's administrative ego can also appear in the form of creating new academic programs or adding new colleges to an institution. I believe this behavior is also partially responsible for the unnecessary and often very expensive institutional mission creep that has become prevalent within higher education today. For example, numerous former liberal arts colleges have added graduate or *career-related* majors such as business, nursing, and education, or they have established weekend colleges for non-traditional students, all in an attempt to maintain or expand enrollments. Similarly, a number of the four-year colleges have changed their identities from colleges to universities or from comprehensive universities to research universities, in an effort to attract a different type of student and to expedite their quest for greater prestige. What senior-level administrators need to keep in mind is what Jim Collins states in *Good to Great*, "anything that does not fit, we will not do. We will not launch unrelated businesses. We will not make unrelated acquisitions. We will not do unrelated joint ventures. If it doesn't fit, we don't do it Period!" (2001, p. 134). If the administration is true to the mission of the institution it will follow Collins' guidance and not add programs simply to create a highlight that can be added to one's curriculum vitae. Collins notes that new CEOs tend to bring in new programs and will attempt to alter the direction of the previous leader "trying to make a mark with his own program" (p. 179). Too often, trying to make one's mark disregards the current institutional mission, which is ultimately bad for the institution.

Being humble and controlling your ego will most likely help you forward the institutional goals and ultimately make you a more successful administrator. Collins (2001) mentions that "a Level 5 Leader blends extreme personal humility with intense professional will" (p. 21) and Sousa and van Dierenfonck (2017) indicated that "humble leaders showed the highest impact on follower engagement regardless of their hierarchical position ... for leaders in high hierarchical positions, the moral virtue of humility seems to strengthen the impact of their action-oriented leadership the most" (p. 13). Keeping yourself humble may present some challenges, but it can serve you well in higher education.

Another aspect of higher education, the concept of shared governance, can play a role in the management of one's ego and maintaining one's humility. As Mitchell and King (2018) state, "[shared] governance requires the sublimation of individual and collective egos, with clear rules to put aside distracting questions about who has too much power" (p. 22). Higher education institutions are composed of multiple divisions and departments, creating an interdependent system, and this interdependent system requires individuals to cooperate and collaborate with others to accomplish goals. This cooperation and collaboration more often than not requires individuals to recognize their dependence upon others to move their goals or agenda forward which requires one to be humble, thereby keeping one's ego in check.

I believe Collins (2001) said it best – people who "could never in a million years bring themselves to subjugate their egoistic needs to the greater ambition of building something larger and more lasting than themselves," may appear to be successful in the short term, but will be exposed for their poor decisions in the long run (p. 36). It is unfortunate that these leaders are more concerned about leaving a legacy than the institutions they are leading.

NARCISSISM

This is one trait you were probably not expecting to find on a list describing successful leaders. While initially this may seem repulsive or incongruent with leadership success, remember that there are successful leaders with whom you may disagree and/or perhaps even personally dislike. In their article *Narcissistic CEOs and executive compensation*, O'Reilly et al. (2013) state that "[n]arcissists present a puzzle to students of leadership. Many of the characteristics that make them problematic (e.g., self-confidence, grandiosity, exploitativeness, and persistence) can, under the right circumstances, also make them successful" (p. 228). In *Narcissism in organizational contexts*, Campbell et al. (2011) provide a definition for narcissism that is quite enlightening:

> It is useful to think of narcissism as containing three components: the self, interpersonal relationships and self-regulatory strategies. First, the narcissistic self is characterized by positivity, "specialness" and uniqueness, vanity, a sense of entitlement and a desire for power and esteem. Second, narcissistic relationships contain low levels of empathy and emotional intimacy. In their place, there are (often numerous) shallow relationships that can range from exciting and engaging to manipulative and exploitative. Third, there are narcissistic strategies for maintaining inflated self-views. For example, narcissists seek out opportunities for attention and admiration, brag, steal credit from others, and play games in relationships. When narcissists are successful at this, they feel good – they report high self-esteem and positive life satisfaction.
>
> (p. 269)

Pfeffer (2015) indicates that, in psychology research literature, narcissism has been defined as:

> a grandiose sense of self-importance; arrogant behavior or attitudes; a lack of empathy for others; a preoccupation with fantasies of unlimited success or power; belief in one's special unique status including a fixation on associating with high-status people or organizations; an unreasonable sense of expectations or entitlement; and desire for excessive admiration from others, among other characteristics.
>
> (p. 70)

I am confident that everyone reading this book can think of at least one person with whom you are acquainted, perhaps worked with or for, who fits many, if not all of the descriptors listed in these two definitions of narcissism. And I am equally as confident that not all of the individuals you have identified are or were terrible leaders, in fact many of today's high-profile corporate and political leaders exhibit many of these behaviors. Campbell et al. (2011) indicate that social psychology research has identified a strong connection between organizational and political leaders and narcissism, while the research literature on leadership has not given this relationship much attention.

O'Reilly et al. (2013) also mention that "on the positive side, narcissists are more likely to be seen as inspirational, succeed in situations that call for change, and be a force for creativity" (p. 219). This sounds a great deal like a charismatic or perhaps a transformational leader. Pfeffer (2015) claims that "immodesty can help people attain leadership positions in the first place and then, once in them, positively affects their ability to hold on to those positions, extract more resources ... which may seem counterintuitive" (p. 72). Additionally, Pfeffer goes on to show that research indicates narcissists demonstrate four key characteristics; energy, dominance, self-confidence, and charisma, which tend to be associated with leader effectiveness as well.

According to O'Reilly et al. (2013) "the long-term negative effects of narcissistic leaders may in part result from those leaders' inability to develop a cohesive team" (p. 227). Leaders, within whom this trait is dominant, tend to surround themselves with *lap dogs* and *floaters* because they do not want to be challenged nor do they wish anyone around them to appear smarter than they perceive themselves to be. Their lack of concern for others and their focus on themselves make them less likeable but not necessarily less successful. Additionally, O'Reilly suggests that narcissists, while less agreeable, "may be more skilled in navigating organizational politics than those who are more agreeable and higher on empathy" (p. 227). It has been suggested that narcissism, while quite common among entrepreneurial leaders, is not a cause of success, but when one is successful the narcissistic trait tends to become readily apparent (Lovric and Chamorro-Premuzic, 2018).

NICE/LIKEABLE

The old adage *nice people finish last* is obviously not a truism. While there are times in which being nice can be somewhat detrimental – after all, how many times have you heard someone say "s/he is just too nice?" – it is also accurate to state that being nice or likeable can help some individuals attain positions of power. As Pfeffer (2010a) points out "Being nice to people can be effective because people find it difficult to fight with those who are being polite and courteous" (p. 98). Gilley (2006) suggests that being nice to others is an underutilized but very effective approach to accomplishing one's goals. Even Machiavelli in *The Prince* notes that "he who is highly esteemed is not easily conspired against." Moreover, when individuals are nice to us we may feel the need to reciprocate and in turn be nice to them. This reciprocity rule (Bolton and Ockenfels, 2000; Ouchi, 1980) can have both positive and negative consequences. Social science literature suggests that we tend to like people who like us, we gravitate toward people whom we believe we know well, and we typically like people who bring us good news (Pfeffer, 1992).

Throughout the literature in business, psychology, sociology, and other disciplines, authors discuss the positives and negatives of being nice. On the positive side, "the social influence literature is rife with demonstrations of the positive relationship between our fondness for a person and the likelihood of compliance with his or her request" (Cialdini and Goldstein, 2004, p. 598). Essentially, the more we like someone, the more likely we are to comply or respond favorably to their requests. Additionally, Cialdini and Goldstein point out that "physical attractiveness, a predictor of interpersonal liking, has been demonstrated to influence responding in a number of domains" (p. 598), suggesting that the more attractive we perceive someone, the greater the prospects we will respond positively to him or her. For example, reflect back upon a few times you were asked to perform a task or serve on a committee that was above and beyond your position's duties and responsibilities. Did the attractiveness or appearance of the individual asking you to serve influence your decision?

On the negative side, according to Pfeffer (2010a), "nice people are considered warm but niceness comes across as weakness" (p. 87). This sentiment was reinforced by President Dan Mahony (Winthrop University) when he was cautioned that people often "misinterpret kindness for weakness." This suggests that one may need to balance being nice with being assertive or firm – in other words you do not have to come across as mean when you are being firm but you also want to make sure that you do not appear to be too soft or weak when you are being nice.

PLANNING AND SETTING CLEAR GOALS

Successful leaders have a tendency to establish goals and stick with them. This does not mean that one cannot be flexible (also a trait that is valued). It instead implies that leaders should continue to stay focused on their career goals and plan accordingly, understanding that there may be a few detours along the way. During your career you may find there to be a slight disconnect between your personal or career plans/goals and those of the institution for which you work. This is quite common and, therefore, should not cause alarm, but rather a simple recalculation of your path.

Within higher education there is no single path to power or to powerful positions. On the student affairs side of the operation vice-presidents can come from a wide variety of academic disciplines and they may have worked in several functional areas or may have spent their career in a single area. In academic administration it is a bit more focused, in that academic administrators typically move through their respective disciplinary tracks as faculty then become department chairs or school directors before moving into more senior and broad-based roles such as academic deans or provost positions. If one aspires to be the president or chancellor of an institution, again, there is no single path, but rather multiple paths that permit individuals to develop the skills necessary to be successful.

During individual meetings with staff, I would oftentimes ask, "where do you want to be in three or five years?" I believe that as a supervisor it is just as important for me to help my staff achieve their career goals as it was for me to achieve my own. If staff members were focused and had thought about their path I would try to assign duties or recommend opportunities to help further them along their path. This kept the individuals engaged in their work while indirectly supporting the goals of the unit and me as the supervisor.

During your administrative career you will likely partake in several strategic planning sessions, at the departmental, divisional, or institutional level. Higher educational institutions love to plan and it seems that, with every change in senior leadership, institutions have the need to develop a new plan. Strategic or long-range plans are typically expected to last five years or until there is an administrative change at or near the top. With these changes you will need to review your individual plan to see how it fits with the revised institutional direction. Figure 5.1 gives a few questions to help you sort out the new environment.

> Are the institution's goals and objectives in line with your personal values and beliefs?
> How has the new plan impacted the priorities set for your area?
> How has the plan impacted the institutional priority of your area?
> How has the new plan influenced staffing and budgeting priorities?
> Is your position stable?
> Is the position to which you aspire in jeopardy?
> Is your mentor still with the institution?

Figure 5.1 Individual Plan and Institutional Direction

It is also important to understand that as an administrator you need to set goals that are appropriate for your institution, its mission, and its current faculty and staff. This is best done by involving a wide variety of stakeholders in the process. President Tressel of Youngstown State mentioned in a conversation that "the planning process is a way to educate for tomorrow and it is important to let everyone know we want your input so we have to provide a way for them to interact with the process." President Tressel also made a comment that demonstrated his commitment to establishing institutional goals rather than personal goals:

> In my first meeting with the strategic planning steering committee, I came in with my legal pad and sat down. I said to them "this is your process and here are my ideas here for review." Then I passed around a blank sheet of paper. I told them "I'm 65 and you're 45, you have a lot of years left so this plan is for your future not mine." I wanted them to take ownership.

Rather than imposing his views, he chose to let the strategic plan develop from the faculty, staff, and administrators. The institutional plan does not have to be your plan and in most instances it is much better if the plan is developed with significant input from others within your institution. You need to be your own planner to plan your career and help create institutional plans, but you do not have to impose your plan on an organization that neither wants, needs, nor benefits from it.

TOLERANCE FOR AMBIGUITY

Leaders and individuals seeking powerful positions, especially within higher education, need to have a high tolerance for ambiguity. Pfeffer (2015) notes that

> many, possibly most, leadership roles are ambiguous – there is uncertainty about what the leader should do, uncertainty about who would be best in that position, and frequently even a lack of clarity about how people are performing in their leadership roles.
>
> (p. 72)

Additionally, Gilley (2006) points out that being comfortable with ambiguity is a requisite of being a successful negotiator, which he believes is an important skill for any leader.

Abraham Zaleznik's (1998) discussion of chaos and leadership relates directly to this discussion of ambiguity. He suggests that

> leaders tolerate chaos and lack of structure [read ambiguity] and are thus prepared to keep answers in suspense, avoiding premature closure on important issues ... seldom do the uncertainties of potential chaos cause problems. Instead, it is the instinctive move to impose order on potential chaos that makes trouble for organizations.
>
> (p. 87).

Finally, you will find that most good administrators will delegate responsibility and in doing so expect the subordinates to have the requisite knowledge and skill set to complete the task(s) assigned. However, what good administrators won't do is tell you *how* to accomplish the task(s) or give you step-by-step instructions. That is for *you* to determine. These ambiguous directions give you the opportunity to problem solve and to use your critical thinking skills. If you need to be told *how* to do it, your supervisor might as well do it herself.

TOLERANCE OF CONFLICT

In any social organization, conflict is unavoidable and if addressed appropriately, conflict within the institution can result in a healthy organizational culture. Disagreements are a natural part of institutional life and doing one's job. What is important is how you handle the conflict. As Brass (2002) states "power is more likely to be exercised and visible when conflicts exist ... Researchers agree that interdependence is a necessary condition for the exercise of power" (p. 140). In exercising your power during a conflict you do not have to belittle your colleagues nor do you need to prove them wrong. Exercising your power can come in the form of listening to their thoughts and ideas and generating thoughtful constructive feedback. A key to successfully dealing with conflict is to remember that the *conflict is with the idea or action not with the person*. This can be incredibly difficult to do, but it can be a goal of your interaction.

Tolerance of conflict does not mean that you are looking for a fight nor does it means that you retreat from disagreements and simply give in to avoid a conflict. If you continually shy away from conflict you will lose respect from supervisors, peers, and subordinates and you risk losing what, if any, power you may have had. Similarly, if you are consistently creating or causing conflict you may be labeled as someone who is difficult to get along with, which can jeopardize your future career within that institution. You will need to be assertive and perhaps, on occasion, aggressive to ensure that the group looks at multiple sides of the issue and to ensure that your points are heard.

In a supervisory role you will hopefully have the opportunity to select some or all of the individuals who report to you. In selecting this group you must ensure that you do not simply hire *lap dogs* as surrounding yourself with yes people does not help further an institutional mission. As an administrator and institutional leader, you need to surround yourself with bright and inquisitive individuals with whom you can dialogue around ideas with the intent of generating alternatives to the path you suggest. These types of conversations can at times be a bit uncomfortable for those with a low tolerance for conflict. However, encouraging these healthy disagreements will more often than not result in a much better decision and most likely a comprehensive plan for implementation and moving the unit or institution forward, benefitting internal and external stakeholders.

TRANSPARENCY

When one hears the term *transparency* what is really being asked for is honesty, integrity, and an open decision-making process. I believe that transparency is the basis on which trust is established and "trust is the foundation of all forms of influence other than coercion" (Hill and Lineback, 2011, p. 128). Working for someone you trust is of utmost importance. You want to have confidence in your supervisors and trust that the information being shared by your supervisor is accurate and provides much of what is necessary for you to be able to perform your duties and responsibilities. Additionally, you want to trust that the information you share will be passed along up the chain of command, unless you asked it to be kept in confidence.

Inspiring trust as an administrator helps create a work environment that is more productive (Pfeffer, 2015). Leaders who are transparent tend to be viewed as having integrity and are trusted by their subordinates, making it more likely the leaders will have support for their ideas. If people believe they have a say in the decision (buy-in) or decision-making process they are more likely to support the decision, even if they initially disagreed. If people do not trust you they will not be motivated or inclined to follow you. You must establish trust before you can become a leader with the power to shape an institution (McLemore, 2014). Establishing a climate of trust begins by being transparent in your decision-making processes which in-and-of-itself is risky (Kramer, 2009).

When communicating with stakeholder groups, omitting part of the information is not being transparent. Partial truth does not equate to being transparent and, unfortunately, too many administrators omit information critical to the decision-making process with the intent to guide the discussion to support a decision consistent with their own views. This type of omission does not engender trust. On the contrary, once people learn of the omission or learn all of the facts, the confidence in the administrator begins to erode.

Transparency is also important when communicating with your external stakeholders. Higher education is a trust market. Students are unable to conduct an evaluation of the educational services they receive until after they have been delivered. Being a *trust market* also means that students and their families must rely on the institutional representatives' expertise, honesty, and integrity when making their decisions (Kretovics, 2011). If potential students and their families as well as other stakeholders do not trust the information being presented or the individuals making the presentation, they will be far less likely to commit personal resources toward your institution. This makes it critical for you, as an administrator, to establish trust in you, your staff, your unit, your institution.

Collins (2001) proffers four practices he believes lead to the creation of a work environment grounded in trust and transparency:

- Lead with questions not answers
- Engage in dialogue and debate, not coercion
- Conduct autopsies without blame
- Build *red flag* mechanisms – turn information into information that cannot be ignored – refer to demographic shifts and international enrollments

Another practice that can also lead to creating trust and ultimately transparency among your staff is empowerment (see below). Yukl (1989) mentions that "the need to empower subordinates and develop a sense of ownership for what goes on in the organization echoes the emphasis on power sharing, mutual trust, and participative decision-making" (p. 279). Practicing these will not ensure a transparent environment but they are definitely a great start in helping you establish your credibility within your institution.

CAN YOU BE TOO HONEST AND TOO TRUSTING?

There is no doubt that being honest is an admirable trait that engenders confidence and trust in a leader. You were most likely conditioned as a child to tell the truth and as you grew older you most likely heard the phrase "honesty is the best policy." I agree and believe that taking the moral high ground and acting ethically without compromising your integrity will help you become a better administrator. However, you will experience times when you believe honesty may not be the best policy for your career. For example, a common mistake that is made by inexperienced administrators and managers is assuming that, when your supervisor asks for thoughts and opinions on the decision/topic at hand, s/he really wants an honest answer. In many instances s/he is looking for affirmation and support, not your honest opinion. You will need to determine what your supervisor really wants and what compromises you are willing to make before deciding on your course of action, inaction, discussion, or omission.

> During my tenure as the senior student affairs officer at a small college, the president stopped by my office to ask about a recent decision. He explained his decision then asked what I thought. My response began with the question "do you really want my opinion?" I asked him that question three times before giving him my honest opinion. Needless to say, it was not what he wanted to hear, so he made it very clear that my comments were not of value as he proceeded to leave my office. This signaled the beginning of the end of what had been a good working relationship.

By telling the boss what she wants to hear or reinforcing the decision you could improve your standing with her, but at what cost to you? While helping people feel good about themselves can help you create a little power within your unit it may also lead you to a career as a Lap Dog, to not think or innovate on your own, to compromise too much of your own self.

On trusting others, many of us take the initial approach of trusting the other until we are proven wrong. This approach has its risks because there are many others who practice the converse. Regardless of which approach you take, you must be prepared to work with others who do not share your beliefs. Kramer (2009) believes it is possible to be too trusting because, as he states, our "inflated sense of our own judgment makes us vulnerable to people who can fake outward signs of trustworthiness ... and our readiness to trust makes us more likely to make mistakes" (p. 72). Perhaps more importantly, our readiness to trust makes us easier targets for the less scrupulous among us. These less scrupulous individuals will oftentimes use your trusting nature against you. Kramer (2009) also believes that we need to temper our trust to help protect ourselves from those who would prefer to take advantage of our openness (see Figure 5.2).

Additionally, this relates to what was previously stated in Chapter 4 about commitment and people's willingness to continue promoting a bad decision because they refuse to believe a bad decision was made and, because the decision was a failure, by extension all those involved in the decision are failures. As Pfeffer (2015) notes, "lying helps people attain powerful positions ... powerful people lie more often and with more ease. ... Thus, powerful people – leaders – are able to lie more successfully, and they do so" (p. 115). Therefore, you are encouraged to view most decisions with healthy skepticism. I also encourage you to reflect upon what Renè Descartes stated centuries ago, "the senses deceive from time to time, and it is prudent never to trust wholly those who have deceived us even once" (www.brainyquote.com/).

ATTRIBUTES AND TRAITS OF SUCCESSFUL ADMINISTRATORS

- Know yourself – two buckets; those who readily trust and talk freely about beliefs and impressions, and those who are skeptical of others and their motivations, intentions, and potential actions.
- Start small – keep risk sensible (small) in the early phase of relationships. Shallow risk, small but productive behaviors to communicate a willingness to trust.
- Write an escape clause – have a clear plan to disengage and hedge your relationships
- Send strong signals – **most of us tend to underinvest in communicating our trustworthiness** to others, because we take it for granted that they know or can readily discern our wonderful qualities of fairness, honesty, and integrity.
- Recognize the **other person's dilemma** – have empathy for others and try to understand their perspective
- Look at roles as well as people – high levels of trust can come from depersonalized interactions (swift trust) or trust in the role of the individual. Role-based trust
- Remain vigilant and always question – **once we've made a decision, we tend not** to revisit it as long nothing seems to have changed. (this is important to be mindful of when there are personnel changes.)

(Kramer, 2009)

Figure 5.2 Kramer's Rules for Developing Professional Relationships

UNDERSTANDING OTHERS

If you hope to positively influence others it is best that you understand them – their issues, their needs, and their motivations. Pfeffer (1992) discusses *sensitivity to others* as a trait, but I believe *understanding others* captures the essence of this trait. This is not the same as being empathetic, but rather it means paying attention to others and being observant. If you know what is needed (sometimes wanted) by your various constituency groups and you know what motivates them, it becomes easier to develop a strategy to help meet their respective needs. If you do not understand these groups it is very easy to offend them, thereby making it far more difficult to accomplish your goals and objectives.

The president of Edinboro University (PA), H. Fred Walker is an example of someone who truly did not understand one of his more important stakeholder groups. *The Chronicle of Higher Education* reported that President Walker referred to the Edinboro faculty as "obstacles to be worked around" and as a group with which "he could never reason." These comments, once reported publicly, generated a student-driven letter calling on Mr. Walker to resign, which he did less than a week after his ill-thought remarks. Had Mr. Walker been more sensitive to the faculty and taken the time to understand their needs, he may have chosen different terms to describe them or perhaps an entirely different approach to the situation at hand.

Another president's public comments didn't result in an early departure but did result in a lasting bitterness among students and faculty. A former president of Kent State University received a bonus of $70,000 at the end of his first year in office. When asked by a student newspaper reporter about accepting such a bonus during a time of increasing tuition and record high student debt, he remarked that it amounted to less than $.10 per student so it didn't make sense to donate it back to the institution. This reinforces what Pfeffer (2010a) says about individuals in powerful positions – "those with power pay less attention to those who are less powerful" and they are less likely to watch what they say and do and tend to be more concerned about themselves than about the feelings of others (p. 202).

If you are a good listener, as noted previously, you will naturally take the time to understand your stakeholder groups and, therefore, will be more likely to have a positive influence on their behaviors.

ABILITY TO EMPOWER OTHERS

Empowerment is a term used frequently in organizational behavior literature. Unfortunately, this is often confused with delegation. Delegation is giving subordinates the responsibility to complete a task or set of tasks, while empowerment is giving subordinates or colleagues the power to make decisions that impact their work lives. By empowering others, the administrator is giving away power to gain power. I believe Maxwell (2013) caught the essence with this:

> Many leaders don't want to share responsibility with others because they don't want to lose any of their power ... As you develop people and empower them to lead, their territories expand and so does yours .... You cannot become an effective Level 4 leader unless you are willing to let go of some of your responsibilities.
>
> (p. 102)

Elizabeth Allen's concept of *Power-to* was defined in Chapter 2, as the ability of an individual actor to attain an end or series of ends. According to this definition, the terms "empowerment" and "power-to" are essentially synonymous (p. 34). This then circles back to the idea of gaining power by giving it away through empowerment. You can increase your organizational power by empowering those beneath you in the hierarchy, letting them fully participate in the decision-making processes. Bassam Deeb, President of Trocaire College, looks at empowerment through decision-making as an opportunity to help staff gain a better perspective about the institution and the problem at hand ...

> the ability to look at the scenarios ... they'll bring an issue to the table with two or three different scenarios and I will say have you looked at it from this perspective ... after a while they realize there are more venues than they thought about ... it does prolong some decisions and sometimes people will delay bringing it in then say I have vetted it three different ways and we're ready to go and I say no, no we're not ... no matter how much exposure and training you have there are always situations that come up that are a little more nuanced than what you've seen before, you have to have an internal process in place to enable you to deal with whatever situations get thrown in front of you.

CONCLUDING COMMENTS

According to Jim Collins (2001) character attributes are considered more important in the long run than education, specialized knowledge, or previous work experience. This reinforces the importance of understanding your strengths and limitations with regard to the attributes discussed above. As an administrator and leader, it is not critical for you to demonstrate all of these attributes, or even the majority of them, but you must be able to demonstrate the ones needed by your institution or it may be difficult to maintain your position. It is, however, important to remember that having all of the traits above does not guarantee your success as a leader or administrator. These traits are only effective if your followers are confident in you as a leader and believe you are capable and competent (Sousa and van Dierenfonck, 2017). Many of today's leaders do not exhibit the above-mentioned traits and abilities, but give the perception that they have them. It is this perception that Machiavelli discusses in *The Prince*, the importance of appearance or creating a perception among one's followers, "it is unnecessary for a prince to *have* all the good qualities I have enumerated, but it is very necessary to *appear* to have them."

McLemore (2014) believes that the majority of organizational leaders are intelligent and have the ability to engender trust among their followers. This trust is important because, as Pfeffer (2015) notes, there are a great number of successful leaders who are skillful in misrepresenting and distorting reality (p. 126), which may work in the short run but will diminish credibility and has the potential to foster a toxic work environment.

REFLECTIVE QUESTIONS

For each of the attributes listed, rate yourself on a scale of 1–6 for each, with 1 being low and 6 being high.

1. Which are your three strongest attributes?
2. Which are the three attributes you believe require the most work to attain?
3. What is your perception as to how your co-workers and subordinates would rate you on each?
4. What attributes have you noticed in other leaders in your organization?
5. How have your attributes contributed to your success?
6. How have you seen others' attributes contribute to their success?

Chapter Six
Using Power to Accomplish Your Goals

Unlike other resources like time and money, power as a resource is not quantifiable, meaning there is no fixed amount of power which once consumed is gone. To some degree, power is limitless and is able to be used over and over again. Power can be taken away only by those who have bestowed it upon you, i.e. your supervisor (delegation), colleagues, subordinates, students, or other stakeholder groups. In your role as an administrator there are several tactics that you can use (or identify them being used) to aid in the accomplishment of your goals and objectives.

USING POWER

In an environment of interdependence such as higher education, the creation and use of power to accomplish one's goals is of great importance. Simply being good at what you do is not enough to impact other departments or divisions. You must recognize that when you do not have direct authority (*Legitimate Power*) you will need to use your political skills and your ability to develop one or more of the other types of power (see Chapter 2). Pfeffer (2010b) mentions that to build power you do not need extraordinary talent or amazing brilliance (p. 227). Sometimes, it is simply a matter of timing; you can acquire power by being in the right place at the right time.

If you have worked at a college or university, you undoubtedly are aware that these institutions are filled with very bright people, many of whom fail to accomplish their goals on a regular basis. They do not fail necessarily because they are incompetent (although many are) but rather in many instances this failure can be attributed to their inability to recognize power tactics being employed throughout their institution and/or their inability to properly employ power tactics to their advantage. As an administrator, it is important for you to fully understand what you have gotten yourself into. To do this, you must first listen and observe before jumping into the fray. The more you understand about the political and power structures of your college/university (not the same as the organizational structure) the greater the likelihood of your success.

In the previous chapter, several sources of power that transcend institutional type, location, or tax status were discussed. In this chapter, we will look at strategies that permit individuals to use what power they have attained or to create the perception they are powerful individuals. To be a great leader one must take risks (Zaleznik, 1998) and incorporating the tactics in this chapter into your administrative leadership style requires a certain amount of risk.

When to Use Power

Power can be used to resolve conflicts among members of any organizations and the more diverse the roles within an organization the greater the likelihood there will be conflict. As mentioned earlier, there are few organizations that have greater role differentiation than in higher education (Chapter 3). Faculty are specialized in minute areas within greater disciplines (biology, molecular biology, cell biology, etc.) and even within student affairs and administrative services we have witnessed an incredible division of labor with the creation of more and more specialized functional areas. When deciding to use the power that you have it is best to consider using it when the task at hand is vital for your success. Decisions that involve issues critical to you and your department/division within the institution like reorganizations and budget allocations are most likely to bring out power tactics (Pfeffer, 1992).

The sections that follow briefly describe several tactics that can be employed to demonstrate one's power over others. Using them effectively can help forward one's agenda or help undermine someone else's agenda. Understanding the context or framing the issue helps determine which tactics may prove more useful.

FRAMING

How issues and problems are perceived is entirely dependent on where the individuals are situated within the organization i.e. positioning and context are everything. Tversky and Kahneman (1981) suggest the framing of acts or outcomes can influence their desirability or acceptance. This was reinforced in a study three years later by Bazerman (1984). What appears to be a crisis at one level within an institution may be perceived as a minor inconvenience or perhaps even a positive outcome by other units within the same institution. And from a perspective outside the institution, an external stakeholder may be asking why the topic is even being discussed. For example, the unexpected resignation of a very popular supervisor in a support unit can create a great deal of anxiety and confusion for the staff. However, senior administrators overseeing this unit in the organization may see this as a perfect opportunity to change the direction of the unit in question or perhaps to implement a new administrative structure. Ultimately, the unit in which you are located within the hierarchical structure of the institution will indeed *frame* your view of the institution. This is due to the amount and type of information that is accessible as well as the opportunities for you to connect with other members of the institution's administration. Or, as Pfeffer states "how we look at things affects how they look [to us]" (p. 187).

This section will discuss several *framing* tactics Pfeffer (1992) identified and a few new ones that can be used to frame your proposal, argument, agenda, etc. in an effort to make it look more desirable to your colleagues – *Commitment, Contrast, Scarcity, Timing, Delaying,* and *Language.*

Commitment

When individuals openly support an idea, decision, or action of another, they are making a commitment. Once this commitment has been made, it becomes easier to ask more of them. Daniel Brass (2002) mentioned, "persuading a person to take a small step (action) can quickly lead to a committed path of related actions leading to a larger goal" (p. 148). That is why it is common for institutional leaders to continue allocating resources to ongoing projects that may appear destined to fail. In U.S. higher education, we have a tendency to support and respect individuals who stick with their decisions. There are numerous examples of business or government leaders who have stood by failed products or policies long after the death certificate had been signed. Pfeffer (1992) reports that "studies have found that subjects facing failure escalate their investments, committing more resources to endeavors that aren't doing well," hoping to salvage their efforts and save face with their colleagues. Think of gamblers who believe that the next card or roll of the dice will change their luck, throwing good money after bad. Or when a university devotes resources to a department that had failed or perhaps outlived its usefulness decades earlier.

This can be used to develop power by getting people to commit to or *invest* in you. Once you have the support of your supervisor or colleagues, they will not want you to fail because they do not want to be seen by others as backing a loser. Institutions will continue with programmatic efforts for which no evidence exists to support their success. Whether that be a summer reading program, the use of a new technology, or the implementation of a new major; those who supported the endeavor do not want to give up hope. Similarly, this is precisely one of the major reasons that administrators in higher education have difficulty terminating poor employees, they feel a sense of commitment. After all, the thought is, "if I hired these people they must be good." As Jim Collins (2001) states, "when in doubt, don't hire – keep looking" (p. 54).

> During the search process for an academic dean you notice the list of finalists being brought to campus and recognize the name of someone who has not had a good reputation in the field. You follow up with a colleague at the person's current institution and find out the individual had been terminated for cause. You bring this to the attention of the search committee but much to your dismay the individual is hired. After a bumpy start you bring up the individual's past to the provost, only to be told that everyone deserves a second chance. On the one hand this does appear to be somewhat compassionate, but on the other hand could it simply be a justification for a poor hiring decision?

Contrast

Whether an idea is good or bad/acceptable or unacceptable depends on to what it is being compared. As Pfeffer (1992) states "what is expensive or inexpensive, what appears reasonable or unreasonable, is profoundly affected by what we have just experienced" (p. 190). For example, your institution just spent a few million dollars on a new software platform designed to reduce costs in (fill in the blank). Now that you have the new software you should be able to persuade the powers-that-be to pay tens of thousands of dollars on consultants to train staff how to use it. After all, what good is the technology if no one knows how to use it?

The power behind *contrast* is the idea of presenting the more expensive part of a project first, then introduce the less expensive items which in turn seem *not so bad* by comparison. There is greater likelihood that the department will receive full funding if you can get the most expensive portion funded first. Institutions are not going to leave a brand-new building unfurnished.

Another way to use contrast to your advantage is showing that your proposal is very reasonable when compared to other possibilities. This is used quite often in budgeting proposals – ask for a lot more in hopes of getting what you need. For example, if you are hoping to receive a funding increase for a new program or service it can help your cause if you benchmark your costs with similar or aspirant institutions who are doing what you are proposing, but they are doing it in a more costly way. Your proposal can look quite promising compared to the others.

Scarcity

How many times have you seen advertisements for an item that states *while supplies last* or *limited time offer*? Even though there may be plenty to go around, the purpose of this approach is to create the image or perception of *scarcity*. In the U.S. and much the western world, we have been conditioned to value something if it is perceived to be scarce, e.g. gemstones, rare coins, luxury items, or almost anything labeled as a *special edition*. This is directly connected to the economic principle of supply and demand. If the demand for an item is greater than the available supply the price for the item will increase. That is, when an item is perceived as scarce, i.e. if the supply is low, the price will increase and so will the desire to possess it.

Within higher education we see this play out in our admissions processes and practices. Institutions that have *highly selective* admissions or specific majors/programs that have a limited capacity, admitting a small number of students each year, tend to be more desirable than institutions or programs that are open admission. Another area where scarcity can play out is in the hiring or perhaps negotiating processes. If a job applicant or current employee has another job offer this can be used as leverage to negotiate for additional salary or benefits. Again, the perception is that, if something is difficult to obtain, or scarce, it must be valuable and worth pursuing.

The concept of scarcity may explain why so many institutions seek external consultants to help address problems even though there may be one or more individuals on the campus who are equally qualified. Menon and Pfeffer (2003) explain it this way – "internal knowledge is more readily available and hence subject to greater scrutiny, while external knowledge is more scarce, which makes it appear more special and unique" (p. 497). They continue: "once knowledge was internalized, it was seen as less valuable … an internal idea that was undervalued when it was inside was seen as exciting and desirable when an external firm developed it" (p. 504). The old adage "you cannot be a prophet in your own land" holds true in higher education.

Kanter (2010) cautions that, within organizations, scarcity can breed resentment or dissention among the staff. She believes that managers and administrators can unwittingly encourage the development of powerlessness by limiting the information available to peers and subordinates. Lack of transparency in decision-making can also create a lack of trust in the administrator or administrative team. Therefore, when employing scarcity as a strategy with regard to information/data sharing, you must be fully aware of the potential unintended consequences to the long-term cohesiveness of the team/group.

Timing

The colloquial phrase "timing is everything" appears to hold true in many instances of decision-making in most organizations, and particularly on college and university campuses. How an issue is framed significantly affects how it is viewed (Pfeffer, 1992) and as Vecchio (2007) points out "the nature as well as the timing of information given out can have strong effects on others' conduct" (p. 78). Pfeffer breaks the concept of timing down into several parts which are relevant to college and university administrators; order of consideration, deadlines, and delaying.

Order of Consideration

It is only natural that the order in which things are presented impacts how each item is viewed. This is because people are prone to making comparisons so the person who controls the agenda not only controls what gets discussed, that person also controls the order of consideration which in turn impacts all participants' perceptions. How the agenda is structured can greatly enhance your ability to accomplish one or more of the desired outcomes you have set forth. Much like the concept of contrast, decisions made early in the meeting will have an influence on items to be discussed later. For example, putting *weaker* proposals first will make subsequent proposals appear to be even stronger, and therefore likely to receive a more favorable response. This can result in earlier items drawing out more discussion, and if they are rejected, people have a tendency to be a little softer on later proposals. Additionally, there may be a sense of fair play, suggesting the presenter should receive something for the effort, making it more likely that later proposals will receive more favorable treatment.

Likewise, items toward the end of the agenda may not receive the same attention because oftentimes people want to leave. I have seen this play out in hiring decisions as well as admissions decisions – the closer you are to a deadline, the more likely you are to make a decision more rapidly and without the rigor of previous decisions. Institutions that have not met their admissions numbers in June or July will be much more lenient than they were with similar files back in January and February. Jaques (1994) identifies another tactic with regard to agendas, which is to schedule the discussion of a potentially controversial topic when the individuals who are opposed happen to be out of the office, perhaps at a conference or on a consultancy. If there is little or no opposition to the proposal it has a much greater likelihood of succeeding.

Deadlines

The use of deadlines can be another strategy which helps move a proposal forward. During a meeting, if the discussion about your proposal appears to be in your favor, you can press the issue and state that a decision needs to be made today. Since there won't be enough time to thoroughly discuss the topic, you may stand a better chance of having your proposal approved.

> This sometimes happens with employment decisions when consulting firms are involved. The consultants pitch a candidate and indicate that if you don't act fast you will lose the opportunity and will have to start over, which would effectively kill the position for that year. The committee, not wanting to have to start over, makes the decision to hire the individual and, in some cases, several months later wishes they had waited.

Finally, timing plays an important role when initiating a change on campus such as a new curriculum or a new technology tool. Being on academic calendars and knowing that the typical institution enrolls more students in fall than in spring or summer, it may not be in the best interest of students, faculty, or staff to pilot a new technology platform or tool during the fall semester. Most technology roll outs will have a soft pilot in the spring term, a broad pilot in the summer, and a formal release in the fall. Waiting to implement the change gives the technology staff time to work out the bugs in the system so the fall release can go as smoothly as possible. On the curricular side it is more often than not a full-scale roll out in the fall because that is the more traditional start time. Understanding the timing of a change is very important for generating acceptance for the proposal and for helping to minimize the complications or unintended consequences.

> Recently, we have witnessed a number of college closures, primarily for financial reasons. It is important to observe the timing of many of these announcements, usually several weeks into the academic term. It is no coincidence that the announcements came after most of their students had paid their tuition. Had the news of trouble come prior to the start of the term the institution would have run the risk of students transferring to another institution, creating an even greater financial problem. Timing really is everything.

Delaying

As a tactic or power play, delaying can be used in a few different ways. The most common delaying tactics are: making someone wait for you, postponing a decision, creating a task force or study group, and placement of items on an agenda. These approaches can be quite useful for someone trying to assert his/her power or when someone wishes to avoid making a decision. They can also create problems for the administrator if used too frequently.

Making someone wait for you, or your unwillingness to wait for others, suggests to them that you are more important or in a position of power. This waiting game tactic is best used sparingly and usually is most effective with peers or subordinates and can be dangerous if used with those above you in the hierarchy. If overused, playing the waiting game can damage one's reputation; in civilized society, it is rude and inconsiderate to others. While you may be demonstrating power to those in attendance you may soon find that fewer and fewer people will arrive on time or even attend your meetings in the future.

> I worked for a dean who was notorious for making faculty and staff wait. I cannot recall a time when this individual ever made it to a meeting on time, even those that he initiated. Needless to say, after a year or so of witnessing this behavior, most people started to show up late as well, ultimately creating a culture of inconsideration amongst the faculty and staff.

Another form of making people wait can take place when an individual is asked to complete a task or project and agrees to do so but states a time frame that is not what the requestor intended. For example, stating, "sure I will be happy to help out and take that on, but I won't be able to start for two weeks because of other projects already in the queue." The individual is not verbally declining to help out, but by delaying the start of the project may render his/her cooperation moot.

The second approach is to postpone or simply delay making the decision. This can be an effective way to end a discussion or to effectively kill an idea. The longer you draw out the requisite discussion of the proposal, let alone its implementation, the greater likelihood that proponents will tire or get distracted and move on to another idea. In organizations that use Robert's Rules of Order, members can table the idea. In such cases by tabling or not making a decision you have essentially decided against the proposal.

> I recall a colleague discussing a situation in which she was seeking an increase in salary because of a significant change in her responsibilities and workload. After several months of performing the extra duties she approached her immediate supervisor requesting an increase in salary to accompany the increase in workload. The supervisor indicated he would look into the possibility. After a few weeks passed my colleague again approached her supervisor and was told he had to talk with his boss, the director, and that it may take a little more time. After a few more weeks she decided to talk with the director and was politely told that it was a decision for her supervisor and not the director so she should follow up with her supervisor. When she went back to her supervisor, he told her that director was leaving the institution soon and he would need to wait until the new director was hired which could take a little longer. Six months later she was still waiting for her raise and the search for a new director had not started.

The third approach mentioned is assigning the idea or project to a study group or a task force. Pfeffer suggests that the most effective method of delay is to "call for further study or consideration" (1992, p. 231). In many instances, decisions are time sensitive, so calling for further study extends the conversation beyond the time limit, which stops the idea from moving forward. While task forces or study groups are common in higher education, an administrator wishing to stop the momentum of an idea can use this tactic. Additionally, once the report is submitted there can be additional delays in bringing it up for further discussion or in the final decision-making process.

The fourth approach in which I have also seen the delay tactic used is similar to the order of consideration discussed under the *timing* section above. However, in this delay tactic the driving force is not to discuss it. Here, the person in charge of a meeting puts a controversial topic at the bottom of the agenda knowing that there will not be enough time to fully discuss it or perhaps to even broach it. Toward the end of the meeting, s/he will acknowledge the importance of the item and say "to ensure enough time to properly discuss we will make sure it is on the agenda for the next meeting," at which it once again appears at the bottom. This type of delay will most likely make the topic irrelevant by the time it actually does come up for discussion.

Finally, a word of caution, you must recognize that, even when you choose not to decide, you have still made a decision (attributed to Neil Peart) and that decision by default is the status quo. Therefore delaying or postponing keeps the status quo in place, which may be preferable to the leader, but it limits or perhaps eliminates discussion, and discussion is important to ensure a quality decision is being made.

Language

Language can create perceptions of the speaker, giving him/her power over his/her audience. As Hill (1978) stated – "[w]ords and phrases hold power – otherwise advertising and propaganda would be useless" (p. 28). The power of language is not restricted to marketing techniques. Pfeffer states, "the language people use and how they construct presentations and arguments help determine their power" (2010a, p. 139) and he goes on to suggest that those with power interrupt and those without get interrupted. This reminds me of a scene from the movie *Darkest Hour* in which Neville Chamberlain and Winston Churchill are having a somewhat heated exchange and Churchill blurts out "don't interrupt me while I am interrupting you." Churchill was definitely asserting his power over Chamberlain.

Within higher education, language is an essential and remarkable tool and the longer you are in this industry and the more institutions you work for, you will recognize that, like every other industry, we have our industry-specific vernacular. For example, the position title of provost, or how institutions refer to their set of common courses that students take, are unique to higher education institutions. As members of the academy, we have the privilege to be working with some of the brightest people on earth, many of whom enjoy the English language and its nuances. A well-crafted phrase can change the direction of a conversation or help initiate a new campus-wide initiative. However, a poorly crafted or an ill-chosen phrase can cause problems or perhaps spell doom for the offending individual.

An example of how word choice impacts the way the messages are received comes from a new president's first year at a university. In this case, the new president had been visiting each college to introduce himself and provide a brief talk as to his vision for the university. When addressing the faculty from the College of Education, he began to talk about the importance of recruitment and retention of students by telling the faculty "you need to do more to increase the number of *tuition bearing units* in the college." This reference to students as *tuition bearing units* was perceived as insulting and started what was to become a strained relationship between the faculty and the president for the duration of his tenure. Had he been more thoughtful in his word choice or been more perceptive of the members of this particular college, and made a simple alteration to the choice of his words, the message may have been far better received and easily could have conveyed respect for students and the faculty, perhaps resulting in a little more respect for him in return.

> One of my favorite examples of a clever turn of a phrase came when a provost addressed the faculty senate about some significant administrative changes on a campus, for which a committee recommended *not* moving forward. The provost stated that the "committee did not give us a green light nor did they give us a red light, but rather an amber light, therefore, it is important for us to proceed with caution." This paved the way for the proposed structural changes at the institution.

More costly examples, as reported in the May 2018, of *Inside Higher Education* (*IHE*), happened when the provost of San Diego State University resigned after an email he sent became public. According to *IHE* he was invoking *karma*. He stated in that email

> you willfully sought to harm or hurt me, may my Lord Jesus Christ ensure that you reap what you sowed … [and] you are showered with unending curse and harmed, hurt and visited by evil a million fold in everything you do throughout the rest of your life

The power of the words he chose cost this provost his job. Word choice does have an impact.

Finally, an egregious example of word choice comes from the now former president of Mount St. Mary's University. It was reported that, while referring to underprepared and underperforming students, he suggested to the faculty that they "stop treating them as 'cuddly bunnies and drown the bunnies'" (Mangan and DeSantis, 2016). He later apologized for his statements, but the damage was done and he received a vote of no confidence from the faculty and ultimately resigned a few months later.

Obviously, not all phrases are inflammatory. Within the administrative ranks of higher education institutions there are always words or phrases that are trending. Sometimes we borrow them from business sectors and in other cases they truly belong to higher education. I would like to take a look at two that have been trending for several years and have varying levels of importance depending on institutional type, reputation, or location. First let's look at the term *best practices*, then there will be a brief review of *retention*.

The Myth of Best Practices

Best practices is a special case for the use of language. This phrase has become commonplace in administrative meetings and is usually brought up by someone putting forth a proposal for a new process or policy. The individual proposing the policy provides little or no evidence demonstrating that the practice works any better than what presently exists, but instead states "we need to adopt this policy or process because it is a best practice." The implication is that there is no better process or policy, therefore, your institution should adopt this practice and change its process(es) as quickly as possible or risk being left behind. It is nothing short of amazing that a college or university would change a process based solely on the new process being called a *best practice*. I believe that the term should be eliminated from our lexicon and replaced with *common practice*. At some institutions, the term is used to mean *a practice currently used by an aspirant institution*. In reality, I contend there really is no *best practice* for *all* institutions.

You may find that when administrators want to limit, or in some instances halt the discussion about a proposed change, they will oftentimes invoke the *best practice* term as if to say: if other institutions do it we too should be doing it. This type of warped logic has brought many cumbersome and burdensome policies and procedures to too many institutions.

When we look to other institutions for ideas, we are hoping to make an improvement in a current practice(s), and in most cases we look to a group of aspirant or peer institutions because we make an assumption that these institutions must actually be doing things better. What we should be doing is looking at processes in a variety of institutional types, as well as in different

> When your supervisor or colleague uses the term **best practice** it indicates:
>
> a) He just returned from a national conference
> b) She read an interesting article in a professional journal
> c) He wants your institution to look more like an aspirant institution
> d) She wants your institution/unit to look more like her previous institution
> e) All of the above
> f) Any combination of the above

Figure 6.1 Best Practices

industries, to see how others approach the topic at hand. In many instances, what you will find is that your institution is actually doing quite well and adopting another institution's practice or process will not significantly improve yours. Figure 6.1 is a One-Question Quiz about best practices.

The Retention Myth

First, it is important to understand that retention is *not* a problem and never has been a problem in any institution of higher education. A declining or low retention rate is a *symptom* of one or more problems within the institution, not *the* problem. Typically, if an institution has a situation that is being characterized as a *retention problem,* what it really has is a problem of someone or some group not doing their job properly or there is a job that is simply not being done at all. Students leave colleges and universities for a wide variety of reasons including: lack of financial resources, lack of motivation, mental health/personal issues, the institution does not have the right major, lack of engagement, and the list goes on. It is difficult for an institution to determine where the problem lies until it can be ensured that everyone is doing their job properly, which should be the starting point of every retention committee.

Diagnosing the root cause of a lower than desired retention rate is a long-term process and there are no quick fixes that will deliver sustained increases in retention, regardless of what the latest consulting guru may have told you. Too often administrators return from a conference or have just read an article about a retention success story and attempt to implement similar programs. If it were that easy every institution in the country would have already achieved their desired rate. Instead of spending money on the latest *retention solution*, I suggest that it is more prudent to make sure that the faculty and staff at your institution are *doing the things that need to be done* and doing them well, rather than worrying about how you are being perceived by other institutions.

Realizing that this takes time, you will need the support and buy-in of those above and below you in the hierarchy. Even though it may not be a *common practice* (yet), conducting program reviews of each administrative and student support unit may be the appropriate place to begin.

Damning by Faint Praise

This idiom has been around for quite some time and continues to hold true today in higher education. This is used when you do not want to say something negative nor do you wish to speak highly of the individual or situation. This could come in a meeting where a colleague is discussing a recent event/activity and states to the person in charge, "you have done a great job considering the talent you have to work with." This looks like a compliment on the front end, but is actually a criticism of the staff responsible for the event. Another way *faint praise* can be hurtful is in references for employment. When calling for a reference, one often listens or looks for what is not being stated or what is being stated using *faint praise* instead of glowing feedback. For example, if someone were to state "he has done remarkably well for someone of his ability," the first part of the statement is a compliment, but the second part undercuts it and implies the individual has limited ability.

Finally, when I think about the power of language today what jumps to mind is Kellyann Conway, Counselor to the President of the United States, when she coined the phrase *alternative facts* and how that term has been used to obfuscate the misdeeds of powerful people. Another term that has become popular since 2016, is *fake news* which currently permeates the daily Twitter feeds or presidential rallies. These terms are used to redirect individuals' thinking. I am sure that there will be numerous psychological studies on the impact of these phrases in the near future, which can be further discussed in the next edition of this book.

GAINING POWER BY GIVING AWAY POWER

The literature is replete with articles and books on delegation, mentorship, empowerment, however, it is rare to see these terms connected to power or politics. In reality, powerful administrators will often give up part of their power by delegating responsibility and authority to others within the hierarchy. This is what Elizabeth Allen (2001) calls *power-to*. I believe it is a given that effective administrators cannot do everything by themselves. Therefore, by extension, to be effective, one must delegate and empower one's subordinates and/or colleagues. To be confident in delegating the authority along with the responsibility, a supervisor must trust her subordinates will act in the best interest of the institution.

Kanter (2010) suggests that giving employees more control (empowering them) over their situation leads to increases in productivity. This is also reinforced by Maxwell (2013) when he discusses Level 4 and Level 5 leaders and how they need to empower others in the organization so the organization can continue to develop the next generation of leaders. According to Maxwell (2013) Level 4 leaders empower others and develop them until they become leaders, while Level 5 leaders concentrate on developing other leaders who are willing and able to develop other leaders.

If you are in a position of power and choose not to delegate to or empower those who report to you, there is a danger of developing a sense of powerlessness within your division/institution. Rosabeth Kanter (2010) believes that within any institution the sense of "powerlessness is corrosive and destructive" (p. 39). Wherever power and politics are present so is powerlessness. Therefore, it is important to realize that by delegating and empowering you create a more engaged and functional environment. I believe Maxwell (2013) summed it up nicely, stating

> Many leaders don't want to share responsibility with others because they don't want to lose any of their power ... [however] As you develop people and empower them to lead, their territories expand and so does yours ... You cannot become an effective Level 4 leader unless you are willing to let go of some of your responsibilities.
>
> (p. 102)

Institutionally, one of the better examples of empowerment is the use of decentralized budget models like Responsibility Centered Management (RCM). RCM is a budget process that empowers the units responsible for generating the revenue by giving them the authority to distribute the revenue, creating a direct link between responsibility for and authority over the budget process (Kretovics, 2011). The primary purpose of this approach is to push the decision-making and prioritization processes to the units that generate the bulk of the institution's revenue, thereby empowering them. In an effective RCM environment the central administration is giving up some of its power over the revenue with the hope that the individual RCM units will be more entrepreneurial and increase overall revenue, creating more power due to the larger institutional budget.

When administrators empower their subordinates they demonstrate trust and confidence in those individuals, which in turn will create self-confidence and ownership amongst those subordinates. As Maya Angelou said, "people will forget what you said, people will forget what you did, but people will never forget how you made them feel" (www.brainyquote.com). Therefore, when you can help your subordinates feel good about themselves through empowerment, you will help craft a reputation that can increase your power within the institution.

PERCEPTION MATTERS

Machiavelli states that "everyone sees what you appear to be, few experience what you really are," therefore you should "appear as you may wish to be" (*The Prince*). This underscores the importance of creating a perception of an individual who holds power. Other authors echo this sentiment, suggesting that impression management through self-presentation and confidence help successful people reach their powerful positions (Hill and Lineback, 2011; Leary and Kowalski, 1990; Pfeffer, 2010b; Tiedens and Fragale, 2003; Vecchio, 2007). According to Leary and Kowalski, "conveying the right impression increases the likelihood that one will obtain desired outcomes and avoid undesired outcomes" (p. 37). One such desired outcome may be power within one's organization or network.

As a leader, if you want to have power, others must believe you possess power. Therefore, you will need to develop an image and reputation of a powerful leader. This can be accomplished by having others publicly acknowledge you as an effective leader/manager, because people "see what we expect to see – imputing to successful individuals qualities that we think are associated with success, even if such qualities aren't actually there" (Pfeffer, 2010b, p. 12). In some instances, with whom we associate can give the perception of power (Referent Power). The more you are seen with powerful leaders, the greater the likelihood you too will be seen as powerful. Tiedens and Fragale (2003) observed what they call motor mimicry, which is when individuals will begin to dress and even move like those they admire. This suggests that individuals desiring power may begin to dress, talk, and act like those whom they perceive as having power.

Creating a positive impression is important because, as noted by Gardner and Martinko (1988), impression management is "potentially related to individual success and promotability ... and [these] behaviors may be an important influence mechanism for leaders in generating support for their actions" (p. 321). Pfeffer (2010b) noted that social science research indicates that "people engage in behavior that helps make their initial impressions of others come true ... cognitive discounting – once people have formed an impression of another, they disregard any information that is inconsistent with their initial ideas" (p. 151). Simply stated, people see what they want or expect to see and they tend to look for evidence that supports their initial impressions. Thus, if you can shape other's impression/perception of you, you have the opportunity to "influence other's behaviors in desired ways" (Leary and Kowalski, 1990, p. 37).

CONCLUDING COMMENTS

The tactics mentioned above can be effective in helping forward your agenda or to further a cause, or they can be equally effective in destroying a cause. I recommend they be used sparingly and that when implemented, their use needs to be well thought out and well executed. Colleges and universities are social organizations in which administrators must be able to establish collaborative relationships that transcend the silos, ignore the fiefdoms, get past the pettiness and other structural barriers that may exist. To do so, it is important to understand that there will be times when you will have to work with difficult or untrustworthy individuals while trying to accomplish your goals. In these situations you must learn to put your differences aside and work to accomplish the task at hand and achieve the desired outcomes.

If you use any of these tactics too frequently or predictably the effectiveness of the tactics and by extension of yourself will diminish. Similarly, if your use of power is perceived as vindictive or retaliatory you run the risk of creating a reputation that can hinder your long-term success. While organizations may have short memories, people don't and it is the people with whom you work that permit you to be successful.

When you are new to a campus or are newly promoted to another administrative position, there are a few questions you should ask yourself before you begin to act on your new-found power.

- Who controls the financial resources that I will need to accomplish my goals?
- Who controls the allocation of space, i.e. rooms, buildings, and grounds that will be necessary to cultivate in order for me to be successful?
- Who controls the flow of information necessary for appropriate decisions to be made?
- Essentially, on whom do I need to depend in order to accomplish my goals?

These questions will help you frame your situation and give you a better perspective on the institution as a whole. Remember, regardless of the power you believe you have amassed, you should always assume that there are others in the organization with more.

REFLECTIVE QUESTIONS

1. What power tactics do you find yourself using in your current university role and to what level of success?
2. What power tactics have you seen/do you see effective/powerful leaders using and to what level of success?
3. Give an example of a time when you were a victim of one of the above-mentioned strategies.
4. Have you ever used power to accomplish a goal?

CASE SCENARIO

A politically powerful college (with a strong budget, and in good favor with the provost and/or president) is using an expensive service that is centrally funded, so it does not impact their revenue; however, there is pressure to reduce the central budget and consolidate to universal services across the institution wherever possible. All other colleges use a different resource that is notably cheaper, easier to support and to maintain. The politically powerful college argues that their added services expense is justified as it creates an ideal student experience; also, switching to a commonly applied service to save money would be insufficient for their needs, and would devalue their degree programs. Nonetheless, a change in this service has been mandated by the Provost's Office.

With regard to the aspects of using power to accomplish your goals (e.g. commitment, contrast, scarcity, timing, delaying, the myth of best practices, etc.), how do you approach this college and proceed to change the service in question?

Chapter Seven
The Power of Internal and External Influencers

This chapter will take a look at several internal and external influencers of higher education institutions that may not initially come to mind when discussing power on a campus. Below, I briefly describe the power of these influencers and their potential impact on institutions. Whether it is the power of external consultants or the influence of intercollegiate athletics, senior leaders along with mid-level administrators need to understand that positions not shown on the organizational chart can wield power and influence the allocation of institutional resources.

THE POWER OF EXTERNAL CONSULTANTS

The use of external consultants in higher education has become common practice. Consultants are hired to assist institutions with marketing, fundraising, developing master plans, assessment activities, strategic planning, and hiring mid- to senior-level administrators (see search consultants below) among others. Consultants visit our campuses and provide a perspective that can be valuable in solving problems, jump-starting new initiatives, or simply providing a different approach to the way faculty or staff conduct their daily activities. However, in some instances consultants may make recommendations for change without understanding the institutional culture or context. This section is not meant to condone or dispute the use of consultants, rather to point out the power that they can wield on a campus.

Valuing External Knowledge

Like managers in most organizations, and as mentioned earlier, administrators in higher education tend to place greater value on external knowledge rather than internal knowledge, reinforcing the adage – *one cannot be a prophet in one's own land*. The preference toward and use of outside consultants is somewhat related to the concept of scarcity mentioned in Chapter 6. As you recall, if something is perceived as scarce or in limited supply, people have a tendency to place more value on it and perceive it as more desirable. Simply because we have access on a regular basis to persons with the desired knowledge or expertise, there is a tendency to place a lower value on or have less appreciation for the contributions those individuals can make. Menon and Pfeffer (2003) summed it up nicely: "[m]arket competition makes knowledge from external competitors seem more valuable, while organizational competition makes knowledge from internal competitors seem less valuable" (p. 505).

> I worked at an institution interested in making improvements to its campus environment. The institution hired a consulting group to come in and assess the current physical environment and make recommendations for improvements needed to increase student engagement. Once on campus, it became apparent that the consultants brought in were using the principles outlined in a book that happened to be authored by a faculty member on that very campus. Even though the faculty member was one of the most recognized experts in the field, the institution chose external knowledge instead of the actual source of that knowledge.

The above is one of many examples in which an institution has overlooked its internal expertise, gravitating to external knowledge for solutions. Colleges and universities need to do a better job of assessing the talents of their staff and faculties prior to reaching out to external sources. Utilizing internal consultants can be a very cost-effective way to solve institutional problems and it may also help gain support of faculty and staff. Additionally, the current faculty or staff member who could serve as the consultant has a vested interest in the outcome because of her/his employment relationship with the institution.

Change Consultants

As institutions look at changing a process or procedure, it may be prudent to bring in consultants from outside of the institution. As noted by Lorenzen (2009) "the opposition to change may be based on good reasons, or generated by those same people who oppose all change initiatives. Leaders are at greatest risk when they attempt to make changes" (p. 83). External consultants can oftentimes moderate that risk. If an actual change does need to take place, external consultants can be a great starting point as they can look at what is currently taking place more objectively than the current staff do. Sometimes it is difficult to propose a change to the way you have always done it. For example, if your admissions yield has been declining the past two years, chances are that continuing to do what you have been doing is not going to work. Bringing in someone (or a group) from a more successful institution could help provide new ideas that the current admissions staff might not have considered.

Unfortunately, what happens all too often with external consultants is that an administrator or administrative team feels the need to make changes, so they bring in a consulting team to make recommendations for changes that in many cases have already been determined but not disclosed. The consultants are brought in to recommend (support) the desired change, which is then adopted by the administrators responsible for bringing in the consultants. In many cases, these recommendations are not in the institution's or students' best interest. In some instances, it is driven by the administrative ego (see Chapter 4) and in others, by the consultants. Too many national consulting firms, especially in the recruitment and retention areas, market themselves as consultants when in reality they are simply marketing a prepackaged set of solutions.

> A large regional public institution had a decentralized graduate admissions system with three distinct graduate schools on the campus. A new provost was hired who began promoting the idea of a single, centralized graduate school, suggesting it was a way to streamline the graduate admissions process making it easier to recruit a higher quality graduate student. To reinforce the plan, the provost invited a team of consultants to assess the situation and help provide some direction. After a two-day visit on the campus, the consulting team provided a report documenting the advantages of the current system along with a few opportunities for improvement. The bulk of the report was quite complimentary about the decentralized system, especially its ability to respond to and admit students in a timely manner. However, the final recommendation from the team of consultants was to consolidate the graduate schools because that was the *best practice* at larger research (aspirant) institutions and because according to the team, "bigger is better." The provost used the consultant's report as evidence as to why the change was necessary.

March and Cohen (1974) would classify this as an example of garbage-can decision-making, where solutions go in search of problems and with this, one finds that decision-making does not follow ordinary institutional processes nor rational logic, leaving the institution no better off, and in some instances worse off, than prior to when the consultants arrived.

Previous experience supports Jeffrey Pfeffer's (2010a) contention that external consultants can be handy because, if the proposed changes don't work out as anticipated, they can be blamed for not achieving the goals. And if the changes meet or exceed institutional expectations, then you look good and increase your power base because, after all, you were the one to bring them to campus.

THE POWER OF FREE SPEECH

In the United States, free speech is a constitutionally protected right and is considered a foundational value of higher education and we have an obligation in higher education to uphold this freedom for as long our institutions exist. If speech is silenced or the free and open exchange of ideas is discouraged, how can we expect our students to engage in critical thinking or critical discourse? Ultimately, free speech helps to balance the power for those whose voices have been limited in other ways.

Recently, free speech has become hotly contested on many campuses throughout the country. There have been numerous speakers who have been shouted down for their views or prevented from speaking because of protests on a campus. It seems as though each week one can read an article in *The Chronicle of Higher Education, Diverse Issues in Higher Education*, or *Inside Higher Ed* that details an issue of speech being repressed or discouraged on an institution's campus. Here are just a few examples.

Scott Jaschik reported (April 18, 2019) that Middlebury College called off a speech to be given by a controversial figure due to the threat of protests and the college's concern for the safety of students and faculty at the college. Two years earlier there was a similar situation in which a controversial speaker was shouted down on the campus. Cynthia Miller-Idriss and Jonathan Friedman (December 5, 2018) reported in *Diverse Issues in Higher Education* that

> [h]undreds of hate incidents have taken place on college campuses over the past two years, from nooses hung on trees, to a 77 percent increase in White supremacist propaganda during the 2017–18 school year. Anti-Semitic acts have seen a particular surge in the past month, as swastikas have been carved in pumpkins, stamped in the snow, and painted on a Jewish professor's office walls, to name

just a few examples. "It's unsettling at best, it's terrorizing at worst," said Lecia Brooks of the Southern Poverty Law Center ...

According to an article in *The Chronicle of Higher Education*, Emma Pettit (August 30, 2018)

> Southern Illinois added language to its code of conduct prohibiting university athletes and cheerleaders from showing any sign of activism while in uniform – a decision that ran afoul of the First Amendment ... After an outcry, though the university rescinded the new ban ... Southern Illinois wasn't alone in restricting its athletes' abilities to protest during sporting events. Last year Colorado Christian University told athletes to stand for the national anthem. When Eastern Michigan University caught wind of a planned protest at a football game, it played the national anthem a half-hour before game time instead of right before kickoff. When players on the University of Arkansas at Fayetteville's women's basketball team took a knee, Republican legislators criticized the students and threatened to cut the university's budget.

It has gotten to the point where the President of the United States believed it necessary to step in and issue an executive order. The order entitled "Improving Free Inquiry, Transparency, and Accountability at Colleges and Universities" designed to ensure free speech remains a priority for colleges and universities. Two excerpts from *The Chronicle of Higher Education* provide a context for what the executive order is attempting to do (Thomas, 2019).

> ... seeks to promote free and open debate on college and university campuses. Free inquiry is an essential feature of our nation's democracy, and it promotes learning, scientific discovery, and economic prosperity. We must encourage institutions to appropriately account for this bedrock principle in their administration of student life and to avoid creating environments that stifle competing perspectives, thereby potentially impeding beneficial research and undermining learning.
>
> (p. 1)

> Section 2 (a) encourage institutions to foster environments that promote open, intellectually engaging, and diverse debate, including through compliance with the First Amendment for public institutions and compliance with stated institutional policies for private institutions.
>
> (p. 2)

To many, the order simply reinforces the First Amendment, but to others it signifies an institutional challenge to be more receptive to some of the conservative views that recently have gained in popularity. This was highlighted by Nicholas B. Dirks, the former UC Berkeley Chancellor, when he wrote an October 28, 2018 piece for *The Chronicle of Higher Education* discussing the fallout from Milo Yiannopoulos' visit to Berkeley in February 2017.

> Those on the left who have sought to silence offensive or dissenting views have provided an easy target for this kind of state intervention. By rejecting the procedural commitment to free speech, protesters on the left have undermined its substantive value, which will inevitably come back to haunt them as a precedent to censor their own views ... The university as an idea stands resolutely in contrast to the like-minded bubbles of insular and uniform thinking that increasingly make up the public sphere, especially on the Internet.

College and university leaders are in a difficult position, protecting free speech on their campuses and also trying to protect their students from harm and their physical facilities from damage. It seems that politicians, donors, the media, and almost anyone with an opinion have weighed in on this issue. When hate speech comes to campus another element is now involved and how leaders respond becomes even more challenging. In an article by Jamie Rogers (November 1, 2018), Eddie Cole an Assistant Professor at William and Mary provided the following advice to today's leaders

> Responses that do not strongly condemn the content of hateful acts can add a sense of institutional indifference to these already vile incidents, particularly in the eyes of those targeted. They also mistakenly position free speech against hate speech, assuming that protecting free speech means there are constraints on denouncing hate. This is categorically wrong.

How institutional leaders address free speech on their respective campuses will impact their tenure at those institutions. Mishandling of a demonstration or controversial speaker can hasten one's departure and can also have an impact of other institutions, especially public institutions.

THE POWER OF SOCIAL MEDIA

The use of social media has transformed communications throughout the world and within higher education. The expectations of access for, and/or to everyone and immediate responses has never been greater. With students, faculty, staff, and other stakeholders using social media such as Twitter, Instagram, and Facebook, it can be challenging to stay abreast of the events of the day. Institutional leaders are caught in the middle, attempting to provide reasoned responses while still trying to respond in a timely fashion. Dan Mahony, President of Winthrop University, mentions some of his frustrations with the use of social media:

> there is an expectation that presidents need to react to everything going on in the world. With the current administration in DC Tweeting on a regular basis people expect more of an immediate response to everything ... If I respond to others it would just be my personal view ... People want an immediate reaction but it takes us time to figure out what is going on. If you react immediately you may have it wrong – frankly, that's the reason I am not on Twitter. I do other social media that does not require an immediate response

It seems that, as an institutional leader, you will need to decide for yourself as to how accessible you or your office will be to your constituents. The question you may get is, if the President of the United States can tweet throughout the day, why can't a college or university leader?

THE POWER OF THE SEARCH PROCESS

Within institutions of higher education, I believe there is no decision with greater long-lasting effects than that of a hiring decision. Whether hiring faculty, staff, or administrators; institutions spend significant resources (money and time) to bring in talented individuals who help fulfill the stated mission of the college or university. As Collins (2001) wrote in *Good to Great* – "people are not your most important asset. The right people are" (p. 13). The key to one's success as an administrator is to ensure that the right people are the ones who get hired. The largest percentage of institutional budgets is typically tied up in its employees' salary and benefits, emphasizing the importance of making the right decision. When looking closely at the hiring process on most campuses there are several key players who have the ability to utilize their respective power to influence the hiring decision.

When deciding to fill a vacant position, you will first need to make a decision whether to look internally within your current institution, or to conduct a national or regional search. This decision should not be taken lightly. On the one hand, an internal candidate knows the institution well, its people and its processes, and you can also assume that the individual believes in or at least supports the current mission, vision, and values of the institution. On the other hand, you know more about the internal candidate and have witnessed the individual's strengths and limitations, giving you more direct knowledge of a potential fit. Once the scope of the process has been determined, you will find three key *positions of power* in the search process of which to be mindful – the hiring manager, the search committee chair, and the committee members. Additionally, for many senior level searches there may be a preference to look outside the institution, which then may result in the hiring of an executive search firm to direct the process.

Hiring Manager

The hiring manager will be supervising the new hire and typically provides the overall leadership for the search. The hiring manager will be responsible for selecting the search chair and potentially other committee members, establishing a timeline for the search, determining the scope of the search (local, regional, or national), developing or approving a position description, and approving the advertising plan. Each of these decisions can have an effect on the quality and diversity of the applicant pool, giving the hiring manager power over the hiring process.

From an institutional perspective, because of the responsibility and power these hiring managers have, it is important to train and support them through the process to hire staff or faculty. Every institution should have a brief training process for hiring managers, be they faculty or staff, to ensure a smooth and as bias-free process as possible. The duties and responsibilities during a search process are very different than one's day-to-day administrative or teaching responsibilities.

Committee Chair

The chair of a search committee, may be the hiring manager, or in most cases, is the individual who represents the committee to the hiring manager and to others within the institution. Depending on the particular search policies or procedures at the institution or within the unit, the search chair may be involved with selecting the other members of the search committee, thereby influencing which voices from within the institution are going to be heard during the search. Regardless of the position level, the committee membership is important and the chair should ensure that the committee is structured to find outstanding candidates. Depending on the charge from the hiring manager, the chair of the committee may also be responsible for, or involved with, the development of recruitment materials, screening/evaluation tools, and interview questions for candidates.

As a search process progresses, the committee chair will determine the process for narrowing the applicant pool to those who will be invited for telephone/Skype (first round) interviews and those who will progress to an on-campus phase of a hiring process.

The committee chair will lead or guide the discussions of candidates and can have significant influence over the decision to advance or remove a candidate from further consideration. How the chair introduces a file can set the tone of the conversation or review of each candidate. The chair can be positive, lukewarm, or negative depending on his/her attempt to steer the committee to the desired recommendation.

Another power dynamic can come about if there is a committee member with whom the chair disagrees. The chair has the ability to determine when committee meetings are scheduled and, if desired, can schedule them at varying times when some individuals cannot attend. Therefore, the input of those committee members is limited to written feedback only, which, most likely will be summarized by the chair.

Committee Membership

Many staff and faculty shy away from volunteering to serve on search committees, viewing it as *unnecessary service*, which takes away from their primary duties and/or scholarship activities. When examining committee membership from a power perspective, shying away from such responsibilities can be a grave mistake. Being on a search committee that hires a dean, vice-president, or president can be very beneficial. Earlier, in Chapter 3, the concepts of doing favors and reciprocity were discussed; both of those can come into play if you are on a search committee. Oftentimes, the individual hired will feel a sense of obligation to those on the committee; after all, members of the committee were somewhat responsible for bringing the new hire to the institution. This sense of reciprocity can give you access to the individual in a powerful position that others at your level will not have; you are familiar to the new hire and you will be viewed positively because you were part of the team that recognized the talent or expertise of the individual. Helping bring an individual to the campus initially places you in a favorable light. Additionally, by agreeing to serve on the committee, you will be viewed as doing a favor for the hiring manager because there are times when it can be quite difficult to find people willing to serve on searches. Also, serving on a search committee can make you feel good that you are contributing in a positive way, but it can create an unspoken debt, which, if needed or wanted, can be collected by you at a later date.

External Bias When Hiring Senior Staff

Similar to the use of external consultants, there are senior-level administrators who prefer to hire candidates from outside their respective institutions. They tend to believe that, in order to make a change or to bring in new ideas to progress forward, the institution needs to hire *new blood* from the outside. This logic is fascinating because these are the same individuals who insist on *benchmarking* practices with other institutions or like to implement *best practices* borrowed from other institutions. In both cases, the ideas are coming from the outside, so why then do they also need to hire personnel from the outside to bring in new ideas? Collins contends that

> the evidence does not support the idea that you need an outside leader to come in and shake up the place to go from good to great. On the contrary, going for a high-profile outside change agent is negatively correlated with sustained transformation from good to great.
>
> (2001, p. 31).

Additionally, having searched the literature, I have found no evidence that outsiders/external hires make better leaders within higher education. Bozeman et al. (2013) did find that department chairs hired from outside the institution were *perceived* as having greater power than internal hires and that increased power is based solely on their status as an outsider.

Search Consultants

In recent years, a fourth power player has emerged on the scene and has been able to acquire a great deal of power and influence in the hiring process, especially when recruiting at the senior levels of administration – the search consultants. Gagliardi et al. (2017) note that just over 71% of college and university presidential searches between 2014 and 2016 used executive search firms. This is significantly higher than the 51% between 1996 and 2000. Using consultants or executive search firms when hiring for positions at the director/dean level or above has become the norm for mid-sized and large institutions, and more recently, even some small schools have jumped on this bandwagon.

While I am not convinced the use of such firms is good for institutions or for higher education in general, I don't see this trend changing direction

THE POWER OF INTERNAL AND EXTERNAL INFLUENCERS

- Institution sends out a request for proposals or directly solicits a firm
- Firm(s) present their proposals as to what they provide before, during, and after the search. This typically includes:
  - Assisting the development of promotional materials (position profile)
  - Assist with the development of screening tools/methods
  - Solicitation of applicants including specialized advertising
  - Scope of search – *confidential* or *secret* (usually for presidential) search
  - Screen applicants so the internal committee sees only highly qualified applicants
  - Review candidates with internal search committee
  - Conduct or assist with background checks of selected candidates
  - Assist the internal committee in narrowing to final pool
  - Arrange for the off-site/airport interviews
  - Assist in salary negotiations
  - Provide a guarantee not to re-recruit your new hire for a period of X years
- Firm is selected
- Firm creates position profile and begins recruiting
- A search consultant will guide the search committee through the candidate screening process, narrowing the pool to a manageable number (10-15)
- Airport/off-site interviews are conducted with the candidate pool
- Finalists are selected and invited to campus
- Recommendation is made to hiring manager
- Offer extended (firm will often help negotiate the contract)
- New hire begins employment

Figure 7.1 Executive Level Search Process

anytime soon. Since it looks as if these firms are here to stay, it becomes more important to understand how they operate and the implications for power on your campuses. Figure 7.1 gives a generic example of a search process for a senior executive position when using a search firm. Understanding how these firms conduct the search process will give you a better understanding of the power the firms have in determining who the senior level administrators are at our institutions. While the institutional hiring authority may have the final decision-making power, the quality of the candidates is determined by the search firm.

While the exact steps may vary slightly, depending on the type of institution and the level of position for which the search is being conducted, the search firm is the driver behind the process and not the internal search committee.

Before agreeing to a contract with a search firm, the institution's officers have a responsibility to ensure that the firm will be acting in the best interest of the institution. This means the institution should determine what the firm's responsibilities will be, and what role the firm will play in the recruitment and screening of applicants. A few questions to consider are listed in Figure 7.2.

Ideally, once the contract has been signed, the search consultant(s) will work closely with the institution's key internal stakeholders to understand

- Is the financial commitment a fixed amount or variable depending on the salary?
- What are the contingencies for a failed search?
- For previous placements by the firm, how many at the level for which you are searching stay six or more years? Less than four years?
- What kind of institutional support is required?
- How will the firm determine the scope of the search?
- How will the firm handle applications?
- How will the firm ensure candidate confidentiality, especially with regard to public records requests at public institutions?
- Is there a conflict of interest with the selected firm – Was the hiring manager hired in a search conducted by the firm?

Figure 7.2 Questions to Ask

the duties and responsibilities of the position; the traits, characteristics, and abilities desired in the candidates; and the institution itself. Most often the search consultants hired will meet with key personnel individually to discuss their perceptions of the institution, the unit for which they are recruiting, and the qualifications necessary to be successful in the position. Individuals such as the hiring manager, administrative peers and subordinates to the position being recruited, and if appropriate, the current position holder, will be among those interviewed by the search consultant. Additionally, members of the search firm will oftentimes hold open forums or large group meetings to gather information from other members of the institutional community. This data gathering is completed to provide the members of the firm information necessary to develop a prospectus or position profile. This profile, created by the outside search firm, is then used as a marketing tool to promote the position (and institution) and to aid in recruiting potential applicants. The typical profile will contain information about the institution, the community, and details about the position itself.

Most, if not all, institutions will have an internal search committee that will be responsible for reviewing the files and conducting the initial/screening interviews, however, the power belongs to the search firm. Consider this, it is the search firm that will draft the position profile, place any advertisements, solicit and collect the applications, and perform the initial paper screening of the candidates. In most cases, the search committee will see only the applications the outside search firm deems appropriate. Many firms do an excellent job of creating the *impression* of stakeholder involvement while all the time ensuring as little actual input into the search process or the vetting of candidates as possible.

When presenting applicants or potential candidates to the internal search committee, committee members need to pay special attention to the word choice of the search firm's representatives making the presentations. For example, firms often show their bias toward certain candidates in the pool when introducing them to the committee by providing glowing comments and highlighting accolades or by using faint praise and questioning abilities or motives. For example, toward a positive bias you may hear something similar to:

> We really like this person; she has what it takes to be successful in this role ...
> Great candidate, incredible set of skills and very engaging personality ...
> There aren't many as well qualified as ...
> This one is a no-brainer, and I am sure you're going to want to talk with ...

Or, when they look to discourage further conversation of a certain candidate, they may say something like:

> Very interesting, but not sure if he has the scale or scope you're looking for. Probably a better fit at a different type of institution ...
> Really enjoyed talking with her but not sure how she will fit in this position. Perhaps with a few more years of experience ...
> A non-traditional candidate who may take a while to get up to speed and may not be acceptable to faculty ...
> Great experience, but not sure if he understands the higher education environment ...

It is important for members of the institution's search committee to do their due diligence and ask the search firm's representatives specific questions about each applicant or potential candidate.

Search firms actively promote two types of searches – confidential and secret. These approaches to conducting a search are described below to help you gain a better understanding of how they may impact stakeholder perceptions when used on your campus.

Confidential Searches

The trend in higher education today is to use a *confidential search* for positions at the academic dean and vice-presidential level, although there are still a few institutions that use this process for presidential searches as well. In these searches, information about applicants is held by the search firm and not reviewable by the public. The search consulting firm is responsible for collecting information about the potential candidates and presenting that information to the search committee. Oftentimes, the identities of candidates who progress to the off-site/airport interview stage are subject to disclosure. Additionally with these searches, finalists are invited to make a public appearance on the campus. Those invited to campus will participate in a round of interviews with internal and in some cases, external stakeholders. On many campuses the candidates can be expected to participate in an open forum and respond to questions from audience members in a townhall format. This allows the campus community and others to feel a part of the process and in some instances provide an evaluation of the individual candidates. See Figure 7.3 for the common steps in confidential and secret searches.

Secret Searches

At the presidential level, the trend is to conduct *secret* searches where the consulting firm and the internal search committee are the only parties involved in the process until the recommendation moves forward to the governing board. Some unique twists may be involved, especially at public or other institutions subject to open records requests (Figure 7.3). With the guidance of the search firm, the committee will narrow the pool to a usually predetermined number who will be invited for airport/offsite interviews. After airport interviews, the search committee will narrow the pool further, typically two to four semi-finalists, who are recommended to the governing board. The board, with guidance from the search firm, completes the process and hires a new president. In most secret search processes, the search officially ends when a *sole finalist* is brought to campus and announced as the institution's new president.

These *secret* searches directed by executive search consultants often leave most institutional stakeholders out of the decision-making process. The rationale most often given for the *secret* search is that candidates are worried that exposure could jeopardize their status at their current

- First, the search firm may not require any official applications so when a public records request comes in for a review of the applicant pool the only files available will be from individuals who submitted letters and CVs *directly* to the Human Resources Office. Technically, the candidates to be reviewed by a search committee are persons of interest *not official* applicants. In many instances the only official applicant to be interviewed is the sole finalist.
- Second, the internal search committee does not receive letters of interest or CVs to review because none were officially submitted. The materials reviewed will be public documents found on the web (individual home pages, LinkedIn profile, etc.). Again, this is so no official records can be requested.
- Third, no minutes or official notes are taken when the internal search committee meets.
- Finally, when narrowing down the pool everything is done orally or candidates are labeled in such a way that no outsider could identify anyone being considered.

The theme here is that nothing official or identifiable is written down so there are no official public records to be requested.

Figure 7.3 Steps in the Process of a Secret Search

institution. However, if the search firm is performing its due diligence, they will have checked references, on and off the list, before an invitation to campus is made. By checking references, the individual's candidacy is now *public* at their home institution, making the secrecy argument moot.

As an aside, the vast majority of college and university presidents and institutional governing boards realize that several of their senior executives aspire to higher-level positions within the academy. With that said, it should come as no surprise when a senior vice-president, provost, or dean is announced as a finalist at another institution. Also, it speaks volumes about the relationship between a subordinate and supervisor when the subordinate is fearful about communicating her aspirations for a higher-level position.

Part of a supervisor's role, at any administrative level, is to help subordinates achieve their career goals while they in turn help the supervisor achieve the institutional goals. One of the most flattering events is when a subordinate receives a promotion or is wooed away by another institution's competing offer. This should be viewed as reinforcing the initial decision to hire that person. If other offices or institutions are not interested in the personnel you have hired, then why are you?

In my opinion, the movement toward *secret searches* is not in the best interest of higher education. These types of searches contribute to a climate of mistrust between the powers-that-be and the rest of the institutional community and other stakeholders. The only people who gain from a secret search are the consulting firms.

In these searches, the firm does not have to publicly disclose the list of applicants/candidates nor are they compelled to disclose their recruitment or screening processes. This permits the firms to *recycle* candidates from one search to another and the institution has no way of knowing how many other times these individuals have been actively involved in trying to find another position. All too often, these firms seem to be looking for individuals who are in search of a title rather than a position at your institution. It is that type of individual who rarely commits to the institution and the local community, which is *why* it becomes important to check the longevity of the firm's placements and whether or not the firm will give this information will tell you quite a bit about that particular firm.

Higher education is an industry that values shared governance and transparent decision-making. The utilization of executive search consultants and conducting *secret* searches is antithetical to everything for which institutions of higher education stand. At the end of the day, it is very important to understand that members of the executive search firm are getting paid by the search not by the effort expended or the longevity of the successful candidates (after the contractually obligated period). They do not have to work with these candidates on a daily basis. You and your faculty and staff do, so make sure you invest the time necessary to make the best hiring decision possible based on the information/evidence you have. After all, there are no more important decisions than personnel decisions.

Finally, it is important to note that a problem with many search consulting firms is their guidance to conduct rather narrow searches. This is usually in regard to limiting advertising of executive level positions, thereby restricting the quantity (and arguably the quality) of applicants in the pool. Unfortunately, this also has the potential of limiting the diversity of the applicant pool by discouraging non-traditional and underrepresented candidates from applying because they are not already in the firm's *virtual Rolodex*. This was highlighted by the presidential search conducted at the University of South Carolina. The pool of candidates reviewed and the finalists brought to campus lacked diversity, which prompted the students and faculty to raise questions in protest. The university acknowledged the concerns raised and declared a failed search, agreeing to start the process over. Had this process been more open from the start, the lack of diversity would have been exposed much earlier and could have saved the university time and money by addressing it before bringing finalists to campus.

THE POWER OF INTERCOLLEGIATE ATHLETICS

If your institution has an intercollegiate athletics program, whether it participates in Division I, II, or III of the NCAA or if it participates in NAIA competition, you will most likely find that the athletics program's sphere of influence is far greater than one would expect based on the number of students it affects. Mitchell and King (2018) suggest that "strategically, presidents and boards ignore college sports at their own peril … In public and internal battles between presidents and athletic coaches, the power of the athletic office can be significant" (p. 112) and should not be underestimated. While serving as president of the Ohio State University, when asked if he was intending to fire the football coach after the coach was found in violation of NCAA rules, Gordon Gee quipped "I hope the coach doesn't fire me." Intended to be humorous, there was also a bit of concern because problems in high-profile athletics programs can spell the end for university presidents. Ultimately, presidents are responsible for everything beneath them in the organizational chart and that includes intercollegiate athletics, regardless of how much money it brings in to the institution.

In the last decade we have seen several presidents either step down or get fired in the aftermath of an athletic scandal including: Graham Spanier,

Penn State University (2011); G. Holden Thorp, UNC Chapel Hill (2012); R. Bowen Loftin and Timothy Wolfe, University of Missouri (2015); James Ramsey, University of Louisville (2016); and Kenneth Starr, Baylor University (2016), to name a few. In some cases it may not have been entirely due to the athletics problems (e.g. Timothy Wolfe, University of Missouri System), but for several it was a direct response of a president not acting in accordance with university policies and or the law. More recently, Wallace Loh, President, University of Maryland at College Park announced his resignation effective June 2019. This followed the death of a football player in the summer of 2018 and the subsequent investigation which, according to *The Chronicle of Higher Education*, "was a damning report" indicating a toxic culture within the athletics program. Initially, the athletic director and football coach were placed on administrative leave and several of the University's regents pressed President Loh to reinstate the head coach of the football team. While still the president, Mr. Loh decided to terminate the coach's contract, acting in direct contrast to the recommendation of several regents, including the chair. This then led to a *crisis in leadership* and resulted in the resignation of James Brady, chairperson of the Board of Trustees.

The details behind the athletics scandals have shown the power that an athletics department and, in particular, high-profile coaches can wield. In several instances it has also shown how little oversight the NCAA really imposes over these high-profile programs. Two brief examples demonstrating how athletic departments use their power to influence academics come from Auburn University and the University of North Carolina at Chapel Hill.

Auburn University

According to Jack Stripling (2018), Auburn University was advancing an athlete-friendly curriculum demonstrating "how the athletics department exerts influence on academic matters." Stripling goes on to discuss how "email and other communications obtained by *The Chronicle* suggest an openness among Auburn's academic leaders to tailor a curriculum for the specific benefit of athletes." On the one hand, the university appears to be trying to create majors to accommodate the busy training schedules of today's Division I student athletes. On the other hand, the university appears to be trying to make it easier for athletes to enroll in a major that has a greater likelihood of allowing them to remain eligible to play their respective sport.

The fact that the discussions being held at Auburn were described by Stripling as private and they were attempting to create "new majors that would best serve a small but high-profile segment of the student body" demonstrate the power and influence of the athletics program. To me, this is also an example of a university placing its athletic interest ahead of its academic mission.

University of North Carolina Chapel Hill

Perhaps the best example of the power of athletic programs comes from the decision by the NCAA not to sanction the University of North Carolina for its lengthy history of academic fraud, which in my opinion was unconscionable and clearly demonstrates that the NCAA has little control over high-profile Division I college athletics programs (www.chronicle.com/article/In-UNC-Case-No-Watchdog-for/241448). The failure of UNC to maintain any semblance of academic integrity in its athletics department, while an embarrassment to higher education, indicates just how money influences decision-making. Money over academics is truly front and center at institutions with *big-time* college sports and this scandal at the University of North Carolina at Chapel Hill is a blatant example of that prioritization. Either NCAA Division I athletics needs to end the charade of the *student athlete* in these big-time college sports programs or the individual institutions should take control and put the student in the spotlight, instead of the revenue-generating athlete. These are supposed to be extra-curricular activities. However, now with policies like *one-and-done* in men's basketball, they are nothing more than feeder teams for professional sports or reincarnations of the gladiator sports of the Roman Empire – entertainment. Unfortunately, I believe this entertainment has the power to self-perpetuate.

As discussed in Chapter 3, the ability to generate revenue or control resources can be a symbol and a source of power in higher education institutions. If an institution's budget is indeed a financial representation of its values, one will be hard pressed not to see the power held by intercollegiate athletics on many campuses across the country. The money involved in the high-profile athletics programs, especially in the so-called Power Five Conferences, can be mind boggling. The Knight Commission on Intercollegiate Athletics has an interactive database that provides users financial information on revenues and expenditures for public institutions in the NCAA's Division I of intercollegiate athletics (http://cafidatabase.knightcommission.org). When reviewing the revenue generated by some of these programs, one can see how money has influenced the power dynamics at the institutional level. Surprisingly, even at institutions where the athletics program annually loses money, a disproportionate level of power can still be found within that institution.

THE POWER OF POLICIES

In general, there are three types of policies in most colleges and universities – health and safety, efficiency and effectiveness, and what I call lack of trust. First, health and safety. These policies are often determined by law and put in place so staff, faculty, and students do not injure themselves or others during the normal course of conducting business or related activities. For example, policies direct how chemicals are stored or handled in laboratories and in maintenance and custodial departments. Similarly, institutions will have policies in place governing student conduct on campuses and when participating in institutionally sponsored activities. Second, institutions enact policies to help employees work in more efficient or effective ways. For example, there are policies that determine the scheduling of classes and the utilization of campus buildings, which prevent multiple classes scheduling the same space or the under-utilization of prime spaces on campuses. Additionally, institutions have policies regarding student registration for classes. Finally, lack of trust. These are the policies that require multiple signatures on forms or that require certain employees to *clock in and out* of work. Many of these policies were enacted because one or a few individuals' behavior earned a lack of trust from their respective supervisors. It is this latter group of policies that typically create inefficiencies in the workflow process. Instead of dealing with the individual who created or has become the problem, it is unfortunate that higher education administrators tend to craft a policy to prohibit *all* others from said behavior in the workplace. Administrators can use their legitimate power to restrict, and in some instances, direct the behaviors of the staff in their respective units. A word of caution here, just because you can, does not mean you should. If supervisors do their jobs and supervise and train their staff well, many of the policies in these manuals become unnecessary.

Enforcement of Policies and Exceptions

When looking at the policies of our respective institutions we must constantly ask ourselves *why* a particular policy exists. On many campuses, policies are overridden on a regular basis with exception after exception, rendering said policy virtually ineffective. For example, on many residential campuses, the housing office will have a policy prohibiting room changes within the first week or two of classes. However, it is quite common for institutions to make *an exception* when parents call complaining about their student's living conditions (you fill in the reason).

When you start to see numerous exceptions to the same policy, it becomes important to ask yourself and your colleagues, "why does the policy exist?" All too often we discover that we really don't know why the policy is in place and it is simply the way we have always done it, which really does not justify its existence or is not an acceptable response. Another common response is, "because my supervisor said we have to do it this way." I strongly encourage you to use what power or influence you have to *push back* a little on policies that, on the surface, don't seem to make sense. For example, several institutions have a policy in their graduate schools that require graduate students to apply for a leave of absence when they wish to stop out. On the surface, this seems to make sense for students. However, if one is a part-time student who needs to take a semester, or a year off due to a family situation or who simply wants to stop for a break, but intends to graduate within the allotted time, one would rightfully question, do we really need a form for that? In so many instances it just creates unnecessary work for the student and the advisor. Is the policy in question designed to help the students or to help staff and administrators? Exceptions to policies should be just that, *exceptions*, not common practice.

THE POWER OF RANKINGS

The numerous national and international rankings, now a permanent fixture of the higher education landscape, may cause some confusion among more mobile students – international students and domestic students looking at institutions more than 200 miles from home. The important point to note with regard to rankings is that they are so ubiquitous and methodologically flawed (Kretovics, 2011) they have rendered themselves almost meaningless to potential students and academics alike. After all, the median distance that students travel to attend postsecondary education is slightly less than 100 miles (Mattern and Wyatt, 2009), so spending too much time on rankings may not be the best use of time for the vast majority of institutions because the target market is relatively local. The value seems to be more for marketing purposes and self-promotion than for any other value. "What rankings measure offers insight into the hegemony of particular values and practices in contemporary universities and into the role of state policies and practices in discourse, resource allocation, and power relations" (Pusser and Marginson, 2012, p. 93).

Toma (2012) mentions that rankings encourage institutional leaders to engage in mission creep, stating that institutions are "seemingly obsessed with moving to the next level. Their common goal is legitimacy through enhanced prestige" (p. 118) and he goes on to state "[p]ositioning for prestige is the standard strategic direction chosen across higher education ... Prestige is to higher education as profit is to corporations" (p. 119). Toma's comments are reinforced by Pusser and Marginson (2012):

> Rankings are exceptionally effective in legitimizing prestige-seeking behaviors while excluding other goals ... Rankings foster a policy environment that facilitates state-managed quasi-markets and new public management reforms designed to secure state influence and augment performance using accountability, audit, and quality assurance techniques.
>
> (p. 117)

This quest for prestige, to advance in the rankings, has institutions concentrating on admissions selectivity, reputation among peer institutions, and endowment dollars; not the quality of instruction, or the educational outcomes of graduates. Institutions have resorted to efforts to increase their applicant pools, so they can in turn reject more applicants, thereby becoming more *selective*. An unintended consequence of the ranking-game is that most rankings prioritize institutions that use financial aid to recruit academically talented students and penalizes institutions that attract low-income, at-risk, and underserved students (Volkwein and Grunig, 2005). Another unintended consequence is that institutions are now more focused on collecting *comparable* data rather than *assessment* data, creating a *culture of comparison* (Pusser and Marginson, 2012) rather than a culture of assessment. Institutions have become more concerned about retaining students than understanding what or if students have learned. These media-generated rankings "reflect prestige, a concept sufficiently amorphous as to lose most of its meaning when one tries to describe the difference between two institutions with similar profiles but ranked twenty places apart" (Zemsky, 2005, p. 284).

Even though institutional leaders decry the use of rankings within higher education, many still want to ensure their institution or program receives some recognition. This has led to numerous instances of institutions *gaming* the rankings or in some instances, simply submitting false information. In February 2018, Scott Jaschik reported that the University of Florida and the University of South Florida both submitted incorrect data regarding the dollar amount of grants awarded to their respective College of Nursing. Additionally, he also reported that Sam Houston State University exaggerated the research expenditures for its College of Education. In August 2018, eight other institutions were also found to have submitted erroneous data. More recently, Jaschik (2019) reported that the University of Oklahoma had been supplying false data regarding the percentage of alumni who donate to the institution for almost twenty years. In all cases, the institution or specific college was removed from the *U.S. News and World Report* rankings for the time period in question.

Unfortunately, what is occurring in many institutions is a reprioritization of resources creating a new attitude amongst administrators – what gets ranked gets funded! Rankings have far too much power in higher education. While higher education professionals encourage high school counselors not to perpetuate the use of these rankings, it remains a significant challenge for higher education to eliminate their use because institutions continue to tout their respective ranks on their websites and in their marketing materials. This hypocritical behavior can be stopped by the perpetrators themselves – college and university presidents. Until this group decides not to comply with rankings requests, I believe institutions will continue to waste money on unnecessary practices.

THE POWER OF DONORS

In Chapter 4, it was noted that one's ability to control access to or possession of resources was considered a source of power within a college or university. This also holds true for some external stakeholders such as donors and a few of the large grant funding foundations such as Lumina, and Bill & Melinda Gates, as they control financial resources in the form of potential contributions to an institution. Additionally, foreign governments can also have an influential role, such as the Chinese government's sponsorship of Confucius Institutes on numerous U.S. campuses. This flow of outside dollars can be very enticing and difficult for a college or university president to pass up and also a hardship when these resources are rescinded.

In many, perhaps most cases, donors are not trying to influence the curriculum or administrative policies but simply trying to help students through scholarship or by providing resources for building new facilities or renovating current ones. However, there are some that do make it clear that they want to have a say in what students are learning or who is teaching. It is up to the institution's leadership to determine if the goals of the donor are compatible with the vision and mission of the institution. For example, Confucius Institutes are sponsored by the Chinese government's Office of Chinese Language Council International (Hanban) and according to Guttenplan (2012) the Chinese government is attempting to influence how Chinese language is taught and what parts of Chinese history should be avoided. *The Chronicle of Higher Education* reports host institutions typically receive $150,000 to help defray start-up costs and receive $100,000/year to support faculty or programming.

Additionally, the institution receives teaching materials from Hanban. Another example of a controversial contributor is the Charles Koch Foundation. In 2016, the foundation contributed over $50 million in grants to 249 colleges and universities (Basken, 2017). Basken also reports that the foundation has been accused of trying to influence research on campuses and for funding "politically tinged work on other campuses" such as the Center for the Study of Free Enterprise at Western Carolina University (Schmidt, 2016).

In most cases, money donated to an institution of higher education will arrive on campus with some strings attached. Sometimes it is simply a naming right, or it could be to create a targeted scholarship, or it could be for a politically motivated speaker series; regardless, there will be strings. Some strings are more institution friendly than others and it is the responsibility of the institution's senior leadership to ensure that those strings don't pull the institution in a direction that will compromise its core beliefs/values. It is important not to let the power of the purse override the power of the institutional mission.

POWER OF THE PARADOX

The Abilene Paradox, coined by Jerry Harvey in 1974, refers to a group or team's inability to manage agreement. Harvey contends that, in every organization, we spend a great deal of time and energy addressing the issue of conflict management, but completely fail when it comes to managing agreement. Not to be confused with group think, the Abilene Paradox describes a situation in which no one within the group wants to pursue a particular course of action and for individual reasons no one is willing to voice their disagreement. Although introduced decades ago, Harvey (1988) believes this paradox may still be the greatest source of organizational dysfunction – "the inability to cope with (manage) agreement, rather than the inability to cope with (manage) conflict, is the single most pressing issue of modern organizations" (p. 17).

To illustrate the paradox in action Harvey describes a situation in which his wife, his in-laws, and he were relaxing at his in-laws' home in Coleman, TX, when his father-in-law suggested driving to Abilene for dinner. Everyone agreed and off they went in an unairconditioned car on a 53-mile journey for dinner at a recently opened cafeteria. Upon their return, hot and tired, one-by-one they all confessed that they did not really want to go but agreed to do so because they did not want to disappoint the others. Hence, the paradox, everyone agreed to do something that, individually, no one actually wanted to do. Harvey suggests that this happens in organizations all too frequently and as a result the institution pursues a path that is contrary to what the individual members believe to be in the institution's best interest.

Harvey (1988) identifies the following six characteristics that are present in the Abilene Paradox:

- Members of the team/group individually agree in private as to the nature of the group situation or problem.
- Members of the team/group individually agree in private as to the next steps required to resolve or cope with the problem at hand.
- Members of the team/group *fail* to accurately communicate their thoughts and desires to others, leading one another to misperceive the current situation.
- Using inaccurate information, the team/group makes collective decisions that are contrary to what they really want to do, resulting in actions that are counterproductive to the team's/group's intentions.
- The counterproductive actions result in team/group members experiencing frustration, anger, irritation, and dissatisfaction with the team/group and its direction.
- If team/group members fail to manage their agreement, the dysfunctional cycle repeats itself with increasing intensity. (p. 16)

Harvey analyzes the paradox using the metaphor of a map and he points to five landmarks on the map along the road to Abilene. These landmarks (Figure 7.4) help us better understand why so many teams/groups take actions that are counterproductive and very often counterintuitive. How many times have you or a colleague stated – "it sounded good at the time" or "I can't tell the president (or other senior administrator) that"?

- Action anxiety – thinking about doing what is believed to be the proper course of action creates undo anxiety.
- Negative fantasies – a belief that confronting the issue will result in embarrassment, loss of prestige, their position, or an increase in health concerns.
- Real risk – every decision or action has consequences, some positive, some not. There are risks to taking a stand but how likely are the negative outcomes?
- Separation anxiety – it is understandable to fear the unknown so sticking one's neck out may risk alienation from those with whom we work the closest.
- Psychological reversal of risk – the failure to take the risk results in the fantasized risks becoming an actuality.

(Adapted from Harvey, 1988)

Figure 7.4 Landmarks on the Road to Abilene

Agreement management is different from conflict management. However, failing to manage agreement may eventually result in actual conflict which "stems from the protective reactions that occur when a decision that no one believed in or was committed to, goes sour" (p. 29). Instead of perpetuating the dysfunction of the team/group by continuing down the road to Abilene, it is incumbent upon every member of the team/group to identify and confront the issue at hand. You cannot rely on institutional leaders to point out the inconsistencies in direction or strategy, because much of the time it was their idea or comments that started the group down the road to Abilene.

The surest way to avoid trips to Abilene is for the senior leadership to develop an institutional culture where questioning decisions and having reasoned debate is preferred to blind obedience. In the parlance of Chapter 2, institutions need more *Counter Balancers* and *Athletes* and fewer *Lap Dogs* and *Floaters*. I believe it is much easier to manage conflict within an institution than it is to manage agreement. Sometimes a simple question such as "are we really sure this is the best approach?" or "remind me again, why are we doing this?" can help us avoid Abilene. Therefore, if you have developed a culture that accepts conflict as a part of a well-functioning team, you will be less likely to travel to Abilene. However, if by chance you find that your group/team has wound its way to Abilene all is not lost. You have to recognize that everyone was party to this unfortunate road trip and it will most likely take everyone working together to find your way back home. The leaders (formal or informal) must ensure that the blame game does not erupt and that the focus becomes returning home rather than finding fault. Remember, the effective use of power is doing the right thing, the right way, for the right reasons.

CONCLUDING COMMENTS

This chapter shared several sources of *powers* that can be found on campuses, which directly affect colleges and universities across the country. Factors such as your institutional type, its financial situation, and your position within the institutional hierarchy will determine the degree to which these individual powers impact you or your unit. Identifying these and other influences on your campus or within your system will assist you in becoming more conscious that power does not reside within the organizational structure only. It is incumbent upon you to understand the influence of these powers and how they can be used to your advantage or minimized to reduce any negative effects.

REFLECTIVE QUESTIONS

1. Of the powers listed above, which ones have the most significant impact on your current role?
2. How have you seen donors influence institutional priorities?
3. In what ways do rankings influence policies or practices at your institution?
4. What additional powers are present on your campus?

Part III
Politics and Decision-Making

Chapter Eight

Politics and Political Behaviors

Tip O'Neill, former Speaker of the U.S. House of Representatives, stated that *all politics is local*. While he was referring to elected government officials and referenced the local nature of the issues of the day, his statement is also quite accurate in depicting organizational politics and political behavior within higher education. The concepts of power and organizational politics are interrelated and much like with power, organizational politics and developing political savvy can be viewed as positive influences within an organization's decision-making structures (Pfeffer, 1992; Gilley, 2006). In their writings, Jeffrey Pfeffer and Jerry Gilley also promote the idea of successful leadership, requiring the understanding of internal politics and the development of political knowhow. According to Gilley (2006), one must become a political navigator; which is an administrator who is competent and a master of the political interaction. This is also supported by the research of Herdlein et al. (2011) "more than 94% of respondents indicated that political knowledge and skills were either essential or very important" for senior level administrators within higher education (p. 49).

Gilley (2006) suggests that whenever two or more groups within an institution pursue differing goals, or the institution's goals are unclear or ambiguous, the environment will be ripe for politics. This seems to be a perfect description of the internal environment of almost every college and university in the United States. As noted in Chapter 3, institutions of higher education are comprised of structurally diverse administrative and academic units with differing goals, all competing for scarce resources, and in the process spawning political environments like no others. Gilley also mentions that, when it is difficult to assess effectiveness, or in the case of higher education learning outcomes, an environment is created that fosters organizational politics. Therefore, it is all but guaranteed that colleges and universities are perfect breeding grounds for a political environment and political interactions.

Institutions of higher education are *trust organizations* with collegial relationships that are political in nature, and I contend that you will be hard pressed to find more political environments than institutions of higher education. Scarce resources, competing interests, frequent changes in leadership, and administrative and academic silos all contribute to the political climates existing on our campuses. As your colleagues engage in party politics, it is incumbent upon you to understand their tactics and strategies, and to be prepared to engage in and/or defend yourself against said tactics. You will need to fully understand the politics of the internal and external environments in order to take appropriate actions. In the following paragraphs we will explore political interactions, political navigation skills, and political savvy.

POLITICAL INTERACTIONS

Gilley (2006) defines a political interaction as a "conversation between you and one or more individuals designed to achieve a desired result while simultaneously meeting the interests and needs of all parties" (p. 5). This type of conversation is a process in which you use your political or interpersonal skills to guide your colleagues to a mutually beneficial decision. During these interactions, you need to be aware that there will always be a power differential between the parties involved (Wolfe and McGinn, 2005), making it critical that you assess and understand the motives and desires of your colleagues so you can avoid outcomes that are too one-sided, which do not benefit you or your unit. In negotiating these interactions you may find yourself assuming the role of a facilitator or the helping professional who encourages your colleagues to identify and reflect upon their goals. "The primary purpose of political interactions is to assist others by helping them understand their concerns, expectations, thoughts and fears" (Gilley, 2006, p. 8). Remember, political interactions are not by nature negative or destructive, instead these relationships or discussions should be viewed as attempting to discover a win–win scenario.

In every higher education setting, nearly all interactions between administrators can become a political interaction. To ensure these interactions are effective and productive, it is advantageous for you to control the conversation and its direction. This does not mean that you dominate the conversation, but rather shepherd it along so it does not get hijacked or redirected or become one-sided. To control and direct the conversation requires a skill set common amongst many helping professionals (Figure 8.1).

POLITICS AND POLITICAL BEHAVIORS

- Actively listen to what the others are saying
- Paraphrase and summarize to help others recognize their needs and expectations
- Utilize coaching and facilitation skills
- Help others identify and reflect upon their motivation for achieving the stated goals
- Assist with conflict resolution
- Inspire a shared vision
- Help to look for alternatives or new opportunities

(Adapted from Gilley, 2006)

Figure 8.1 Skills for Directing a Conversation

Gilley also believes that a positive political interaction permits all parties involved to work collaboratively and accomplish their goals while encouraging mutual respect among the participants. This positive outcome is referred to as self-esteeming, which Gilley defines as "the sum total of how people feel about themselves as a result of a political interaction" (p. 10). Also, as discussed earlier, if you can help others feel good about themselves, it will increase your personal power in that situation, possibly invoking the *reciprocity rule* (Cozby, 1972).

One of the primary reasons that political behavior turns toward the negative is that the individuals involved are fearful of the uncertainty that lies ahead (Gilley, 2006). Uncertainty Reduction Theory suggests that "there is a human drive to reduce uncertainty, to explain the world, and to render it predictable" (Bradac, 2001, p. 456). Additionally, the theory states "that high levels of uncertainty will result in information seeking [behaviors] ... and that as communication increases, the level of uncertainty decreases" (Kramer, 1999, p. 306). During challenging or turbulent times, uncertainty will increase, and if communication does not increase to counteract this uncertainty, there is greater likelihood of negative political behaviors. Kanter (2010) noted that when budgets are tight the stakes tend to increase and that power and political behaviors increase as well (p. 39). Institutions that have developed a *culture of fear* or that have a disproportionate use of *Coercive Power*, will have an increase in negative political behaviors. These negative political behaviors can have long-term detrimental effects on individuals and organizations. As Jaques (1994) describes, "the victim of a master politician is seldom initially aware that they have been targeted until the damage is done" (p. 16). It has also been documented that "higher levels of perceived politics inside organizations are associated with reduced job satisfaction, morale, and organizational commitment, and higher levels of perceived politics are also correlated with higher intentions to quit" (Pfeffer, 2010a, p. 213).

Additionally, to improve your prospects of becoming an effective politician within your institution you will need to understand the political influence tactics described by Yukl and Tracey (1992) in Chapter 1 (see Figure 1.1). These tactics are used to help those being influenced to commit to or at least comply with the decisions made during the interaction. The worst-case scenario is that the interaction leads your colleagues to resist the decision.

Political Navigation

To become a successful administrator you will need to develop at least a minimal understanding of a few leadership and management principles and practices and how they relate to your role within your current institution. While this knowledge is necessary to become an effective administrator, I believe it is not sufficient in and of itself. Gilley (2006), Pfeffer (1992), and many others suggest that you will need to develop additional skills to help you navigate the political landscape of your institution effectively. First and foremost, you must reframe your thinking by utilizing "political thinking skills" (Gilley, 2006, p. 86) as noted in Figure 8.2.

As with any skill set, developing them does not come without practice. Once developed, these skills become part of your *tool kit* to be used as needed; but remember, using them does not ensure success as a political navigator. However, these skills will definitely equip you to perform better in difficult situations and put you in the position to become a more effective administrator. As you can see, one of the most important skills you can

---

- Listen carefully to others' requests
- Ask questions appropriately (open ended vs closed ended)
- Think before you act or react
- Filter suggestions and recommendations through a defined philosophy of interpersonal relationships
- Understand your role during engagements with others inside and outside of the institution
- Possess the courage to recommend solutions that are appropriate but may not be popular
- Analyze all requests as requests not as commands (regardless of the source)
- Maintain consistent guiding principles to ensure your credibility

(Adapted from Gilley, 2006)

Figure 8.2 Political Thinking Skills

develop is that of listening. Simply put, successful administrators are good listeners because listening is powerful, and in my opinion, the most important skill for administrative success. Therefore, good administrators will spend more time listening and less time talking.

Gilley (2006) believes that there are specific behaviors that a political navigator exhibits that are a direct result of acquiring the above-mentioned skills (see Figure 8.3). These behaviors help to establish one's credibility within the institution and lay the foundation for a successful administrative career.

Incorporating these behaviors into your administrative life will allow you to establish the relationships with colleagues on your campus that are critical to your success. As Herdlein et al. (2011) found, "there was broad agreement that political activity intensifies with the level of responsibility from entry-level to mid-management to senior-level officers" (p. 47), so it is obvious that these skills and behaviors become more important as your career advances. Through these relationships you will be able to co-opt others into seeing you as successful, which will help you forward your agenda (Battilana and Casciaro, 2013).

Developing Political Savvy

Regardless of institutional type, or your administrative level within your institution, chances are you play multiple roles as leader, follower, contributor, team member, etc. While these roles vary depending on your individual circumstances, there are a few that transcend a divide. Gilley (2006) highlights five key roles that are important to your developing political savvy and being viewed as a political navigator within your institution: relationship builder, assertive communicator, negotiator, organizational expert, and partnership builder.

- *Be predictable and consistent – dependable and reliable*
- *Establish collaborative relationships*
- *Be accurate in your practices – evaluations, budgets, etc.*
- *Meet your commitments in a timely and efficient manner*
- *Express your opinions not emotions (keep your cool)*
- *Demonstrate creativity and innovation*
- *Maintain confidentiality*
- *Be ethical in your treatment of others*
- *Demonstrate integrity in your actions*
- **Listen to and respect others**

(Gilley, 2006, p. 39)

Figure 8.3 Political Navigator Behaviors

First, it is imperative you take time to establish *positive relations* with individuals within your department/unit, across departmental/unit boundaries, and across institutional boundaries. Silos are still plentiful within colleges and universities and unfortunately the larger more complex the institution the greater number of silos present. It is your responsibility to construct or foster the development of an environment of trust and confidence within your department before you can expect *outsiders* to feel comfortable with you. Developing this trust begins with being open and honest when sharing information. There is a stark contrast between departments that *want* to work with you and those that *have* to work with you. It is your responsibility to convince others that it is to their benefit to work with you and your departmental colleagues. This institutional buy-in is valuable in helping you move your agenda forward. Battilana and Casciaro (2013), note that positive relations with and personal connections to "potentially influential fence-sitters and resistors" will help you in forwarding your agenda (p. 833).

Second, you will need to recognize that conflict is part of organizational life, and handling conflict in an assertive manner will garner far more respect and admiration than being aggressive or passive. It is important that you focus on the issues or problems not the people or personalities involved. Being an *assertive communicator* begins with being a good listener and involves direct communication that permits both parties to retain their dignity. Criticizing, belittling, or trying to bully people does not help resolve problems, Rather, those approaches only exacerbate existing problems.

Third, you need to be a formidable *negotiator*. Within every organization, conflict exists, and colleges and universities are no exception. Any time individuals with different experiences and different expectations are put together around a table, in a meeting, or on the same staff/team, some level of conflict will arise. Recognizing this requires an administrator to utilize effective negotiation skills. In order "to reach an agreement each party needs to convince the other to make a concession that he or she would not make absent the influence of the other" (Wolfe and McGinn, 2005, p. 3). To be an effective negotiator, you must be able to separate the people from the problems at hand, focus on common goals not only problems, generate a set of reasonable alternatives, and ensure that the result is based on an objective standard (Gilley, 2006). Gilley further points out that being comfortable with ambiguity is a requisite to being a successful negotiator.

Fourth, your effectiveness within the institution depends heavily on your *organizational expertise*. The better you understand the institution, its people, their needs, and their expectations; the greater likelihood you will be more successful in your endeavors. Before you undertake a project or submit a proposal you need to do your homework. Critical to your success will be an understanding of the bureaucratic and communication channels, who the key stakeholders are, and the institution's culture, along with the mission and goals. As an organizational expert, you will demonstrate knowledge of institutional policies and procedures, and who is who within the departments you will engage. You need to be seen as a problem solver – not as part of the problem. Additionally, knowing the culture and the language of those departments will enhance your credibility.

Finally, as a *partnership builder* you must have strong communication skills, including excellent interpersonal skills (Casey, 2009) and be confident in the work of your department and your individual abilities as an administrator. Partnerships evolve out of strong relationships and are developed within an institution to improve the effectiveness and/or efficiency of the institution. Successful partnerships also increase the credibility of the administrators and staff involved. The development of a partnership needs to be strategic and it needs to be done with the best interest of the institution in mind. To be successful, it is important that you have developed allies who can help you span the various silos present within your institution. These allies will help you create a positive and mutually beneficial environment in which all parties can see the relationship as a positive.

Becoming politically savvy will not solve specific problems but it may help you avoid problems in the future. Figure 8.4 summarizes some of the key components that may assist you in developing political savvy within your institution.

The Importance of Political Savvy
When being politically savvy, you will find that it is important for you to stay above the fray and stay true to your own standards, values, and ethics – maintain your integrity! Peter Jaques (1994) contends that there are two main strategies used by office politicians in an attempt to self-promote at the expense of others within the institution. First, they may use disinformation to place others within the department in an unfavorable light. In many situations, to accomplish this they will use their knowledge of the unofficial or informal communication channels to facilitate the speed at which the disinformation spreads throughout the department (Jaques, 1994, p. 16). The second approach is to introduce a minor or cosmetic change to a practice or process, making it appear to be new and different. They will tout this change as a more efficient or effective approach in an attempt to gain recognition from those in the supervisory positions (Jaques, 1994, p. 19). As you become savvier, you will be able to see these strategies and protect yourself or your department from any fallout.

POLITICS AND DECISION-MAKING

- *Listen more than you speak*
- *Observe and identify the strengths and limitations of others within your institution*
- *Study your institution and learn as much as possible about its culture, mission, its history, and goals by asking questions*
- *Find one or more mentors to help you navigate the institution's politics and power dynamics*
- *Determine whom you can trust*
- *Develop allies slowly and purposefully – share information as appropriate*
- *Form opinions gradually and base them on facts not rumors*
- *Choose your friends carefully – confidents and friends are necessary to keep you grounded and focused on your goals*
- *Be proactive not reactive – anticipate the needs of others and do favors*
- *Make sure you have evidence to support your statements – no facts, make no comment*
- *Do not publicly criticize others – attack problems not people*
- *Don't make statements you are not comfortable seeing on the front page of the student newspaper*
- *Learn to keep a "poker face" that helps to hide your emotions*
- *Don't panic – people need to perceive you as calm and in control*
- *If you lose your cool – you will lose your credibility*

(Adopted from Kretovics, 2011)

Figure 8.4 Developing Political Savvy

Additionally, having this understanding gives you the insight and ability to be more assertive and identify such behaviors to others as needed.

Concluding Comments

Politics is pervasive within institutions of higher education therefore, it becomes important for administrators to understand how to navigate these political environments. Herdlein et al. (2011), indicate their survey results and the research literature reinforce the role of politics in policy formation and decision-making is pervasive (p. 55). This was also brought up by Julius (2009), when he stated "where some encounter difficulty, however, is in comprehending the political dynamics of the decision-making environment" (p. 73). In addition, several authors including Herdlein et al. (2011), Kanter (2010), Pfeffer (2010a), and Julius (2009) identify budget and budgeting issues as one of the most politicized processes in institutions of higher education, believing these processes to be rational and/or straightforward can be a mistake in most organizations. Perhaps this is why Wallace Sayer was famously quoted as stating, "academic politics are so fierce because the stakes are so small" (https://quoteinvestigator.com/2013/08/18/acad-politics/#return-note-7033-10).

Gilley (2006) suggests that "political success begins by identifying the individuals who have something to gain or lose as a result of a political interaction" (p. 13) with you. Those are the individuals who can help you achieve your goals for your department or college. In Figure 8.5 I list a few

POLITICS AND POLITICAL BEHAVIORS

Keep it professional not personal no matter how personal it may seem at the time. You do not want to sink to the level of personal attacks. Once you make it personal you begin to lose credibility and power.

Be politically savvy – understand how and when to ask questions appropriately. Closed ended questions and open ended questions elicit very different types of responses each providing information that can aid in forwarding your agenda

Understand yourself and your institution – conduct **S**trengths **W**eaknesses **O**pportunities & **T**hreats (SWOT) or **S**trengths **O**pportunities **A**spirations **R**esults (SOAR) analyses. (Aspirations – what do you want to look like in the future) (Results – how will you know you have succeeded)

Develop allies – determine who can help you and in what situations they can be best called on for assistance

Do favors – help yourself by first helping others accomplish their goals

Be nice – show kindness to others including those you do not like or do not respect

Be concise – remember the KISS principle (**K**eep **I**t **S**imple **S**tupid)

Be seen as a problem solver not a problem creator – understand how to reach compromise and broker deals

---

Figure 8.5 Keys to Success

keys to success that will assist you in becoming a political navigator which in turn can help you accomplish your organizational and professional goals.

REFLECTIVE QUESTIONS

1. Reflecting on your budget process, what are the most political or contentious aspects?
2. Of the five key roles to developing political savvy, which do you believe to be most important? Why? Which do you need to work on the most?
3. Think of an instance where a political interaction went well. Why was this interaction successful?
4. Think of an instance where a political interaction did not go as well as you hoped. Why was this interaction not so successful? What tactics could you have utilized that could have helped reframe and improve this poor interaction?
5. Identify a professional goal that you associate with a political barrier or difficult situation that you need to navigate in order to achieve this goal. Identify tactics noted in Figures 8.3 and 8.4, and

151

POLITICS AND DECISION-MAKING

   describe how you might apply political thinking skills and behaviors to navigate your way to reaching your goal.
6. Rank your Political Savvy from 6 (high) to 1 (low) in terms of Positive Relationships, Conflict Management, Formidable Negotiator, Organizational Expertise, and Communication Skills.

CASE SCENARIO

You are the Assistant Dean in a college at a large state institution. Over the past year you worked with the Assistant and Associate Dean representatives from the other colleges to craft a new direct admission program to your college, eliminating the preprofessional admissions program beginning this summer. During this first summer of direct admission you are attending a meeting at which the president of the university is addressing the Dean's staff and department chairs of your college. He begins the meeting with typical pleasantries then proceeds to launch into a tongue lashing about how this particular college had cost the university over one half million dollars in lost summer school revenue because of a "unilateral decision to change your admissions criteria."

You know this statement to be inaccurate because, as the author of the new policy, you had worked with the other colleges and the provost to ensure broad-based university support for the plan. This was anything but a unilateral decision. What alternatives do you have in responding to the president's statement? What are the political implications for each of these alternatives?

Appendix

I believe that a book about power, influence, and politics to be incomplete if it does not pay homage to Niccolo Machiavelli. I also believe that Machiavelli's writings have been misinterpreted by most writings on leadership and management. Below, I put the writings of Machiavelli into context and also provide a bridge for his works into higher education leadership in the twenty-first century.

MISUNDERSTOOD MACHIAVELLI

Many leaders and powerful people associate Niccolo Machiavelli with the abuse of power and the nefarious manipulation of others. I believe this to be a misunderstanding of his work because of a failure to consider the time and circumstances of his writings. Machiavelli was not a leader himself but was considered more of a political scientist, counselor, and a diplomat (Fabrizio Ricciardelli, personal communication). Throughout his diplomatic career Machiavelli studied the leadership of others and provided guidance on how to respond based on those observations. His primary writings focused on how rulers acquired power, how they used power to control their principalities, and what was necessary for those rulers to hold on to power during the Renaissance. He was writing from the perspective of an observer, *not* expressing his personal views on power and leadership.

In 1513, Niccolo Machiavelli wrote *The Prince*, in which he was describing the rule of principalities, not republics or democracies. He provided advice on how to be perceived by others as a ruler or leader, so as to maintain authority and control over one's subjects, especially during times of unrest or outright war. *The Prince* was written during a time when the republics and principalities of Italy were protecting themselves from external forces, hoping not to get "sacked" by other nation-states.

It has been called the best cover letter ever written (Ricciardelli) and it is an effort to help a ruler understand how to gain and maintain power. At the time of writing *The Prince*, Machiavelli was living in exile outside of Florence where he had once served the republic as a diplomat. He wrote it in an effort to regain a diplomatic position with the Medici family who at the time controlled Rome and the papacy. *The Prince* was never intended to be a text on leadership or management, rather a documentation of how rulers of the time maintained or enhanced their power. According to Skinner (1981) and Ricciardelli, to understand Machiavelli one must look beyond *The Prince* to the discourses and his other historical/political works. Machiavelli believed that a prince should be the first among equals and should strive to establish horizontal, not vertical power (Ricciardelli).

As a supporter of republics and more democratic power structures, Machiavelli encouraged *ruling for the greater good* rather than the tyranny established in many of the nation-states of the time. He advocated for those in power to listen to and understand the populace and to provide for representation in decision-making from the working class of the guilds. Also, according to Skinner, Machiavelli believed that leaders would be far more successful if they adapted their personalities (leadership styles) to the circumstances at the time, much like the situational leadership theory proffered by Hersey et al. (1979; Hersey and Blanchard, 1982) which advocated that different leadership styles were needed depending upon the maturity level of the group and the task(s) needing to be accomplished. The lower the maturity level of the group, the more direct supervision was necessary to achieve the desired outcomes.

TWENTY-FIRST CENTURY HIGHER EDUCATION APPLICATIONS

To view all of the tactics Machiavelli discusses as completely transferable to today's world is to take much of what he describes out of context. However, if you consider the context in which he was writing I believe you can find a few ideas that have withstood the test of time and can be applied today to the world of higher education. For example, Machiavelli wrote about people being promoted to their level of incompetence, known as the *Peter Principle* today, in 1513 when he stated that

> talent is always suspect. A man attains an elevated position only when his mediocrity prevents him from being a threat to others. And for this reason a democracy is never governed by the most

competent, but rather by those whose insignificance will not jeopardize anyone else's self-esteem.
(www.azquotes.com/author/9242-Niccolo_Machiavelli)

In his writings, Machiavelli is viewed as the first to separate ethics from politics (Ricciardelli), suggesting that leaders have the ability to decide whether to act in an ethical fashion or fall prey to the political decision-making of the time. He discusses leadership and change, decision-making and taking risks, creating perceptions, and the use of external forces to help accomplish one's goals. Machiavelli also writes about the topic of governing, which for higher education today can be interpreted as shared governance.

New Leadership Role/Change

As a new leader, whether promoted from within or brought in from the outside, Machiavelli stresses the importance of "preserving the existing state of affairs" (Skinner, 1981, p. 32). This continuity, albeit temporary, is important to give the current faculty and staff a sense of security and to help the new leader establish a sense of trust among the senior leadership. Taking time to implement change can help obtain commitment from the faculty and staff or at least compliance rather than resistance. In *The Prince*, Machiavelli stresses the importance of leaders needing to be clever like a fox and strong like a lion. Leaders need to be aware of and avoid deception and they must be strong enough to make the difficult decisions necessary to lead complex institutions. Machiavelli (1513, p. 30) continues that

> It should be borne in mind that there is nothing more difficult to arrange, more doubtful of success, and more dangerous to carry through than initiating changes. The innovator makes enemies of all those who prospered under the old order, and only lukewarm support is forthcoming from those who would prosper under the new. Their support is lukewarm ... partly because men are generally incredulous, never really trusting new things unless they have tested them by experience.

This provides a warning that seems to hold true today: quite simply that people, by their very nature, are hesitant or perhaps resistant to change initially. Therefore as a leader you must proceed with caution and use your influence to establish credibility and gain buy-in from as many stakeholders as possible before launching any proposed changes. It is usually wise to start small in order to develop trust among your new staff, which then helps establish confidence in your leadership.

Governance

Machiavelli was a believer in government by the people and as a champion of republics he advocated for more involvement by its people not less. He referred to *good government* which required the active participation of the citizens of the republic. According to Skinner (1981) Machiavelli states that "it is not individual good but common good that makes cities [institutions] great" (p.59). Today, within higher education, this concept is reflected in the shared governance model in most institutions; without the involvement of administrators *and* faculty there is no shared governance. Moreover, for the new leader interested in establishing a legacy, what better legacy than promoting and developing an institutional culture that values strong institutional leadership that engages internal stakeholders and is truly participatory. If it becomes part of the culture it will outlast the leader and live on well into the future. According to Skinner (1981), Machiavelli argued

> that the noblest aim for a far-seeing and virtuoso prince must be to introduce a form of government that will bring honour to him and make him glorious. ... The attainment of worldly honour and glory is thus the highest goal for Machiavelli no less than for Livy or Cicero.
>
> (p. 34)

External Consultants

Machiavelli comments on the use of mercenaries to help Florence fight the war against Pisa. Having no loyalty to Florence the mercenaries proved to be unfaithful and were there for the money not the cause. In my view, many external consultants of today (e.g. executive search firms) are similar to the mercenaries of old, they have no loyalty to your institution, no vested interest in long-term success, and they are doing it for the money. Following Machiavelli's advice, you should not rely on outsiders to solve your problems; it is important for those with a vested interest in the short- and long-term success of the institution to work toward a resolution. According to Ricciardelli, Machiavelli believed that decisions should be made by the *good government* of engaged citizens not by those external to the institution.

Decision-making

Senior level administrators will be confronted with difficult decisions throughout their careers. Some of these decisions could be career ending or at least result in a significant setback. Machiavelli's guidance in this area is to recognize that at times all solutions presented may appear risky and nearly impossible to avoid danger. Therefore, it becomes important to weigh the risks appropriately and act decisively. Similarly, according to Skinner (1981), Machiavelli's "mature political writings are full of warnings about the folly of procrastinating, the danger of appearing irresolute, the need for bold and rapid action" (p. 9). The take-away is that as a leader you are in the position to make the decision and, as noted previously, Machiavelli encourages you to make the choice that benefits the common good rather than the individual.

Creating an Image

Machiavelli believed it was important for rulers/leaders to create an image of an individual who holds power. According to Skinner (1981) Machiavelli mentions that

> most men are so simple-minded, and above all so prone to self-deception, that they usually take things at face value in a wholly uncritical way (p. 62) ... and when it comes to assessing the behaviour of princes, even the shrewdest observers are largely condemned to judge by appearances, isolated from the populace, sustained by the majesty of his role, the prince's position *is such that everyone can see what you appear to be but few have direct experience of what you really are* [emphasis added]
>
> (p. 63)

The implication here is that leaders, especially new leaders, can craft an image of themselves such that their followers will see what they want to see and respond accordingly. Therefore, when you enter into a new position you have the opportunity to become the leader you want to be and the leader the institution desires. You and the institution are starting fresh, but you must be careful not to create an expectation you cannot fulfill. You need to be realistic regarding the persona you intend to create. Machiavelli posited that if a leader could not be loved or revered then he should do his best not to be hated, good advice for today's leaders as well.

CONCLUDING COMMENTS

Those who view Machiavelli as one who promotes the coercive and deceptive side of power take Machiavelli's writings out of context and draw conclusions to imply he advocated the abuse of power. However, it is my hope that reviewing and analyzing his works through a different lens

POLITICS AND DECISION-MAKING

helps you see that, while he was documenting many of those types of behaviors amongst the rulers of the time, he was in fact a supporter of an engaged citizenry and one who believed in government for the good of the people rather than a government over the people.

REFLECTIVE QUESTIONS

1. Machiavelli advocated for customizing your leadership style to the situation and context at hand. Give an example of a time when you modified your leadership style based on the context of a situation.
2. As noted by Machiavelli, how one appears is very important. Describe the "image" you hope to portray to your peers and subordinates. Do you attempt to craft a different image to those above you in the hierarchy? If so, what changes do you attempt to make?

Chapter Nine

Falling from Grace

Every year, notable leaders in almost all industry sectors make mistakes that mark the end of their tenure in that leadership role. In the first section of this chapter we take a brief look at educational leaders who recently self-destructed by making decisions that were not in the best interest of their respective institutions (Scott Scarborough, Akron; Phyllis Wise, Illinois; Timothy Wolfe, Missouri), thereby hastening their departure. In the second section we look at a few examples of senior leaders (Graham Spanier, Penn State; Kenneth Starr, Baylor; Lou Anna K. Simon, Michigan State) who acted immorally, unethically, or perhaps illegally; ending their respective leadership careers. We will look at some of the decisions that set these once respected leaders on a path to an early departure and discuss how administrators might avoid similar circumstances.

Before we examine these missteps, it is important to understand that it is not always the university or college president who makes a significant misstep – other administrators in positions with power make immoral or unethical choices as well. Power is not limited to the central administration or senior leadership and neither is poor decision-making. Here are a few examples of individuals in positions of power who made choices that harmed their institutions while initially benefiting themselves personally.

- During the fall of 2017, the Director and Associate Director of Housing at the University of Florida were arrested for stealing over $470,000 of university funds over a 15-month period.
- The Vice-President for Student Affairs at State University of New York at Buffalo pleaded guilty to stealing $320,000 and the Director of Campus Living admitted to stealing over $14,000 (2017).
- A Director of Student Accounts at Drake University embezzled over $600,000 (2011).

- *The Chronicle of Higher Education* (2009) reported that the Dean of the College of Education and a former student at the University of Louisville misappropriated $694,000 of Federal grant money, resulting in indictments on nine counts of mail fraud, money laundering, and tax evasion.
- According to *The Atlanta Journal Constitution* (2018) a Manager of Central Receiving at Kennesaw State University stole laptops and other technology and sold them on eBay.

In each instance administrators abused their power for personal benefit. Unfortunately, these are but a few examples that highlight problems existing on our college and university campuses. It did not matter that the individuals committing these crimes were in positions considered to be well compensated. Greed plays a major role, or perhaps it is simply an inability to distinguish between what is right and wrong or what is good behavior and what is bad behavior.

PART 1: WHAT WENT WRONG

Three examples follow of decision-making at the executive level that eventually forced these individuals to resign. The purpose of these examples is to demonstrate how some administrators can seemingly lose sight of what skills and abilities helped them to navigate their way through the hierarchy to their executive positions. This failure to utilize their strengths or skill set resulted in poor decision-making, which in turn created or exacerbated problems leading to their resignations.

University of Akron

Scott Scarborough began his presidency at the University of Akron on July 1, 2014, and it did not take him long to start making mistakes, at least in the eyes of many university employees and the Northeast Ohio community. Within his first week on the job he distributed and required his leadership team to sign a *Leadership and Management Principles* document containing 28 bullet points in three sections labeled (1) "In any organization, *success* is a result of," (2) "The Requirements of Teamwork," and (3) "Big Mistakes/ Problems" (see Figure 9.1). It appears that this document was one of his first errors in judgment. It was seen as a demonstration of power from an authoritarian perspective and it did not win much support from within the institution.

Most of what is in the document is not necessarily bad or inappropriate. In fact, many points are seen as being common sense, it was more the

FALLING FROM GRACE

In any organization, *success* is a result of:
- Openly communicating and sharing information with everyone in the organization to create and sustain a culture of trust and group cohesion.
- Solving problems quietly and inspiring hope loudly.
- Always trying to do more with less (see *Less is More* by Jason Jennings).

The Requirements of Teamwork
- Everyone must commit oneself to be a member of the team.
- Everyone must understand who is responsible for the team's final decision.
- Team Members must agree to support the team's final decision after all the thoughts and opinions of team members are heard.

Big Mistakes/Problems
- Failing to serve others with an attitude of humility.
- Failing to pick up trash.
- Failing to maintain an orderly and clean work environment.
- Wasting money or other resources
- Lacking courage to tell people what they need to hear – not what they want to hear.

Figure 9.1 2014 U of Akron Leadership and Management Principles (excerpt)

manner in which this document was communicated along with the requisite signatures of administrators that created a concern. Perhaps of greatest concern about the document was the following statement which appeared above the signature line:

> I acknowledge receipt of the above Leadership and Management Principles, and I understand that they constitute a required code of conduct for those serving in leadership/management position at The University of Akron. If I cannot agree to conduct myself in a manner consistent with these principles, I agree to work with my supervisor to develop a transition plan to another position inside or outside the university. I understand that if I violate these principles, disciplinary action will follow, up to and including termination.

Universities are typically collegial environments with highly educated faculty and administrators who expect to be involved in making decisions, even if just in a consultative or advisory capacity. Mistake number one, Mr. Scarborough chose to *inform* his subordinates rather than *consult* with them.

Mr. Scarborough's tenure at the helm of the University of Akron lasted less than two years. The *Principles* document was just the starting point. In his defense, he did inherit an institution that was experiencing significant financial pressures – his predecessor left the university with an inordinate, some say insurmountable, amount of debt (approaching $500 million) in a period of declining enrollments and reduced state spending. The revenue necessary to maintain the debt payments required the institution to accelerate its growth. Declining enrollments began before Mr. Scarborough joined the university and continued during his term. Unfortunately for Mr. Scarborough, the university's stakeholders saw the financial troubles as his and not his predecessor's. The financial difficulties resulted in a $60 million deficit his first year, requiring swift action – the elimination of over 200 positions and cutting the university's baseball team (to be reinstated 2019–20). Eliminating positions never engenders support from the institution's faculty and staff and most often tends to create a climate of uncertainty, leading to fear and distrust of the administration and an *us* against *them* mindset.

To make matters worse, there was the $556 decorative olive jar purchased as part of Mr. Scarborough's $950,000 renovation to the president's house. Take note, it is usually a mistake to spend money renovating your personal space during your first year on the job – it looks too selfish. Perhaps Mr. Scarborough should have followed his list of principles and realized that "wasting money or other resources" is a big mistake. In an effort to reduce the pressures of ongoing financial troubles at the university, Mr. Scarborough pushed for an ill-fated collaboration with ITT Education Services, Inc. a for-profit technical school which, according to its website (http://itt-tech.info/) discontinued operations in October 2016. Mr. Scarborough was pursuing this with the intention of expanding the university's reach and its online presence in hopes of growing enrollments. This again, was not viewed favorably by faculty or students and was not a viable solution to the financial woes of the university.

Finally, the new president, once again without consulting the faculty, students, alumni, or community, attempted to rebrand the institution as "Ohio's Polytechnic University." Needless to say, this effort was not well received. Then in February of 2016, the faculty voted (50–2) *no confidence* in Mr. Scarborough's leadership, based on numerous concerns, mostly faculty involvement in decision-making. While a vote of no-confidence is not a death blow to most presidencies, this one did signal the beginning of the end for Mr. Scarborough's tenure as president.

In reviewing Mr. Scarborough's brief tenure at Akron, one thing even he agrees with becomes clear – he failed to *communicate effectively*. In an interview with the *Akron Beacon Journal* (2016) he stated: "I think much of the conflict is just miscommunication and we'll take full responsibility for that" (www.ohio.com/akron/news/scarborough-says-he-has-learned-from-mistakes-but-blames-communication-as-the-key-mistake).

Additionally, his decision-making processes came across as autocratic in an environment that cherishes constituent engagement and shared governance. Many of his ideas were not bad ideas, it was the way in which they were communicated that offended people. The perception in the local media and throughout the education community in Ohio was that the decisions were more about Mr. Scarborough than about the University of Akron. Had he learned to submerge his ego (Pfeffer, 1994) and done a better job of listening before deciding, he may have remained the president. Or perhaps this was another example of a new president more concerned about his legacy than the future of the institution.

University of Missouri

Timothy Wolfe became the 23rd president of the University of Missouri system in February 2012. This could be seen as a homecoming for Mr. Wolfe who is a graduate of the university's School of Business. After a successful career in the corporate world where he served in various roles with IBM over a 20-year span and finished his corporate career at Novell Americas as president, he joined the University of Missouri System. He began his tenure as president of the University of Missouri System intending to work with business and political leaders on improving the economic development of the state by increasing the quality of the state's system of higher education. However, he was unable to complete his agenda as his presidency ended abruptly in November 2015.

What led up to Mr. Wolfe's departure was a series of events that began in August 2014, with the police shooting of Michael Brown in Ferguson, MO. This incident sparked protests in Ferguson and around the country, and just down the road from Ferguson is Columbia, MO, home to the University of Missouri. The lack of a university response exacerbated the problem as students expected the university's leadership to take a stand and address the racial tensions surrounding the shooting. During the 2014–15 academic year and into the fall of 2015, several racial incidents took place on the University of Missouri campus which hastened his departure.

One of the incidents took place on October 10, 2015, during the university's homecoming parade when a group of student protesters confronted Mr. Wolfe while he rode in the backseat of a convertible. Wolfe sat silently in the car while the driver attempted to drive around the protesters. Wolfe chose not to engage them in dialogue and according to the Huffington Post did not make a statement about the protest until November 6 (www.huffingtonpost.com/entry/tim-wolfe-homecoming-parade_us_56402cc8e4b0307f2cadea10).

POLITICS AND DECISION-MAKING

Throughout October 2015, there were multiple reports of racial slurs directed toward black students on campus and a swastika drawn with feces was found in a residence hall. On November 2 a graduate student announced he was going on a hunger strike and on November 8 members of the football team joined the protests by stating they "would not participate in any football related activities until Wolfe resigns or is removed" (www.nbcnews.com/news/us-news/missouri-football-players-boycott-protest-president-n459381). These incidents ultimately led Missouri legislators and other politicians to criticize Wolfe for his lack of leadership in addressing the racial problems at the university. The final straw for Wolfe was when 30 members of the university's football team decided to go on strike, garnering more national attention and increasing the calls for him to step down.

According to most news accounts, the university's slow and inadequate responses led to the resignations of President Wolfe and University Chancellor Bowen Loftin on November 9, 2015. Had Wolfe responded in a more timely and forceful fashion he may very well have avoided the campus protests and calls for his resignation. Again, what we see is a failure to effectively communicate. For Wolfe, he needed to take charge of the situation and lead with integrity as he addressed the escalating racial tension. Instead, his limited response to the Brown shooting and the ensuing protests appeared to reflect a president who was distant and did not demonstrate he cared about the climate on the university campus. And remember, perception becomes reality for those watching from the outside and in a polarizing situation, inaction is seen as condoning the events.

University of Illinois

In October 2011, Phyllis Wise took over the helm at the University of Illinois at Urbana-Champaign following the resignation of the previous chancellor amid an admissions scandal involving special consideration given to politically connected or wealthy applicants. Ms. Wise was viewed as an individual who could restore the honor and integrity of the central administration. Prior to joining the University of Illinois, Ms. Wise had honed her administrative skills at the University of Washington where she served as the provost and also interim president. During her four-year tenure at Illinois, Chancellor Wise, like most university leaders, had to make many hard decisions and deal with many challenging situations. She guided the university through the aftermath of the admissions scandal and navigated problems in athletics involving coaches physically and psychologically abusing student athletes. However, it was her decision to revoke a job offer to a controversial faculty member, Steven Salaita, where her chancellorship began to unravel.

In October 2013, Mr. Steven Salaita was sent a written offer of employment from the University of Illinois, for a tenured associate professor position in the American Indian Studies program to begin fall semester 2014. In August, 2014, days before his teaching and research duties were to begin, he was informed that his offer was being revoked. At the September 2014, Board of Trustees meeting, the Board of the University of Illinois voted to uphold the revocation and thereby deny Mr. Salaita the faculty position he had been offered in October the previous year. This decision created quite a stir in the academic community and caused a backlash against the university. Less than a year later Ms. Wise tendered her resignation.

According to university policy, Ms. Wise and the Board did have the authority to revoke Mr. Salaita's job offer. Most in higher education can confirm a line in their letters of appointment acknowledging that the offer is contingent upon approval of the governing board. Typically, a university governing board will approve appointments during a May or June meeting to help ensure a smooth transition into the fall semester. Unfortunately, the timing of the revocation of this employment offer was such that it appeared to have caused significant harm to Mr. Salaita, prompting a legal battle that would uncover other issues at the university.

The biggest problem uncovered was the use of private email accounts by several administrators to discuss university business. The use of these personal accounts called into question the openness and trustworthiness of the administration by casting a shadow on these administrators and their credibility. And being at the top and a participant in the effort to hide the conversations, Ms. Wise accepted responsibility and promptly resigned.

This might have been avoided had Chancellor Wise shown true leadership and done the right thing for the right reasons at the right time. This could have been Ms. Wise lending full support for the hiring of Mr. Salaita while simultaneously taking a stand against what she believed to be his inflammatory rhetoric or for Ms. Wise not to grant permission to hire Mr. Salaita back in October of 2013, and defend that decision to the university community at that time.

PART 2: ETHICS, INTEGRITY, AND MORAL DECISIONS

As you progress through your career you will be challenged by colleagues questioning your decisions and the rationale behind them. Moreover, you will have opportunities to make decisions that may place your integrity in jeopardy or challenge your personal values and morals. I believe that an individual's integrity is of paramount importance and as DeCelles et al.

(2012) suggest, individuals "with strong moral concepts, when given power, will increasingly behave in ways that benefit the common good versus their own interests" (p. 686).

In her book chapter "Leading a university during controversy: Challenges faced by a new president," Dr. Judy Genshaft wrote about her role in guiding the University of South Florida through a difficult time (Genshaft and Wheat, 2004). She remarked:

> Fundamental to an effective presidency is a strong sense of academic and ethical principle, an understanding of the importance of all institutional constituencies to the university's success, a deep comprehension of the symbolic nature of the presidency, and a dogged determination to shepherd the university through the controversy not only intact but strengthened (p. 48) ... The president is the standard bearer for the academic and ethical principles of the institution ... the president must be focused on what is right and must not be swayed.
>
> (p. 56)

Below we briefly look at three examples of high-profile higher education leaders who, in my opinion, did not take to heart what Genshaft or DeCelles discussed in their respective writings. Presidents Graham Spanier, Penn State; Ken Starr, Baylor; and Lou Anna K. Simon, Michigan State all made decisions that led to unethical or perhaps illegal actions. The consequences of those decisions are discussed below. While these high-profile examples involve intercollegiate athletics (which has its own section), more importantly they involve ethical and moral decision-making and demonstrate inappropriate and unethical use of power.

Penn State

During his 16-year tenure at Pennsylvania State University (Penn State), Graham Spanier earned a national reputation as an outstanding university leader. Oftentimes, he was called upon to be a spokesperson for the higher education industry as a whole. Unfortunately, at the pinnacle of his career everything came crashing down and he left Penn State and higher education in disgrace. He was implicated in the cover-up/ignoring of a sexual abuse case involving a former Penn State football coach, Jerry Sandusky. Mr. Spanier's tenure as president of Penn State ended on November 9, 2011 when Penn State's Board of Trustees fired him.

The scope of the Penn State scandal was so widespread that on November 21, 2011, the Board of Trustees hired a Special Investigative Counsel led by

FALLING FROM GRACE

former FBI Director Louis Freeh (Freeh Sporkin & Sullivan LLP) to perform an independent, full and complete investigation. The Counsel's final report detailed the making of this scandal and provided 120 recommendations for university administrators and the Board to consider. Below I have taken excerpts from the Freeh Report to provide a sense of what the Investigative Counsel found during its comprehensive investigation.

> On November 4, 2011 the Attorney General of the Commonwealth of Pennsylvania filed criminal charges against Gerald (Jerry) A. Sandusky involving sexual misconduct with minors between 1998 and 2002. During this time period, Sandusky was either employed or a Professor Emeritus with unrestricted access to the University's football facilities. Additionally, charges were filed against Timothy M. Curley (Athletic Director) and Gary C. Schultz (Vice president for Finance and Business) for failing to report allegations of child abuse to law enforcement or child protective services and for committing perjury during court testimony.
>
> (p. 13)

> ... the most saddening finding by the Special Investigative Counsel is the total and consistent disregard by most senior leaders at Penn State for the safety and welfare of Sandusky's child victims. In addition to Curley and Schultz, longtime Head Football Coach, Joe Paterno and University President, Graham Spanier were accused of failing to protect against a child sexual predator harming children for over a decade.
>
> (p. 14)

> ... the Special investigative Counsel finds that it is more reasonable to conclude that, in order to avoid the consequences of bad publicity, the most powerful leaders at the University – Spanier, Schultz, Paterno and Curley – repeatedly concealed critical facts ... The avoidance of the consequences of bad publicity is the most significant, but not the only, cause for this failure to protect child victims and report to authorities.
>
> (p. 16)

As mentioned earlier, the Special Investigative Counsel made 120 recommendations in eight categories. The first recommendation detailed in the Freeh Report should make a great deal of sense for every institution of higher education to implement. The Special Investigative Counsel recommended:

POLITICS AND DECISION-MAKING

> Organize a [University-led] effort to vigorously examine and understand the [University] culture in order to: 1) reinforce the commitment of all University members to protect children; 2) create a stronger sense of accountability among the University's leadership; 3) establish values and ethics-based decision making and adherence to the [University] Principles as the standard for all University faculty, staff and students; 4) promote an environment of increased transparency into the management of the University; and 5) ensure a sustained integration of the Intercollegiate Athletics program into the broader [University] community.
>
> (p. 129)

As the criminal investigation concluded, several key administrators were convicted including Mr. Spanier. On March 24, 2017, the former president of Penn State was convicted of child endangerment for not taking action when notified by Mr. Schultz and Mr. Curley of the sexual abuse of children perpetrated by Mr. Sandusky. Mr. Spanier was sentenced to four to twelve months, with two months in jail and two months under house arrest and two years of probation (according to Madeline Holcombe of CNN, his conviction was vacated by a Federal Judge on April 30, 2019, www.cnn.com/2019/05/01/us/penn-state-president-sandusky-overturned/index.html).

Based on the information provided in the Freeh Report it is apparent that Mr. Spanier had created an administrative culture that was not conducive to collaborative decision-making. The Report noted that Spanier was "[a] president who discouraged discussion and dissent" (p. 16), which is more common in autocratic or dictatorial organizations and is not conducive to a shared governance model.

Spanier was one of the most highly regarded educational leaders in the United States who ended his career as a convicted criminal, primarily because of his unwillingness to do the right thing. He wrongly chose to use his power to make decisions he believed would protect the university and his legacy as president over the safety and subsequent abuse of children visiting the campus.

Baylor

Kenneth Starr, perhaps best known for his investigation of Bill Clinton's relationship with his intern, Monica Lewinsky, had a distinguished career in law, government service, and as an academic before he became president of Baylor University. He served as the Duane and Kelly Roberts Dean and Professor of Law at Pepperdine University in 2004–2010, then began his tenure as the 14th President of Baylor University, the largest Baptist University in the United States, in June 2010. He was fired from that position in May of 2016 amidst a series of sexual assault scandals which rocked the campus. He was permitted to stay on as Chancellor and Professor of Law but resigned from those positions shortly after a scathing report from a law firm hired to investigate the scandals.

His six-year tenure began its decline in 2013, as several students alleged they were raped by members of the Baylor football team. Students accused the university of not doing enough to investigate the allegations and not enough to protect its students. In August 2015, the university hired Philadelphia-based law firm Pepper Hamilton to investigate the sexual misconduct allegations and Baylor's response to Title IX compliance issues. The law firm found that the university was not responsive enough and, according to Baylor University Board of Regents Findings of Fact document:

> Pepper's findings ... reflect a fundamental failure by Baylor to implement Title IX of the Education Amendments of 1972 (Title IX) and the Violence Against Women Reauthorization Act of 2013 (VAWA) ... the University failed to take action to identify and eliminate a potential hostile environment, prevent its recurrence, or address its effects for individual complainants or the broader campus community (p. 1). Pepper also found examples of actions by University administrators that directly discouraged complainants from reporting or participating in student conduct processes, or that contributed to or accommodated a hostile environment.
>
> (p. 2)

From an outsider's perspective, it appears the university administration was more concerned about protecting the institution's, or perhaps individuals', reputations over the well-being of its students. Similar to the Penn State scandal mentioned above, football had become so important to the university that protecting the football program was of paramount importance. According to the Fact Finding Report, the campus culture had created an environment at Baylor that

> hindered enforcement of rules and policies, and created a cultural perception that football was above the rules. In addition to the issues related to student misconduct, the University and Athletics Department failed to take effective action in response to allegations involving misconduct by football staff. Further, despite the fact that other departments repeatedly raised concerns that the Athletics

Department's response to student or employee misconduct was inadequate, Baylor administrators took insufficient steps to address the concerns.

(p. 10)

The report of Pepper Hamilton uncovered a culture within the institution that was not responsive to the safety needs of its students. The report ultimately led to the resignation of Mr. Starr. The law firm provided the university with over 100 recommendations for improvement in and around Title IX issues on the campus. Additionally, Jake Trotter of ESPN reported that the Big 12 Conference, of which Baylor is part, recently fined the institution for "reputational damage to the conference and its members" (www.espn.com/college-football/story/_/id/25127280/big-12-fines-baylor-2-million-sexual-assault-scandal).

To date, no criminal or civil charges have been filed against Mr. Starr. He left Baylor under a cloud because he failed to hold members of the football program staff accountable for the abusive culture that had been created. Mr. Starr's decision not to intervene signaled the beginning of the end of his tenure at Baylor.

Michigan State

Michigan State University (MSU) and the case of Dr. Larry Nassar is another example of university administrators failing to act responsibly because they were more interested in protecting the reputation of the institution and their own positions of power. According to *The Chronicle of Higher Education*, the timeline of the Nassar abuses are known to have begun in 1997, when a high school student reported to the women's gymnastics coach that she had been assaulted by Larry Nassar. However according to *The Detroit News*, abuses may have started as early as 1992. It was not however until September 20, 2016, that he was fired from Michigan State, after the investigation into sex abuse allegations came to light at USA Gymnastics.

Lou Anna K. Simon came to Michigan State University in 2005, eight years after the first report of Dr. Nassar's abusive behaviors and a decade before he was finally stopped. It is this decade-long gap that fueled the drive for Ms. Simon's resignation. For many, after the fallout from the Penn State/Jerry Sandusky scandal there is little patience for university officials who do not act quickly when sexual abuse allegations are brought forward. Below is an abbreviated timeline of what took place on the MSU campus, beginning with the first Title IX investigation into Nassar's behaviors. Several student athletes testified they had reported Dr. Nassar's

- In 2014, President Simon was informed of the Title IX complaint and police report filed regarding the conduct of Larry Nassar. The Title IX investigation concluded that Nassar's behavior during the *incident in question was not sexual in nature*.

- In 2014, William Strampel, Nassar's supervisor, informs Nassar that he is to have someone in the room with him during any medical exams or procedures.

- December 2015, MSU police detective informs Nassar that based on the 2014 investigation no charges were being filed but she reminded Nassar that he was to have a chaperone in the room during any procedures.

- In September 2016, Dr. Nassar was fired from his position at Michigan State after the news broke regarding the sexual abuse claims involving USA Gymnastics. Shortly thereafter, Dr. Nassar was charged with child sex abuse and child pornography.

- According to a message from the Board of Trustees, in October 2016, MSU retained the law firm of Skadden, Arps to begin an investigation into the Nassar scandal. A few months later, in January 2017, MSU hired another law firm, Miller Canfield to represent the university and conduct a factual review.

- January 2018 calls began for President Simon to resign. On the 18th the student newspaper called for her resignation and on the 19th a member of the Board of Trustees joined in on that call.

- January 24, 2018, Lou Anna Simon resigns as president of Michigan State University.

- November 20, 2018, Lou Anna Simon has been charged with four counts of lying to a police officer.

Figure 9.2 Michigan State Timeline

inappropriate behaviors to employees in the athletic department prior to Simon's arrival at MSU. The first official report did not reach President Simon until 2014 (see Figure 9.2 for a timeline of events).

As one looks at the information about Dr. Nassar's abuses it becomes evident that the culture within the athletic department at MSU, and perhaps the rest of the university, could have been interpreted as one of *looking the other way*. Kim Kozlowski of *The Detroit News* reported that up to 14 individuals who worked at MSU were made aware of one or more incidents of abuse by Dr. Nassar and yet no official actions appear to have been taken to stop or prevent further abuses (www.detroitnews.com/story/tech/2018/01/18/msu-president-told-nassar-complaint-2014/1042071001/). The culture of the athletic department was allowed to fester by the powers-that-be within the institution and it has been shown over the years that organizational culture is typically created or at least reinforced at the top, in this case the president.

As an institutional leader, you are responsible for everything that happens beneath you in the hierarchy, which for President Simon was the entire university. As President Simon noted in her resignation – "As president, it

POLITICS AND DECISION-MAKING

is only natural that I am the focus of this anger." This case will most likely continue for several years before we are fully aware of everything that happened, but it is certain that mistakes were made and some people turned a blind eye to what was occurring around them.

Was President Simon aware of all the issues surrounding Dr. Nassar? As president, is she not entitled to delegate certain authority and responsibilities to subordinates, in this case the Athletic Director, Police Department, and Title IX Coordinator? The answers to these questions are important but not necessarily relevant to who should be held accountable. If this was a single incident it may be understandable that the president was unaware of what had transpired, but it is difficult to imagine that a pattern of abuse for 20 years would escape the view of the executive suite. The first rule of management is that the supervisor is responsible for everything beneath her in the hierarchy. And in this case, President Simon is the top supervisor.

> As of June 30, 2019, the charges against Lou Anna K. Simon remain unresolved.

CONCLUDING COMMENTS

No institution is immune from such behaviors and there is no guaranteed way to prevent these types of abuses by others. The key is for you to ensure you are making the right decisions, for the right reasons, and communicating your decisions effectively. As you progress through your career you will have opportunities to make decisions that may place your integrity in jeopardy. I believe that an individual's integrity is of paramount importance. You must understand that any time you are dealing with issues that involve race, physical or sexual abuse, or abuse of power it is imperative that you

> - If you don't know all of the facts, there is no shame is saying so
> - What you can say emphatically is that your institution is taking the matter seriously
> - The institution has built mechanisms into its structure to deal with such problems
> - You have the utmost concern for the well-being of your campus community
> - This is an opportunity to restate your core values
>
> (Adapted from Genshaft, 2014)

Figure 9.3 Responding to a Crisis

act promptly and professionally – when you are in a position of power you have the opportunity to do the right thing, the right way, and for the right reasons.

Dr. Judy Genshaft (2014), in her chapter "It's not the crime, it's the cover-up (and the follow-up)," gives a few suggestions for institutional leaders responding to a campus crisis (Figure 9.3).

Genshaft also mentions that, as leaders:

> You will not be judged by what you do in the heat of the battle, but by what lessons your institution learned, what mechanisms you corrected, and the follow-up that demonstrates institutions should be continually evolving and perfecting how they manage the complicated human terrain ... the public expects us to be aware of warning signals of an impending crisis, but we don't always see the crisis coming.
>
> (p. 7)

Finally, at some time (perhaps multiple times) in your career you will find yourself in a position to make a decision that may challenge your moral or ethical values. It may be that you are asked to do something that you perceive to be unethical or perhaps even illegal or it may appear that doing the wrong thing seems easier than doing the right thing. When that time arises, it is important for you to use your power and demonstrate your leadership abilities by making the right decision for the right reasons. Remembering what Dorothy Allison said several years ago, "things come apart so easily when they have been held together by lies" (www.goodreads.com/quotes/), should make it a bit easier to tell the truth the first time around. So when you are placed in these difficult situations, a question you need to ask yourself is: "when you wake up in the morning and look in the mirror – do you like and respect the person you see?" It is not necessary to like *what* you see, but rather *who* you see.

REFLECTIVE QUESTIONS

Think of a time in your professional career when you were asked to do something you were not comfortable doing.

1. How did you respond?
2. What were the consequences of your response?
3. Based on what you know now, would you have responded differently?
4. Do you see any common threads between these cases?

POLITICS AND DECISION-MAKING

CASE SCENARIO

As the Senior Student Affairs Officer of a private, residential liberal arts institution you were tasked with chairing a committee on the quality of student life on campus. Your committee prepared a report to be presented to the Board of Trustees at their first meeting in the spring semester. One of the findings called into question the security of the campus and pointed out several problems and potential liability issues. The president orders you to remove that section of the report because he does not want "to air our dirty laundry in public."

How do you respond?

Potential consequences – If you agree, do you compromise your integrity? If you refuse could you lose your job?

Chapter Ten

Paths to Power of the Presidency

The operative word in the title of this chapter is *paths* because as the word implies there is no single path, but rather multiple paths to attaining a powerful position, such as becoming the president of an institution of higher education. In addition to the literature, for this chapter I sought the guidance and input of several sitting college/university presidents. They shared their professional journeys with me and I in turn will share some of their insights with you. Throughout this chapter you will hear from these institutional leaders as they comment on their respective paths to the presidency and what was important for them along the way. The presidents I had the privilege to interview in 2018 are: Dr. Bassam Deeb, President of Trocaire College; Dr. James Gaudino, President of Central Washington University; Dr. Judy Genshaft, President of University of South Florida; Dr. Alex Johnson, President of Cuyahoga County Community College; Dr. Dan Mahony, President of Winthrop University; Mr. James Tressel, President of Youngstown State University; and Dr. Beverly Warren, President of Kent State University.

STATE OF THE PRESIDENCY

In a report for the American Council on Education (ACE), Gagliardi et al. (2017), indicated approximately 85% of presidents in 2016 came from within academe, which emphasizes the importance placed on having experience within the academy in order to lead an academic institution. This report also highlights that 75% of public and 74% of private institution presidents were recruited from other institutions, reinforcing the claims of outsider bias when seeking someone to lead the institution. The data also show that 25% of current presidents were former presidents.

I believe much of this bias can be linked to the extensive use of search consultants, after all, why spend over a quarter of a million dollars to hire someone already working at your institution?

The report provides strong support for the traditional academic paths to the presidency (described below) indicating that 81% of responding presidents had experience as a faculty member (10 years on average) during their careers. That is significantly higher than the 70% in 2011. A disturbing trend is that the average tenure of presidents continues to decline. In 2011 the average length of a president's tenure was 6.7 years, in 2016, the average tenure is now down to 6.0 years. This may, however, be related to the increase in the average age of a president, which now stands at 62.

Gagliardi et al. (2017), highlight three key takeaways from their report. They are listed in Figure 10.1.

Understanding the current state of the position of college or university president provides a context for the remainder of this chapter. Knowing the key issues and challenges outlined helps to provide a frame for the four paths to the presidency and the comments from the seven presidents interviewed for this text.

1) *Diversifying the presidency will continue to grow in importance.*

   With the average age of a president at 62 years old, and more than half (54%) expected to leave their current post in five years or less, this presents an important opportunity to accelerate the diversification of the presidency. However, as noted previously, institutions have been prioritizing experienced presidents, which further skews the pool of candidates toward white men, working against efforts at diversifying the presidency.

2) *State and federal funding will continue to decline in the years to come.*

   Presidents identified budget and financial management (68%), fundraising (47%), enrollment management (38%), and diversity and equity issues (30%)as the areas that will be most important to their successors.

3) *Data-informed decision-making that prioritizes student success will continue to grow in importance.*

   Data suggest that presidents are prioritizing assessment and measurement related to student success and equitable outcomes over other markers of performance and prestige such as rankings, competitive/ external research grants, and tuition/fee costs for students as legitimate performance metrics. Interestingly, only 12% of presidents indicated using institutional research to inform the decision-making process was a future area of importance. This signals a potential disconnect with institutional research offices and functions, and that perhaps more presidents need to awaken to the importance of data-informed decision-making at the institutional level.

   (Adapted from Gagliardi et al., 2017)

Figure 10.1 Key Takeaways

Adapted from Gagliardi, Espinosa, Turk, and Taylor (2017)

FOUR PATHS

Within the higher education literature I have identified four paths that the vast majority of college and university presidents have followed. They are the Traditional Academic, the Non-Traditional Academic, the Non-Traditional Administrative, and the Non-Traditional Non-Academic. These roles are defined as follows.

Traditional Academic Path

- An individual navigates through the faculty ranks then into academic administration, culminating in a CAO or provost position before pursuing the presidency. This is the most often cited path and is considered by most as the traditional academic track.

For the traditional academic path to the presidency, one begins with an assistant professorship at a reputable institution of higher education. Developing a record of scholarship, teaching and service, one will move through the tenure process becoming an associate professor then establishing an area of expertise on one's way to becoming a full professor. Once at the rank of full professor the administrative minded faculty member will seek to establish a record of administrative success. This typically begins at the department chair or school director level, depending on the complexity of the organization. After several years, usually through at least one review cycle, the next step in the process is a move into a dean's position. After several successful years as a dean one will then move into a provost's role (vice-president academic affairs). Then the next step is into a presidency. This was the path taken by three of the presidents interviewed – Dr. Judy Genshaft, President of the University of South Florida, Dr. Alex Johnson, President, Cuyahoga Community College (Tri-C), and Dr. Beverly Warren, President of Kent State University.

For both Dr. Genshaft and Dr. Warren the provost position was the position held immediately prior to their respective presidencies and taking the traditional path was important for gaining a broad understanding of the academic mission of the institution. According to Dr. Genshaft,

> the traditional path is the best preparation to assume the leadership of an institution. Working your way through the faculty ranks (assistant – associate – full professor) then becoming a department chair, dean, and finally provost provides one with the perspective of the academic mission that is paramount to being a university president. The academic mission of an institution is its mission.

POLITICS AND DECISION-MAKING

Dr. Warren agreed and mentioned that having been a faculty member gives one a greater appreciation for life within the academy and Dr. Johnson also believed this path prepared him well for his presidential roles. He was actually serving as a president immediately prior to accepting his role at Tri-C.

Non-Traditional Academic Path

- A non-traditional academic path will stop short of the provost's role, usually ending with an appointment as an academic dean before moving on to the presidency. These deans will usually come from large institutions that utilize a de-centralized budgeting process.

Two of the presidents with whom I spoke used their position as an academic dean as their springboard to a presidency. In both cases the dean role was within a decentralized budgeting model (Responsibility Center Management) in which the dean's responsibilities were similar to those of presidents at small institutions. Dan Mahony, President of Winthrop University mentions that being a president "is not so different from being a dean – the external aspect, budget responsibilities, and working with faculty" closely parallel his presidential responsibilities. James Gaudino, President of Central Washington University, agreed, indicating that the dean's role had prepared him well for the presidency.

Non-Traditional Administrative Path

- Another non-traditional path is non-academic, but still within higher education. This administrative path through higher education will often culminate in a vice-presidential role in divisions such as student affairs, business affairs, or advancement, among others.

Bassam Deeb, President of Trocaire College came from a background in student affairs. He felt quite prepared when making the transition to a president

> The position of president, while symbolically you are the academic representative of the faculty, the job itself has little to do with being the VP of academic affairs ... from a student affairs standpoint, particularly when you are running auxiliary operations, you're self-sustaining, you're dealing with budgets, you're dealing with the

notion of how do you make things work financially while still being service oriented. Frankly dealing with difficult constituents, parents, students, alumni, neighbors, if you run an athletic program, those kinds of [administrative] experiences made it easier to operate within the institution as a president.

James Tressel, President of Youngstown State University, had a successful career in Intercollegiate Athletics as a football coach prior to making the transition into university administration. He was not confident that he had the background to be a president so he had taken an executive position at the University of Akron immediately prior. He met with the leaders of all of the divisions and departments and realized "[t]he more you learn, you find out the similarities and dissimilarities between departments or institutions." It was at this time that the University of Akron president "gave me a couple of books and said 'I think you ought to consider being president.'"

Non-Traditional Non-Academic Path

- These individuals typically come from Corporate America or Politics (State or Federal). Several governors, U.S. senators, state legislators, and corporate executives have maneuvered through the processes to become institutional leaders.

As Pfeffer points out, "people assume that if you are smart enough to succeed in one highly competitive domain, you must be competent in other, even unrelated domains as well" (2010a, p. 220). While none of the individuals interviewed took this path to becoming a president there are many institutional leaders, past and present, who have made such a transition. A few that come to mind are Janet Napolitano, former Director of Homeland Security, former Governor, and former lawyer, has been leading the University of California system since September 2013; Sylvia Burwell, former director of the White House's Office of Management and Budget and Secretary of the Department of Health and Human Services, became President of American University in January 2017; Mitch Daniels at Purdue University is a former Governor for the state of Indiana and has led the university since January 2013. Bruce Harreld became president of the University of Iowa in November of 2015, following a highly respected corporate career, and in that same year, Robert Mong, former editor of the *Dallas Morning News* took over the helm at the University of North Texas at Dallas. Also, in 2018, Astrid Tuminez, former Regional Director for Corporate, External, and Legal Affairs in Southeast Asia for Microsoft, became the president of Utah Valley

State University. These individuals were chosen to lead academic enterprises for their leadership abilities and transferable skills.

The four pathways, Traditional Academic, the Non-Traditional Academic, the Non-Traditional Administrative, and the Non-Traditional Non-Academic, highlighted above are not the only paths, rather four broad categories that describe the majority of the paths taken to become institutional leaders in the U.S. Recognizing that there is no *one path* to becoming a college or university president is important because as you consider the next move along your career journey, you must realize that there may be many side trips you take along the way.

Now let's take a closer look at some of the personal traits/attributes the presidents interviewed believe helped them navigate their respective career paths and those necessary for them to stay in their roles. Not surprisingly, the presidents interviewed mentioned many of the traits described in Chapter 5 as traits necessary to get to the presidency, as well as being necessary to continue serving as an effective president within higher education in the U.S.

GETTING THERE

As you have seen above there are multiple pathways to arrive at a presidency and all of the presidents interviewed followed a path that was best path for their respective careers. James Gaudino mentioned that, while serving as dean, he had a conversation with his supervisor, the provost, about his next step. He believed that a provost position would be the next logical step in his career path. The provost stated: "why do you want to be a provost, that used to be the path but it isn't any more." President Gaudino realized that becoming a president was more about your entire career, not simply your most recent position. He stated:

> I knew from being executive director [of a national association] rather than being a dean. Because as dean I had help from all sides – above and below. When you are president you are at the top of the pile. That's what I was as the executive director, of course the pile is much bigger as president.

I believe Beverly Warren's comment "you need to choose a pathway for the right reasons, one that is right for you, there is no single best path" captures the essence of individualizing one's career path. Dr. Warren went on to say: "there is no one size fits all president … different institutions with different challenges will be looking for different presidents." This sentiment was also shared by Dr. Deeb who stated:

> [w]e talk about institutional fit between the student and the college and I believe there is also institutional fit between presidents and colleges or universities ... there may be times when the institution is trying to solve a problem and it brings in a person to fix the problem then in two or three years off they go ...

During my interviews with these presidents it became clear that many of the personality attributes listed in Chapter 5 (communication, collaboration, humility, and transparency) were important for them as they progressed through their careers and in their presidency. What follow are the traits mentioned by the majority of the presidents interviewed as having been important for them in making it to a presidency.

Authenticity

The phrase *know thyself* comes to mind when people discuss being authentic. Several of the presidents mentioned that you need to know who you are and learn to be comfortable with yourself. This self-knowledge was best articulated by James Gaudino when he was discussing the interview process at Central Washington University:

> One of the reasons they picked me – authentic[ity]. One of the things my wife and I said, which was a gamble, is that we are going to be president and the president's wife 24/7 ... We decided to live an authentic life.

This was also reinforced by Bassam Deeb when he mentioned "I truly believe when you arrive at the position, based on what you bring, your talent allows you to succeed." Essentially, you are successful because of who you are and how you demonstrate that on a daily basis.

These presidents chose different paths through higher education that allowed them to emphasize their strengths. They did not try to change themselves nor did they expect everyone to conform to their beliefs, values, and ideals. Metaphorically, these individuals were like a stream flowing through the forest, the water following a path until it meets an obstacle not willing to move. Instead of forcing itself over the obstacle the water alters its path and goes around it. The ability to let your strengths guide you during your career will most likely take you to the place that best suits your skills and abilities at that particular point. Once in a senior position, the time to change your behaviors and values has passed; this is not the time to try to be someone different, but rather the time to reinforce who you really are. As Beverly Warren stated; "you have to remain grounded in your core beliefs and values. Find your true North and don't change."

Communication Skills/Relationship Building

Regardless of the path taken, the presidents interviewed believed that communication skills were required to develop relationships and in turn, strong relationships were important for navigating the political environments in today's higher education landscape. Whether you are working through the dynamics of shared governance at an individual institution or engaged in conversations at the state or national levels, communication skills and the ability to develop relationships are considered requisites for an effective presidency. Interpersonal relationships and listening skills were the communication skills mentioned most frequently.

I believe that Jim Tressel highlighted the importance of these skills best when he mentioned that to become a president one must be able to build relationships. He stated, "[i]f you want to influence others you need to be influenceable, you have to show others you can listen and develop strong relationships" with a broad spectrum of individuals. For Mr. Tressel, this underscored the importance of listening to those around you. He continued, "when you start a new position, at any level, you need to meet everyone ... it is important to develop strong relationships and to do so you must listen, listen, listen ... "

Bassam Deeb also felt strongly about the importance of relationships and understanding how other view you within your institution:

> in order to be successful I had to allow myself to be exposed to any part of the institution even if it had nothing to do with my daily job and I took that to heart ... no matter what college or University I worked for I would end up being on a committee or task force to solve an institutional problem that didn't always fit with my area that I was in at the time ... it gave me exposure to the finer inner workings of the college or university ... the ability to step away from the job that I am currently doing and allowing myself to be available, builds relationships with people, they viewed [me] not just as a student affairs professional but an institutional colleague ...

Collaboration

To be a successful leader within higher education one needs to demonstrate a level of achievement interacting with various stakeholder groups and diverse individuals to accomplish the goals and objectives set forth. This requires one to be able to work with stakeholders who may disagree with each other and with you. By demonstrating your willingness to collaborate while shaping a shared vision you can set yourself apart as a leader.

Dan Mahony mentioned that "collaboration, not top down decisions allows one to be successful. I had to be clear that this is not my vision, but rather it is our vision." As an institutional leader it is this shared vision that becomes the driving force for the institution. Dr. Warren stressed the importance of "crafting a shared vision ... moving toward a higher purpose for the institution." To craft a shared vision you need to collaborate, which was reinforced by Jim Tressel when he said that "involvement after the fact is detrimental – you need to involve others from the start – collaborate."

Goal Oriented

Several of the presidents mentioned the need to focus on what was happening at the moment. Even with all of the other distractions, they needed to accomplish the task at hand before moving on to the next issue in their unit. Dr. Genshaft put it quite succinctly when she said "I didn't ever say stop. I always focused on the next goal." This goal orientation kept her moving through the bureaucratic structures because of her accomplishments and the recognition she received from others.

Dr. Johnson realized early in his career that "if I did what I was supposed to do I could be successful ... I focused on what I knew needed to be accomplished and completed the tasks at hand." Through this goal orientation Dr. Johnson was able to accomplish a great deal early on and is now on his fourth presidency.

Finally, Dr. Gaudino connected goal setting to institutional change when he stated "I think patience, setting long-term goals, not necessarily published on the website, but setting long-term goals for yourself seeing success incrementally, it takes time to make change." Essentially, if you don't set goals for yourself and the institution, you cannot expect to see change take place.

Technical Skills

All of the presidents interviewed had developed a level of technical or functional area expertise. Whether it was in an academic discipline like Dr. Genshaft (School Psychology) or in a functional area such as student affairs (Bassam Deeb) or intercollegiate athletics (James Tressel), these presidents had a defined area of expertise. Presidents Gaudino and Johnson highlighted technical competence as a given for an individual aspiring to be

183

POLITICS AND DECISION-MAKING

in senior leadership roles. When discussing the search process James Gaudino commented on what he believed to be a given for anyone to make it to the interview stage – some aspect of technical competence in a functional area within higher education. He stated:

> technical competence, they [Board of Trustees] trust the search committee to weed out the people without the experience or skill sets to do the actual work ... they are looking for the person they want to work with, they're looking for that fit ...

Alex Johnson agreed that you must first possess the technical competence or functional area expertise to make it through the recruitment process. Dr. Johnson emphasized the "need to understand how to develop and communicate a vision and you need to understand the strategic planning process." Without that he said, "you won't make it to the interview stage."

Dr. Genshaft immersed herself in the world of academic leadership and became a student of the profession. She believed that technical competence was more than her academic credentials, she needed to demonstrate an understanding of higher education:

> I understand the fundamentals, the foundation, the values, the purpose of higher education, the purpose of tenure, the purpose of writing and research at a research university. Other types of institutions, community colleges, teachers colleges have different missions ... Having grown up in higher education as a professional helped me internalize the core values of higher education and to never trespass those – academic freedom and freedom of speech, you just don't violate those.

STAYING THERE

When asked about differences in the skills necessary to maintain a presidency as opposed to those needed to make one's way to the presidency, four traits/skills were highlighted by several presidents – humility, transparency, trust, and focus. James Gaudino indicated that he really didn't see a difference – "I don't think I see different ones. Particularly as you make your way higher up the ladder, people making decisions become more and more skilled at doing that." Essentially, the skills and abilities needed to navigate the hierarchy are the same as those needed to stay in the presidency, it is how and to what degree they are used that differ. There were two skills/traits from the *Getting There* set that were identified as also being important in maintaining one's presidency: communication and collaboration.

Communication Skills

Not surprisingly all the presidents interviewed agreed that effective communication skills are a must for maintaining your presidency. Whether you are engaging with the governing board, community members, faculty, staff, or students, presidents must demonstrate strong communication skills. Those interviewed believe that for a president to be effective she must be viewed as a good communicator by the various institutional stakeholder groups, internal and external. Communication skills are a must in developing relationships and relationship development is critical to any president's success. As Judy Genshaft stated – "I am a people person … it is all about relationships and you need to work with them to find a win-win … and you must realize the power you have, is the power of persuasion …" Dan Mahony echoed the importance of communication skills, especially listening, in maintaining relationships when he said it is necessary for a president to "be seen as calm and steady, willing to listen to others is important."

Collaboration

Being a president involves working together with a wide variety of individuals from diverse backgrounds and varied interests. Alex Johnson mentions that to "maintain your role as a president it is important to be seen as a strong collaborator." Additionally, Dr. Genshaft states:

> my leadership style is one of collaboration, but I do make decisions. Oftentimes in collaborations you get a committee decision; that is not where I am at. I get everyone's input and I value the input then I explain why I made the decision and try to bring people to consensus.

As the institutional leader, others look to you for guidance not only to solve problems and resolve disputes, but to demonstrate or model *how* to solve problems and resolve disputes. It is important for you to lead by example and demonstrate that better solutions come about through collaborative efforts. Everyone working in higher education recognizes that our institutions are bureaucratic (see Chapter 3) in nature and that this bureaucracy has created silos that can make working across units challenging. If the president demonstrates that collaboration across the institution is encouraged and valued it then becomes possible, as Dr. Warren states: "to create a culture of mutual respect and feeling valued" within the institution.

Submerge One's Ego/Humble

As someone aspiring to be a president or senior leader of a college or university you must already have a record of achievement within your respective fields or disciplines. As an accomplished individual you are most likely comfortable with receiving recognition for your accomplishments. Several presidents suggest that you temper your need for accolades or recognition.

In most leadership texts the authors tend to draw a relationship between being a successful leader and having self-confidence. Each of the presidents I spoke with exhibited a high level of confidence and all of them also understood that they needed to have a sense of humility and a willingness to give credit to others. They recognized that it is not the individual accomplishments of a president that make an institution successful, it is the collective work of different stakeholder groups. For these presidents it was clear that who receives credit is not as important as accomplishing the goals. At the end of the year the board and stakeholders want to see what has been accomplished and how those accomplishments have moved the institution forward.

Dan Mahony discussed how others perceived leadership on his campus and the importance of shifting that view to be a bit more inclusive.

> Many people still have this vision of a leader that when s/he walks into the room like s/he is the biggest person there, the most important, kind of this dominant personality, which is *not me* ... Doing what is in the best interest of the institution means you may have to take a personal hit ... most of the time it is more important for others to shine, they deserve the credit and attention.

For James Gaudino, his institution experienced several successful years and throughout he encouraged others to share in the successes, realizing that the institution is not dependent upon him nor will it collapse without him at the helm:

> our reputation has increased, all of the external markers seem to be showing good things ... Everybody believes they had a voice in shaping things, even if they didn't succeed in getting their way. I think things are better, I can retire tomorrow and say I did my part.

And finally, Jim Tressel combines his collaborative nature with his willingness to share the spotlight when he stated – "As president, you need to involve others, if you can be best at something and make others best at something, you get to stay ... You have to create an environment of shared importance."

This willingness and ability to share the spotlight and to recognize others has served these presidents well and helps each maintain a positive relationship with their respective boards and perhaps more importantly, their institutional stakeholders.

Trust and Transparency

As a leader, if you don't have the confidence and trust of the people around you then failure can't be too far behind. In higher education being open and honest can help any leader in moving an agenda forward as President Gaudino mentioned:

> faculty are very quick to see through duplicity, too smart to be fooled, so you really have to sit down and be completely transparent. Show them everything and say we can change and adapt to this or we can try and resist these forces and we will not be successful ...

Beverly Warren agrees that transparency is important to maintaining the trust and support within the institution. She also provides a word of caution.

> Transparency is important as a president, but there can be a cost to transparency. Some people want to know everything, but sometimes there are things that just can't be shared ... you need to understand what those are and when you can and cannot share.

Jim Tressel highlighted the need to build trust and the importance to have trust in those around you:

> you have to trust others will do their jobs. There is a tendency for others to get out of their lane. You can't have experts in one field telling experts from another field how to do their jobs, that isn't going to work.

ADVICE TO THOSE WITH HIGH ASPIRATIONS

As I concluded my interviews I asked each of the presidents to share a few words of advice to individuals aspiring to become senior leaders in higher education. There were a few themes that stood out to me:

Give it Some Thought

When discussing their career paths, several of the presidents talked about people's perceptions of the importance in taking the next job rather than focusing on what one enjoys doing. As people aspire to move up they sometimes forget that it is a career path and not simply a series of jobs in the same industry. Several references were made regarding one's understanding of what one might be getting oneself into and being sure that is really what is wanted. James Gaudino used the classic phrase "careful what you wish for, you might actually get it" when discussing people's aspirations. Dan Mahony shared that, as faculty progress through the ranks, there is this idea that going from "full professor to department chair is the next logical move." He continues by cautioning faculty, "you may be an outstanding faculty member, but that does not mean you will be a good administrator." Dr. Mahony also has a suggestion for those already in the administrative ranks. As you make your way through the hierarchical structures in higher education it is important that you

> make sure you want the job you are applying for. Sometimes people move up a level beyond where they are happy simply because they think they should move to the next level. Give some thought – you may not want to be the VP and that is okay. Talk to people in those roles about what you will have to give up. People don't talk about that at this level. The presidency is a 24/7 job. I am the president of the university 24/7. I am never Dan. I can't go on Facebook and spout off my opinions about anything, those are things that will come back to haunt you. Some people think you can do whatever you want, it is just the opposite ... because I will alienate half the people no matter what side I take.

Similarly James Gaudino makes it clear that just because you aspire to become a president or other senior leader that may not happen so you need to be prepared for that potential disappointment. He stated one should

> never take a job you would not be willing to retire in. you never know what is going to happen. If I take a job as a dean because it will set me up for the presidency, but I don't really want to be dean, it is a stepping stone ... and it doesn't work out, five and a half, ten, fifteen years of my life are going to be misspent because I am in a job I don't want to be in. Don't suffer in a job in hopes of becoming a president because it may not happen, for a host of reasons.

Bassam Deeb discussed the importance of knowing how you fit with the institution and understanding your limitations before moving into a senior level role.

> I am not a fundraiser so if a time comes when they need a fundraiser, I am not the guy ... I truly believe we all have seasons and the positive side is that there are over 4,000 institutions and so we are bound to find another one that matches our abilities ... you think about the presidents that don't make it past the first three years, invariably it was a bad match ... [here at Trocaire] we are an opportunity college, not open admissions ... we deal with individuals who are first generation or people who have a degree and realize that isn't what they want to do and they need something different ... Buffalo is an immigrant community and more recently a refugee community and I think there is some value in them bringing in someone who shares some of those experiences ... it would not be smart to bring someone [from an elite institution,] if you've grown up in that kind of academic environment you're not going to easily translate, you may have the skill set ... but you will not fully understand the culture ...

Respect the Institution

All too often when new presidents come to campus, they do so with a pre-planned agenda of change for the institution. Typically, this change is met with resistance and as Jim Tressel mentioned "many faculty and staff make the assumption that they can outlast the new leadership as opposed to the attitude of; 'I would like to help make them successful as the new leader.'" He goes on to suggest that, instead of coming to campus with changes in mind, new presidents should "embrace the institution's past, far too many administrators act like nothing was ever done, and well, that is a mistake." Understanding the institution's history will oftentimes put problems into perspective for a new leader.

Judy Genshaft recalled her agenda during her first year as president and how important it was for her to establish rapport within the institution.

> In my first year, along with the Provost, I visited every single department ... it is really important to get to know the departments, the chairs, the dean. This is a learning time ... don't try to make decisions without data. Get to know key members of the community, ask the board, the board has to have faith in you, they hired you.

POLITICS AND DECISION-MAKING

> Get to know them quickly. If the board doesn't support you through tough times it is going to be difficult for you. Get to know your faculty, my first meeting on my 1st day was with the distinguished faculty – they asked me about parking … your first day on campus is very symbolic.

Similarly, Bev Warren spent a significant amount of time during her first year on a "listening tour of the institution." She believed it was important as a new president to "hear the voices of the faculty, staff and students." Dr. Warren went on to develop a strategic roadmap for the institution using the data gathered from the listening tour as the basis for support.

James Gaudino recalls starting at Central Washington University and realizing that he needed to be sensitive to the institutional needs. He mentioned that as president you need to have

> the ability to articulate a vision of the university that is sensitive to the culture of the university … had I come in and said I want to get rid of the graduate programs or conversely I want to start doctoral programs, dramatically changing the mission of the organization, I wouldn't have been able to sell that.

He went on to talk about the role of senior faculty in helping or hindering a new president's agenda.

> They're silverbacks – faculty teaching for 40 years, they have a lot of sway and here comes this guy from the outside who says we have to do things differently, they say hey what is wrong here, what's wrong with my life? As president, you have to have patience and go slowly or you're going to lose the crowd.

Continuing on with the idea of understanding the culture of an organization. Judy Genshaft provided this sage advice to those beginning a senior leadership role in higher education.

> Learn the institution to see what the culture is, you never want to fight the culture. The culture always wins so you have to understand the values of the institution and really focus on the goals and outcomes. Look at culture of the legislature and learn the institution.

While not specifically stating culture, Jim Tressel seemed to be in agreement with Dr. Genshaft when he mentioned that you need to make a whole-hearted try to learn about others and their worlds ... Get to know as much as you can about the university, every department is important. You need a breadth of appreciation for the whole institution and its idiosyncrasies. Learn to appreciate the whole and what everyone else does.

DECISION-MAKING

Depending on one's path to the presidency there are varying levels of and opportunities for individuals to make challenging and difficult decisions. Once at the presidential level the magnitude of the difficulty will increase and one's preparation will influence whether the issue/problem is considered difficult or not. For Jim Tressel it is also important to look at the motivation behind a decision, which is why he put decision-making into perspective when he said: "if you are worried about survival you are more likely to make poor decisions because you are making decisions to make people happy instead of [what is in] the best interest of the institution." Beverly Warren agrees that the *why* behind a decision is important, especially being president of a public institution.

> You need to ask if we [the university] are focused on the collective good. As president, I need to be responsible to and look out for my institution, but I also need to do what is best for the state. We all want our fair share, but we have to balance our wants with the collective good.

Dan Mahony talked about the different roles the president has and what is gained and lost when one has the legitimate power and is now making decisions for the institution instead of a single interest group. Members of the faculty or staff can take a more public stand promoting ideas and perhaps ideals whereas the president, who holds a bit more power and is viewed as representing the institution's position, has choices to make.

> What I get [as president] – is now I am at the table. I can make decisions that impact the university that those who aren't in my position can't make. I give up the public voice I had as faculty because I get to decide on things that make a difference to the institution. As a faculty you can speak out, you have your voice. To me the tradeoff is worth it. But, you have to decide – is the tradeoff worth it for you?

POLITICS AND DECISION-MAKING

Jame Gaudino cautions potential presidents to keep their decision-making power in perspective and not to get ahead of themselves.

> You need to realize that your authority doesn't increase as much as you think, but your responsibility explodes. You're still the CEO, but when you have unions and shared governance, there are a lot of restrictions on what you can do. You can't just impose your will, you're going to have to work with folks, convince them to come along with you but you'll be responsible for meeting all of the goals of the trustees and all of the legislative and public expectations ... there is a bit of a risk that didn't exist at lower ranks, so they have to be willing to take that on ... you really are the person who is going to be blamed if something happens on the campus that gets the media riled, gets the students riled, gets an external movement that gets focused on your campus ... don't put that kind of pressure on yourself ...

Throughout their careers, these presidents were required to make many difficult decisions. When describing the more challenging decisions, it became clear that personnel decisions were the toughest. As new institutional leaders one of the more challenging aspects with regard to decision-making revolved around their lack of context. Being unfamiliar with the history of problems or concerns and not understanding the political dynamics of the institution put them at a slight disadvantage. Frequently, new leaders find themselves at odds with the faculty and staff. Dan Mahony mentioned that "walking into the political environment and saying no a lot, that is tough to do."

When specifically asked about difficult or challenging decisions, several presidents including Judy Genshaft acknowledged that "people decisions are always the toughest." Bassam Deeb talked about personnel issues and how they may vary depending on the individuals involved.

> Almost all of my challenging decisions centered around personnel, essentially sending someone home. I am able to make that decision and to an external person it may seem like it is easy ... to make that decision, it is not. I follow the same process I do with other decisions, I look at things from different perspectives ... Sometimes the person is a disaster and it seems like it might be easier to make that decision ... but with personnel, they are not easy decisions. People say it is because you are looking at that person's livelihood, and that is partially true, but for me it is because there must have been something viable about that individual when you hired them, the

fact that the performance is not where it needs to be and is now at a level you must separate them from the institution. Something went wrong somewhere, maybe it is the individual, but maybe it is not the individual and that is the part that is most difficult for me ... As a president you are relying on the engagement of multiple layers within the organization and you are the final decision-maker.

Dan Mahony agreed that personnel decisions are the most difficult for most any supervisor and that the impact of personnel decisions extends beyond the individuals involved. There is also an impact on the institution – "staff changes are difficult decisions, there is always significant lost time when you make a change ... [as] it takes time to recover." It is for this reason that many leaders have difficulty making personnel decisions, trying to decide if dealing with the current problem is better or worse than dealing with the loss of the individual(s) involved.

ALWAYS THE PRESIDENT

Several presidents mentioned that being a president is a life-changing experience. One of the challenges to becoming the senior leader in a higher education institution, especially coming from the academic side, is that throughout your career you had a specific academic identity as a specialist in your area of expertise. Now as a president you are expected to become a generalist and, to some degree, relinquish your academic identity as a scholar to become an administrator. That can be very difficult for some people. Additionally, as the president you are now asked to give up most if not all of your personal time. It can be very challenging to live in a community where you are quite recognizable.

> The presidency is a 24/7 job. It is not just the 80 hour weeks, but understanding that when there is a crisis it becomes immediate and as president you need to be prepared to respond, regardless of time of day or day of the week ... going to the grocery store for a carton of milk can take 30 to 40 minutes, people stop you and want to talk. You are always the president. You need to find ways to protect your time, if that is possible.
> (Beverly Warren, personal communication)

James Gaudino encourages individuals to do everything they can to understand what and why they are considering a role as a senior leader or institutional president. He suggests that as you progress through your career you need to

> really observe presidents and determine if [you] want the lifestyle, [you] may want the job, but there is a life that comes along with it. And if [you] are willing to live that life ... working six – seven days a week, attending university functions, a theater production, a basketball game on Saturday then a museum opening on Sunday ... You don't really have a private life, you could do it, but you will leave a lot of residue [poor relations with your stakeholders].

For Bassam Deeb his role is a little different because of the size, mission and location of the institution. As president, he sees himself as an ambassador representing his institution...

> We are in a community in which there are 21 institutions of higher education and so there are perceptions about the value your organization has to the community, it doesn't mean they don't value your students or your programs ... there is a pecking order to a degree so the demand on your time will vary depending on what people perceive to be the value placed on your organization ... I am blessed that I have a fairly balanced life, meaning I can go to the store in shorts and not having shaved for a couple of days and it wouldn't matter because most people wouldn't recognize me ... I think if I was in a place where the institution is the center of attention that would be difficult and you wouldn't have the down time you need to stay fresh in the job ... The position is demanding. You have to be at events at which higher education is expected to be represented ... I don't have it as bad as others where they are the center of attention ... The job itself is demanding and being an ambassador you look at the job as a way of life rather than a 9–5 job.

As you consider the path in front of you, perhaps the word of advice from James Gaudino may help you to determine your next few steps.

> if you really want [to be a president], experience as much as you can get involved in the ACE program if you are planning on doing it, expose yourself, get on university committees so you understand how decisions are really made ... get on the finance committee, promotion and tenure, and recognize that presidents mentor people. I wouldn't have this job if it wasn't for Carol Cartwright [former president of Kent State University]. She said "let's talk

about your accomplishments administratively not how many grants you have or articles you've written." She helped me completely reengineer my CV. Having a sponsor, having a mentor is critical. It is hard to do it on your own. Realize the kind of institution you want to be at ...

CONCLUDING COMMENTS

Recognizing your strengths and limitations is a key first step along the path to becoming an institutional president. Connecting what you bring to the needs of an institution is another key step. Several of the presidents talked about different institutional types and differing institutional needs. Maxwell (2013) discusses the characteristics of organizational leaders and one of the keys to success is being "able to cross lines out of their industry or area of expertise to speak with authority. People respect them for who they are and what they represent" (p. 7). This dovetails nicely with what several presidents mentioned regarding the breadth of your experience and your ability to talk with people from different disciplines or different functional areas (Chapter 3).

I believe Bassam Deeb summed it up nicely when he stated:

> college presidents, by definition think they can be presidents anywhere, the ego sometimes can be overwhelming, but the reality is that it is not true. It is often related to your upbringing, your exposure and experiences, what the institution is looking for and therefore, there would be a match. I am a big fan of "every person has a season" ... I am a fit now but I may not be a match in three or five years ... you don't know until you get into the job ... there is a certain level of evolution that can happen in the job but evolution is not sufficient, there is no evolution that can reengineer who you are so that you can be the president for all seasons at that institution ... I truly believe when you arrive at the position, based on what you bring, your talent allows you to succeed in that institution for a period of time ...

Regardless of the path you choose to advance your career within higher education you will need to develop a set of skills and hone certain attributes along the way. There are no guarantees that you will make it to the top of the organizational chart but these presidents would most likely agree it is best that you develop a career path and continue to progress along that path even with diversions along the way.

POLITICS AND DECISION-MAKING

REFLECTIVE QUESTIONS

1. To what position do you aspire? Do you have a plan to get there?
2. How do the traits listed in this chapter parallel or differ from those in Chapter 5?
3. What does it take to become a president?

Part IV
Practical Perspectives

Chapter Eleven

Now What?

The use of power and political behaviors are ubiquitous on college and university campuses. Understanding how they are employed is imperative for administrators and faculty at all levels within any institution. When in a leadership position, by default, you have certain types of power plus access to other types depending on the relationships created with various stakeholder groups. How you choose to exercise the power bestowed upon you, as well as the power you develop, will determine your effectiveness and your ability to develop a collegial environment amongst those you lead. During your tenure within higher education you will be required to make many controversial decisions that will put you at odds with one or more stakeholder groups. In this chapter we will look at some of the controversial topics/areas that tomorrow's leaders will face. According to Kanter (2014), leaders are often measured by how they respond to and resolve problems on their campuses and perhaps in their communities. Therefore, how one addresses these challenges will impact individual careers and, possibly, the future of higher education.

Some of the controversial topics this generation of leaders will face are briefly described below. They include: managing enrollments, free speech, intercollegiate athletics, sexual assault/sexual harassment, mission creep, resource allocation, technology, external forces, among others. An additional wild card, the Department of Education is a political entity that will also have a continued effect on higher education, but that discussion is beyond the scope of this text.

FREE SPEECH

As mentioned in Chapter 6, free speech on today's campuses can be a very powerful tool in forwarding an agenda or creating an environment open to reasoned dialogue about controversial topics. The reason I bring this up

PRACTICAL PERSPECTIVES

again in this chapter is because it can also create some difficult situations for administrators, and how administrators respond to speech on their campuses can impact their tenures on those campuses. If higher education truly is a marketplace for ideas then institutions must be open to hearing all kinds of ideas, even those which some individuals will find offensive.

State legislative bodies and institutional governing boards have begun to weigh in on what should constitute free speech on campus. Conservative student groups want to bring conservative speakers and liberal groups want liberal speakers; each side believes their side holds the truth and they do not necessarily want to listen to those representing a differing point of view. Institutional leaders are being caught in the middle and they must be careful in determining what is free speech and therefore permitted on campus because it is a free speech issue, as opposed to what is university-endorsed speech, which represents the values, beliefs, and morals of the institution. Having controversial speakers on a campus does not mean that an institution endorses that speech, but rather signifies an institutional belief in the importance of its students hearing the message so they can determine for themselves the validity of such speech. Unfortunately, this can be a hard sell to some governing bodies and state legislatures.

MANAGING ENROLLMENTS

Higher education, like most other industries, has ebbs and flows that are impacted by several factors – internal and external. Three of those factors are population shifts, demographic changes, and economic conditions. Because so many institutions have a growth mindset, believing that each incoming class of students needs to be larger than the previous class, admissions offices live and die by population shifts. Currently, within the U.S. we are seeing decreasing high school graduation rates in the Northeast and Midwest as well as population growth in the Southwest and West. These shifts are impacting the size of the pool of potential students, resulting in declining enrollments and numerous campus closures in the Northeast and Midwest, while simultaneously the Western states are adding new campuses and growing enrollments within current institutions. With this new reality, colleges and universities in these regions need to reframe their thinking about institutional size. It may be prudent for institutions in the Midwest and Northeast to take this opportunity to reduce the overall size of the institution, doing so in a very strategic fashion. Institutional leaders need to pay attention to elementary and secondary enrollments in their target markets; there should be no surprises when the number of students graduating changes.

Demographic shifts in student populations continue to occur, signaling a dramatic change in the students served over the past four decades. According to the NCES, in 1980, 16.5% of the students attending degree-granting postsecondary educational institutions were ethnic minorities. In 2017 that percentage was 44%. Today's student body looks very different than it did in the 1970s and 1980s and so should our student support services. These changing demographics have differential effects on institutions, depending on the shifts within their respective markets.

As for the economy's influence; higher education is counter cyclical; that is, when the economy is doing well, potential students have other options (substitutes) and may choose to opt out of postsecondary education. When the economy is struggling or in a downturn, postsecondary education is viewed as a way to develop new skills or update technical competencies that may help individuals improve their employment options.

In this environment it has become important for institutional leaders to understand how external factors influence enrollments. When these leaders set enrollment targets, those targets need to be informed by the realities of the current environment. Presidents who are ill-informed will tend to build budgets based on inflated enrollment projections and subsequently will need to impose budget cuts because of a failure to meet those projections. This lack of foresight creates political problems within the institution and also can begin to erode confidence in the institution's leadership, diminishing the power of said leaders.

RESOURCE ALLOCATION

As institutions of higher education continue to become more reliant on tuition dollars, budgets become more rigid, and with less financial flexibility institutions will see an increase in political activity and a greater reliance on power (Kanter, 2010) to accomplish institutional goals and also a greater likelihood of more risk-averse decision-making practices, which inadvertently limits entrepreneurial activity and innovation. In many of these typical institutional budget environments the focus is on the immediate needs and on short-term expenditure rather than looking at the long-term needs of the institution.

Decentralized budget models like Responsibility Centered Management require senior leaders to give more authority and power to those beneath them in the hierarchy. This takes courage on behalf of the institutional leaders and also confidence that they have the right people in the right positions. In these models, financial decisions are made by individuals closer to the implementation, which can give these individuals a greater sense of accountability and ownership in the decision. If carried out properly, these decentralized budget models have the opportunity to create an environment that encourages and rewards entrepreneurial and innovative approaches to higher education.

MISSION CREEP

In response to budget or enrollment difficulties, more and more institutions are changing their missions, morphing into other types of institutions (see Chapter 3) – liberal arts colleges are becoming comprehensive colleges adding graduate degrees; regional public institutions are trying to become research intensive universities; and community colleges are beginning to offer four-year degree programs. These shifts have been justified by administrators stressing the need to be more relevant or to stay competitive in an ever-changing landscape of higher education. In reality, it may simply be an inflated administrative ego (Kretovics, 2011), leading more and more institutions to become all things to all people. Change does not always equate to progress.

Toma (2012) commented that so many institutions "are eerily similar in vision, in fact seemingly obsessed with moving to the next level. Their common goal is legitimacy through enhanced prestige" (p. 118). The belief here is that more research revenue, more faculty, and more students are best for the institution. However, Lombardi (2013) noted that regional institutions trying to reposition themselves as research institutions tend to underestimate the financial commitment necessary to make such a shift. He warned against such shifts, when stating "research income from grants and contracts never covers the cost of performing the research … most universities are fortunate if they recover half of the audited indirect costs of research allowed by government regulations" (p. 59). So why then do so many of these regional institutions push towards this goal? I believe the most logical explanation is to satisfy the ego of the current institutional leader(s).

Mission creep does not need to continue. Institutional leaders and Boards of Trustees have the power to stop this and to ensure that individuals hired respect and embrace the current mission of the institution. I am not advocating that institutions stagnate or not evolve. I am advocating that an institution hire people who want to be at that particular college or university for what it offers. Too often new institutional leaders (incoming presidents) attempt to reshape their new institution into one that resembles the institution they just left. In cases like this, one must ask, who is more resistant to change? Is it the faculty and staff who really like the institution the way it is or the new leader who wants the new institution to look like the one s/he just left?

INTERCOLLEGIATE ATHLETICS

As noted in Chapter 7, there have been numerous athletic scandals that have created enormous difficulties for specific institutions. I don't see the scandals stopping nor do I see the financial expenditures on athletics being reduced, especially within institutions participating in what has come to be known as the *Power Five* conferences. I believe that the income generated by the revenue-producing sports (primarily football and men's basketball) in these institutions has put institutional leaders in a very difficult position. On the one hand, athletics is supposed to be an extracurricular activity in which degree-seeking students participate. On the other hand, many of the high-profile programs recruit athletes who seek to play professional sports rather than students who intend to graduate. This can put institutional leaders in a difficult position; if they assert their authority over these programs and implement the necessary oversight over the academic mission of the institution, they run the risk of impacting future revenues for the institution. Over the years most institutions with these high-profile athletic programs have made it quite clear that winning is far more important than graduating these student-athletes. Most coaches who lose their jobs will be terminated for losing too many games or violating some NCAA or institutional policy. I cannot recall a coach ever being terminated for not graduating players within a reasonable time frame.

I am a believer in intercollegiate athletics as an extracurricular activity, placing the emphasis on the students and their education, which does happen in most non-revenue-generating sports and at most institutions that do not award scholarships based on athletic ability. Unfortunately, when students are advised not to choose specific majors or certain courses because they are not athlete friendly, I believe that has gone too far. Practice times determine student schedules instead of student schedules determining practice schedules. Athletics should be treated like other extracurricular activities or like student work-study (employment); something in addition to the educational pursuits, not as the purpose for a student to enroll. Colleges and universities need to adopt a student-first mentality for all students and not permit intercollegiate athletics to drive an athlete-first approach.

Institutional leaders need to make a decision as to the importance of revenue-generating sports on their campuses. In order to avoid certain state oversight, three Florida universities have converted their athletics programs to "direct support organizations – a quasi-private status that limits public oversight while granting the department sovereign immunity as a governmental entity" (Jarvis, 2019). They have all of the protections of a state agency but do not have to comply with all of the state requirements.

PRACTICAL PERSPECTIVES

While this impacts a small percentage of institutions in the U.S., these institutions garner a disproportionate amount of publicity which can detract from the overall academic mission and integrity of higher education in general. Perhaps the time has come for these high-profile football and men's basketball programs to divorce themselves from institutions of higher education and create a minor league for athletes who have no intention of pursuing a college degree. Students who enroll in an institution for one or two years to play basketball or football with no intention to graduate would be served far better playing for a salary in a minor league than taking up a seat in a college or university and going through the motions of being a student. Institutions can still have these athletic programs, but with an emphasis on students and their academic pursuits not their draft prospects. For the vast majority of institutions this approach would have little to no impact and for the rest of the student-athletes attending these institutions, they can still participate in the sports they enjoy and receive an education that will prepare them for a future beyond athletic competition.

SEXUAL HARASSMENT/SEXUAL ASSAULT

Higher education has been seized by a number of high-profile cases during the past several years involving sexual assault or sexual harassment. Some of these incidents involved students only, others involved students and institutional employees, and in 2018, the chancellor of the University of Wisconsin at Whitewater resigned shortly after an investigation into allegations of sexual misconduct by her spouse (Zamudio-Suaréz, 2018). The *Me Too* movement has made it more acceptable for victims to come forward with such charges, helping to shed more light on this travesty.

Institutions of higher education and their leaders must establish a culture of moral and ethical behavior in their workplaces, and that culture needs to be modeled from the top down. It never has been nor should it ever become acceptable for individuals in positions of power to coerce subordinates or others with little or no power into inappropriate relationships or to subject them to harassing and demeaning comments.

SHARED GOVERNANCE

Shared governance within higher education in the U.S. has been a point of pride for decades; however, that model of decision-making is now under significant threat. The threat comes from two distinct but somewhat related areas. First, institutions are relying more heavily on non-tenure eligible faculty. During the last few decades, higher education has witnessed a decline in the percentage of tenured or tenure-track faculty teaching in colleges and universities (Ehrenberg and Zhang, 2005). According to the NCES (https://nces.ed.gov/programs/digest/d12/tables/dt12_305.asp) the percentage of tenured and tenure-track faculty declined from 56.2% in 1993–94 to 48.5% in 2011–12. With fewer tenured faculty members the pool of faculty available to participate in governance-related positions becomes smaller.

Secondly, as institutions push for more research activity and scholarly productivity from the ever shrinking tenure-track faculty pool there becomes a disincentive for those faculty to participate in service activities on the campus, of which governance is one. With fewer faculty interested and participating in shared governance there is a danger that the model will shift toward or into an administrative governance approach, leaving the faculty out of decision-making processes.

TENURE

Tenure is far more than guaranteed employment for faculty, it provides faculty the luxury of being able to use their academic freedom to speak freely about their academic discipline and it also gives them the responsibility to speak freely with regard to policies and practices via shared governance on their respective campuses. As tenure-track positions decline as a percentage of full-time faculty, simultaneously, there is also an increase in the use of part-time or contingent faculty (adjuncts).

There will always be a need for part-time instructors on campuses across the country. Some are hired to teach a single course based on a specific area of expertise, while others may be hired due to a slight increase in demand for a course during a particular semester. Unfortunately, what is becoming more common is the hiring of multiple part-time/adjunct faculty to replace full-time tenure-track faculty lines. This has become quite a common practice at larger, research-oriented institutions as a way to reduce costs.

The future of higher education is dependent upon an adequate supply of well-trained full-time faculty. Eliminating tenure eligible positions to save money in the short term has the potential to create a shortage of these faculty in the long term. Eventually, institutions will begin to see a decline in graduate enrollments because of a lack in faculty opportunities and because of the length of time to prepare well-qualified faculty, these declines will limit the availability of faculty in the employment pipeline. The danger here is that these types of shortages are challenging to forecast so, when they do occur, it usually means there will be a period of reduced quality in the education delivered. Therefore, it becomes more critical than ever for the next generation of higher education leaders to re-emphasize the importance of full-time tenure-track faculty and shift resources from contingent faculty to tenure-track faculty lines.

Post-Tenure Review

It seems as though not a year goes by that a state legislative body or other organization calls for the elimination of tenure within public colleges and universities. Thankfully, these calls have not had enough credible support to implement such a policy, but they continue to try. My suggestion here is that state systems or individual public institutions develop a system of post-tenure review designed to hold faculty accountable to a specified balance of teaching, scholarly productivity, and institutional service.

I firmly believe that it will be far better for faculty unions, faculty senates, or other faculty organizations to utilize their power to create or influence such policies before those policies are forced upon them by politicians or voters. While this is a very sensitive topic to many faculty, as current or future administrators, you have a responsibility to at least mention this, thereby warning faculty of the potential of outside influencers impacting their employment within the academy.

TECHNOLOGY

For decades futurists have been predicting a revolutionary change in technology that will disrupt the higher education industry. To date, that has yet to come to pass. This does not mean technology has not had a significant influence on higher education, it has and it will continue to do so. As technology improves and evolves, the ways in which staff and faculty interact with students change. Many of the functions that employees performed on behalf of students are now performed by students (Hoffman and Kretovics, 2004) and it is likely that students will continue to do more on their own on into the future.

Additionally, improvements in technology have made it easier for institutions to collect data about prospective students, increasing institutions' ability to be more precise in their recruitment practices (marketing efforts). Similarly, technological advances have made it easier for institutions to collect data required for accountability and accreditation purposes. A danger here is that institutions will simply collect and report on the data that is easily collected, thereby narrowing their accountability practices instead of expanding them.

Distance Education

Technology in online and distance education has made it easier for some institutions to expand their footprint, reaching students who were not considered to be in their market. However, distance education is still attempting to emulate the face-to-face experience in an online environment, basing teaching pedagogy on the pedagogical approaches most faculty have grown accustomed to seeing in action.

Technology has made it easier to perform certain tasks on campuses, but it has not necessarily transformed the actual tasks being performed. We are still waiting for the disruptive technology that will upset the power structures through a quantum leap in technological innovation that truly transforms what we do, not simply how we do it.

Administrators and faculty need to use their power and leadership to influence the use of technology to create more efficient and effective practices on campuses. I am sure that all of you can think of a colleague or two who never saw a new software program (ERP, LMS, etc.) that they did not love. If these new technologies do not make it easier for students to navigate the bureaucracy, for faculty to improve their pedagogical approach to teaching, or for staff to create efficiencies in their work, the institution should reconsider its purchase.

Social Media

Another example of how technology has reshaped the interaction with students and in some instances, parents, is social media. These technologies have changed student and parent expectations as to administrators' and faculty members' response time to questions or concerns. The expectation is an immediate response to everything, regardless of its level of urgency. This severely limits the time for administrators to craft an appropriate and reasoned response, making it more challenging to resolve an issue before it escalates. Add to this the access to executive-level leadership through these platforms and now an unintended bypass of institutional procedure has been created – go straight to the top, no need to work with entry- or mid-level staff.

If you are on social media, the expectation is 24/7 access. If you are not on social media you may be viewed as a dinosaur, out of touch with this and perhaps the previous generation. Proceed with caution in this area.

EXTERNAL FORCES

Political entities such as Governing Boards, state legislative bodies, and the Federal Government will have an increasing level of influence over colleges and universities for the foreseeable future, primarily as a result of student financial aid and institutional funding formulas, or research grant awards. As enrollment declines in the Northeast and Midwest challenge individual institutions, hastening the closure of some of the smaller private colleges, a few institutional leaders view this as a type of institutional Darwinism – survival of the fittest. However, in some instances, efforts to reduce costs may result in forced mergers between state institutions or between state institutions and community colleges, similar to what has been happening in Georgia. This type of government intervention does not bode well for institutions or their respective leaders.

I believe that college and university leaders should begin or continue to develop partnerships and cooperative agreements with other institutions, especially those in close proximity. In the public sector it does not seem fiscally responsible to have multiple institutions offering the same academic programs within a reasonable commute of each other. Some leaders believe it is not in the best interest of their institutions to collaborate with competing institutions, especially if their institution is on solid financial footing. However, it is always better to act when in a position of power and influence than react when in a position of weakness or desperation. As such, proposing the sharing of resources, both human and physical, can be a powerful way to win support from legislative bodies and other politicians and strengthen some programs.

Another source of external influence comes from corporations and foundations. These organizations like to donate money to institutions to fund special projects or programs. On the surface these may seem like very generous and benevolent organizations. However, they fund what they want, not necessarily what the institution needs. Institutional leaders need to be sure they are utilizing the money to forward the mission of the institution not taking the money just to increase their grant revenue. External entities can exert undue power on institutions that are simply chasing dollars rather than being strategic in their grant applications. This can also lead to *mission creep* as described above.

INSTITUTIONAL LEADERSHIP

McLemore (2014) believes that most people leading complex organizations, such as colleges and universities, are bright and talented individuals. I wholeheartedly agree with his premise, but want to add that tomorrow's higher education leaders will also need to be able to think like non-academics. The days of a president being the academic leader of an institution are ending, if not already over, and it is time for the next generation of leaders to embrace higher education as an industry and each individual campus as a business. Simply put, colleges and universities are in the education business.

I am not advocating that institutions hire leaders from the corporate sector, government, or from other non-profits, although many of those individuals can and do add a great deal to our collective thinking. I am suggesting that individuals who aspire to be institutional leaders devote the necessary time and energy to understanding how to perform the functions of their new administrative positions prior to starting. Colleges and universities can no longer afford to have faculty who become administrators spend their first year in an *on-the-job-training* mode.

The vast majority of faculty have developed an academic expertise, earning a credential that helped them gain entry into the academy. Similarly, most administrators in student affairs or business/administrative services have training in their areas of expertise. Why then, do we have so many senior administrators in higher education with no formal training or academic preparation in administration? Having a record of scholarly publications and presentations in one's academic discipline may be adequate preparation for a faculty position, but it is not adequate to manage a multi-million dollar budget or supervise staff or faculty members. Perhaps this lack of preparation has contributed to the seemingly ever increasing number of administrators on campuses (often referred to as administrative bloat). Could it be that two unprepared individuals are better than one well trained administrator?

There are numerous academic programs that prepare individuals for administrative careers and there are a host of internship/fellowship programs and summer institutes that can help administrator wannabes or newly appointed administrators from the faculty ranks prepare for their new responsibilities. Requiring administrators to be prepared to lead a multimillion dollar enterprise is not too much to ask.

CONCLUDING COMMENTS

The items above are a sampling of the areas where opportunities exist for administrators to use their power and take leadership roles to influence or implement policies and practices that will keep their respective institutions focused on students. Leaders can help develop an institutional culture by ensuring their executive team is well prepared to take on these and other issues of *politics* and *power*.

These leaders also have the opportunity to positively influence higher education in general. It is impossible to help others without helping yourself, so helping prepare the next generation of higher education leaders should be a priority of every senior leader in higher education today. Embrace the future – do not ignore it.

PRACTICAL PERSPECTIVES

REFLECTIVE QUESTIONS

1. Of the topics discussed, which have you seen as having the most significant impact on your campus?
2. How have these topics influenced decision-making on your campus?
3. What do you see as the key administrative issues for the next generation of higher education leaders?

Chapter Twelve

Wrap Up

When you think of *power* and *politics*, view them as tools to help you become a successful leader with the ability to accomplish your goals and objectives within the existing framework of your institution. As with any administrative tools, their inappropriate use or overuse can be detrimental to the administrator, the department or unit, and to the institution. As an administrator one must understand that political behavior and the use of power are not inherently bad. Equally important is that administrators need to ensure they act in an ethical and responsible manner and that the ends do not justify the means. For example, an administrator may complete a project on budget and on time but if it was accomplished through the use of coercive power or by creating a culture of fear, it must not be viewed as a success by the powers-that-be. College and university administrators must do everything they can to ensure that their theories-in-use match their espoused theories and that those theories promote ethical decision-making throughout the institution. Ultimately, if the institution is successful, you as an administrator will be viewed as successful.

As mentioned earlier, there is no single formula for becoming a successful leader within higher education. There are multiple paths to gaining power and working your way into leadership positions within individual institutions. One's administrative personality in conjunction with the type and organizational structure of each institution (Chapter 3) play a role in determining who works their way to the top. The following paragraphs are meant to provide you with some tips to help you navigate the power dynamics in organizations so that you can become a more effective leader.

MAINTAINING CONTROL

Throughout your career you will be placed in a variety of situations that will test your leadership and administrative abilities. It is important that you respond to these situations in a professional manner no matter how intense, frustrating, or confrontational the situation. Few people respect administrators who lose their cool under pressure. During difficult or challenging times, it is important for you to maintain your poker face.

Likewise, if you always appear to be in a hurry or tend to exaggerate the seriousness of the situation you undermine your credibility. As Pfeffer (1992) notes "it is difficult to convince others that you are in control when you race from one (usually trivial) emergency to another" (p. 206). It seems as though those who talk about how busy they are, are often the least busy in the office or unit, but have the ability to have the attention focused on themselves.

COMMUNICATE EFFECTIVELY AND OFTEN

Most leadership books will extoll the virtues of having good communication skills, indicating that effective communication skills are attributed to most, if not all, successful leaders in politics, business and education. As seen in several examples presented earlier, poor communication skills or a lack of communication led to the downfall of several academic leaders. You will want to do everything you can to avoid that same mistake.

Throughout this book, communication skills have been emphasized and listening skills have been touted as the most important communication skill. Therefore, as you make transitions throughout your career, whether you are changing institutions or changing positions within your institution, it will be critical for you to *spend more time listening and less time talking*. You will need to understand the hierarchical structures, communications networks, and power structures of the institution before you can legitimately propose changes. This requires effectively listening to others.

Frequent communication with subordinates helps to build a trusting relationship and is a great starting point for empowering others. When presenting a proposal or proposing a change, the more people know and understand the less likely they are to fear moving forward and the greater likelihood they will follow you and/or embrace the stated mission. If individuals believe or perceive that they are part of the decision-making process they tend to be more accepting of the decision/outcome. This is not the same as buy-in for the *decision* but rather for the *process*. If it is perceived as inclusive and fair people will be more comfortable with the implementation.

FINISHING

To be viewed by others as an effective leader, you will need to demonstrate that you know how to accomplish goals, i.e. finish what you started. This means being knowledgeable of the institution, its policies, procedures, its people, and the distribution of power. When tasks need to be accomplished, complete them. Don't wait for others, take responsibility and finish the job before moving on to the next project.

You will need to lead by example and that means you will need to *spend more time doing and less time complaining*. Additionally, as an institutional leader, you will need to be more focused on the long-term prospects of the institution and/or your unit. All of your short-term actions should be designed to help accomplish long-term goals. Focusing on short-term goals only will lead to unintended consequences that may ultimately compromise the long-term prospects of the institution.

Additionally, as Maxwell (2013) points out, "personal success does not always translate into team success. Leadership is defined by what a person does with and for others" (p. 81). This requires you to collaborate and cooperate with others and to give credit where credit is due. It is not about you, it is about accomplishing the goal(s).

RESOURCE CONTROL

A resource can be defined as anything that you or someone else believes holds value, and as mentioned in Chapter 6, the more resources you have or control the more power over others you can have. Additionally, the units or departments with fewer resources tend to express concern when decisions are made without an opportunity for their voice to be heard, while the units with greater resources tend not to be as concerned, unless of course, they are asked to reallocate some of their resources to other units.

Understanding how resources are allocated at your institution and knowing who within the hierarchy controls or influences the process can help you in your quest for acquiring more resources and, thus, more power. Therefore, if you aspire to positions higher on the organizational chart you will need to think about how each position you take helps you gain control over more resources. As discussed earlier, the more resources you control, the more power at your disposal.

HIRE AND SUPERVISE WELL

It has been said that in any organization people are your most valuable resource. I believe this to be a truism for institutions of higher education; without high-quality people it is impossible to deliver a high-quality education. As an administrator there is no more important decision made by a supervisor than a personnel decision – hiring or terminating employees (Kretovics, 2011). When hiring faculty and staff, remember to hire people

PRACTICAL PERSPECTIVES

who think differently from you and from those already on board – have the courage to hire more *athletes, counter-balancers*, and *collaborators* not *lap dogs, pundits*, and *singers* (see Chapter 3). Hire people who have a passion for the work at hand and people who want to be part of your department, unit, or institution.

It is far better to hire individuals who do not require external motivation, but instead are driven by intrinsic rewards. Putting the right people in the proper positions will create a trusting environment that encourages and promotes individual responsibility. As Teddy Roosevelt noted over a century ago, "the best leader is the one who has sense enough to pick good people to do what he wants done, and the self-restraint to keep from meddling with them while they do it" (www.brainyquote.com/quotes/theodore_roosevelt_137797). Also, recognize when it is appropriate for someone to leave the institution. Don't perpetuate the practice of shifting problem individuals from one department to another. If they truly are dysfunctional within the institution it is better, if at all possible, to remove the person from the institution. Collins (2001) pointed out, "letting the wrong people hang around is unfair to all of the right people" (p. 56).

SELF-ASSESS

Being honest with yourself about your strengths and weaknesses can be very difficult – people have blind spots and also have a tendency to overestimate their abilities. As you progress through your career, you will need to find a way to ensure you have an accurate assessment of yourself as a leader. Maxwell (2013) stresses the importance of self-awareness and encourages individuals to know themselves before attempting to lead others. The best way to minimize your blind spot(s) and to increase the accuracy of your self-perceptions is to ask for feedback. Asking a trusted colleague for honest feedback will help you understand yourself and how you are perceived by others. Most often there is a marked difference between self-perception and others' perception; recognizing these differences and addressing them through self-improvement or professional development plans can help position you for new opportunities.

The more you understand your strengths and limitations the better prepared you will be to present yourself in a favorable light, which in turn can help increase your power within the institution. As noted earlier, Machiavelli discussed the importance of creating a positive perception, suggesting that the more you know about yourself the better equipped you will be to craft the image of the leader you want to be and the leader the institution seeks.

BE THE LEADER YOU WANT TO BE

Being a successful leader does take more than crafting a positive image. You must also be capable of carrying out the tasks at hand and actually becoming the leader that others perceive you to be. As you progress through your career and through the hierarchical structures in higher education, you will come across a wide range of leaders and administrative personalities. You will witness behaviors you believe to be worthy of emulation and you will experience those you hope you will never encounter again. You should strive to incorporate the habits and styles of those you admire the most into your leadership behaviors, but without changing your core beliefs and values.

As a leader you will have ample opportunity to use your power to influence others in their decision-making processes. Additionally, you will find yourself in numerous situations where you are called upon to respond or react to unpleasant or perhaps inappropriate situations. How you choose to use your power when responding will partially define you as a leader. In times like these remember: it is as easy to show kindness and respect as it is to act with disdain and irreverence.

CREATE AN INSTITUTIONAL CULTURE

Many institutions of higher education do not have an organizational culture and many institutional leaders confuse *school spirit* with institutional culture. It is the responsibility of institutional leaders to develop an institutional culture, but many decide not to pursue this because it can be a very challenging goal and it can be very time consuming. Culture cannot be created by talking about it. The change has to begin with institutional values and shared beliefs creating a semblance of homogeneity (Van den Steen, 2010). This means that the institution must be viewed, internally, as stable and consistent in its mission and vision. Employees need to be committed to the institution and the institution must been seen as valuing longevity, because homogeneity tends to be stronger in institutions that have a longer history and where faculty and staff are involved in making more important decisions. Therefore, institutions that have mid-level and executive leaders with strong beliefs and a commitment to the institution will have an increased likelihood of developing a stronger institutional culture by imbedding leadership processes into said culture (Yukl, 1989).

DEPART WITH DIGNITY

All good things must come to an end, and so as your time in your position or perhaps career winds down it is important to depart with dignity, leaving behind a unit or institution that is better off because you served. As mentioned earlier, being an effective leader is not about leaving a legacy, rather it is about doing the right things, the right way, for the right reasons. If you do this your legacy will take care of itself – the department, division, or institution will be better off because you served. It is incumbent upon you to develop your network and allies so that when it becomes necessary for you to leave the institution you will be leaving friends behind. This is possible even when you are departing at the request of your supervisor. Unless you have done something unethical or illegal you should be in a position to control the narrative of your departure and in doing so you are able to depart with dignity.

There may be times when you do not leave the institution on the best of terms or perhaps you have been asked to leave. You must maintain your professionalism and reputation because that follows you wherever you go. If you leave on bad terms you will most likely struggle to find welcoming opportunities at or above that level for quite some time. Let's take a look at an example of how *not* to depart. Earlier, we looked at a few examples of senior administrators who were forced out of their positions for a variety of reasons. However, the situation of Timothy Wolfe's departure from the presidency of the University of Missouri System will stand as one of the most embarrassing in recent memory. Not because of the actions he took leading to his departure, but rather how he responded after he had left the university. A few months after resigning he sent an email to "Friends" that took several jabs at the university's leadership and a Missouri State Senator, among others. He concluded this letter with a call to action, asking his friends to call or email board members to assist him in resolving his ongoing dispute with the university. He believed he was due more money and wanted his friends to pressure the institution and the state to pay him what he believed he deserved. This type of letter, while it may make you feel good at the time, is not how you want to be remembered. When leaving an institution under a cloud it is best for you to keep your dignity and refrain from making disparaging remarks about the institution, especially if you hope to obtain employment in the future.

Whether you hand in your resignation or are handed your letter of resignation, you have the power to control your departure. You can choose to make it a public process or perhaps keep it a private one. Much of this depends on your *administrative personality* and the impetus behind your leaving. I recommend that you maintain your dignity and leave the institution with grace.

CONCLUDING COMMENTS

The world of higher education in the United States is more complex than it was 50 years ago and I believe it a certainty that it will become even more complex in another 10 years. The national, state, and local political environments continue to become more divisive, creating ever more challenges for individual institutions of higher education and its leaders. Every few years the winds of change seem to blow across our institutions as the political landscape shifts around us. To address these changes, leaders will need to reflect upon and learn from the past, but also to be future oriented, "seeing what could be – and helping to make it a reality[which] takes vision, imagination, skill, and commitment" (Maxwell, 2013, p. 96).

Ultimately, it is important for tomorrow's leaders to question everything! If leaders do not use their individual and collective power to question what we are doing and why we are doing it then why would subordinates? Questioning is the easiest way to prevent your unit, your institution, or higher education from taking an unnecessary trip to Abilene.

References

Abbott, T. E. (2009). Keeping your library on the right (correct) side of campus politics. In Fritts, J. E. (ed.), *Mistakes in academic library management: Grievous errors and how to avoid them* (pp. 1–10). Lanham, MD: Scarecrow Press.

Allen, E. (1998). Rethinking power. *Hypatia*, 13, 21–40.

Allen, E. J., Gordon, S. P., and Iverson, S. V. (2006). Re/thinking practices of power: The discursive framing of leadership in *The Chronicle of Higher Education*. *Review of Higher Education*, 30, 41–68.

Andersen, E. (2013). 21 Quotes from Henry Ford on business, leadership and life. Retrieved from: www.forbes.com/sites/erikaandersen/2013/05/31/21-quotes-from-henry-ford-on-business-leadership-and-life/#2aaade31293c

Association of Governing Boards of Universities and Colleges (2016). *Shared governance: Is OK good enough?* Washington, DC. Retrieved from: www.agb.org/reports/2016/shared-governance-is-ok-good-enough

Balderston, F. E. (1995). *Managing today's university: Strategies for viability, change, and excellence*. San Francisco, CA: Jossey-Bass Publishers.

Basken, P. (2017) Think you know what type of college would accept Charles Koch Foundation money? Think again. *Chronicle of Higher Education*. Retrieved from www.chronicle.com/article/Think-You-Know-What-Type-of/242103

Bass, B. M. (2007). From transactional to transformational leadership: Learning to share the vision In Vecchio, R. P. (ed.), *Leadership: Understanding the dynamics of power and influence in organizations* (2nd edition, pp. 302–317). South Bend, IN: University of Notre Dame Press.

Battilana, J., and Casciaro, T. (2010). Power, social influence and organizational change: The role of network position in change implementation. *Academy of Management Journal*, 53, 1–8.

Battilana, J., and Casciaro, T. (2013). Overcoming resistance to organizational change: Strong ties and affective cooptation. *Management Science*, 59, 819–836.

REFERENCES

Bazerman, M. H. (1984). The relevance of Kahneman and Tversky's concept of framing to organizational behavior. *Journal of Management*, 10, 333–343.

Birnbaum, R. (1988). *How colleges work: The cybernetics of academic organization and leadership*. San Francisco, CA: Jossey-Bass Publishers.

Bolino, M. (1999). Citizenship and impression management: Good soldiers or good actors? *Academy of Management Journal*, 24, 82–98.

Bolton, G. E., and Ockenfels, A. (2000). A theory of equity, reciprocity, and competition. *American Economic Review*, 90, 166–193. Retrieved from: www.jstor.org/stable/117286

Bozeman, B., Fay, F., and Gaughan, M. (2013). Power to do ... what? Department heads' decision autonomy and strategic priorities. *Research in Higher Education*, 54, 303–328.

Bradac, J. J. (2001). Theory comparison: Uncertainty reduction, problematic integration, uncertainty management, and other curious constructs. *Journal of Communication* (Sept.), 456–476.

Brass, D. J. (2002). Intraorganizational power and dependence. In Baum, Joel A. C. (ed.), *Blackwell companion to organizations* (pp. 138–157). Malden, MA: Blackwell Publishers.

Campbell, E. K., Hoffman, B. J., Campbell, S. M., and Marchisio, G. (2011). Narcissism in organizational contexts. *Human Resource Management Review*, 21, 268–284.

Carney, D. R., Cuddy, A. J. C., and Yap, A. J. (2010). Power posing: Brief nonverbal displays affect neuroendocrine levels and risk tolerance. *Association for Psychological Science*, 21(10), 1363–1368.

Casey, A. M. (2009). Communication a two-way street. In Fritts, J. E. (ed.), *Mistakes in academic library management: Grievous errors and how to avoid them* (pp. 11–17). Lanham, MD: Scarecrow Press.

Cialdini, R. B., and Goldstein, N. J. (2004). Social influence: Compliance and conformity. *Annual Review of Psychology*, 55, 591–621.

Cohen, A. M., and Brawer, F. B. (2008). *The American community college* (5th edition). San Francisco, CA: Jossey-Bass Publishers.

Cohen, M. D., and March, J. G. (1974). *Leadership and ambiguity: The American college president*. New York: McGraw-Hill.

Collins, J. (2001). *Good to great*. New York: HarperCollins Publishers.

Cozby, P. C. (1972). Self-disclosure, reciprocity and liking. *Scoiometry*, 35(1), 151–160.

DeCelles, K. A., DeRue, D. S., Margolis, J. D., and Ceranic, T. L. (2012). Does power corrupt or enable? When and why power facilitates self-interested behavior. *Journal of Applied Psychology*, 97, 681–689.

REFERENCES

Dirks, N. B. (2018). How colleges make themselves easy targets. *Chronicle of Higher Education*. Retrieved from: www.chronicle.com/article/How-Colleges-Make-Themselves/244921

Dixon, N. M. (1998). The responsibilities of members in an organization that is learning. *The Learning Organization*, 5(4), 161–167.

Ehrenberg, R. G., and Zhang, L. (2005). Do tenured and tenure-track faculty matter? *Journal of Human Resources*, 40(3), 647–659.

Freeh, Sporkin, and Sullivan, LLP (2012). *Report of the special investigative counsel regarding the actions of The Pennsylvania State University related to the child sexual abuse committed by Gerald A. Sandusky*. July 12. Retrieved from https://scholar.google.com/scholar?hl=en&as_sdt=0%2C36&q=Report+of+the+Special+Investigative+Counsel+Regarding+the+Actions+of+The+Pennsylvania+State+University+Related+to+the+Child+Sexual+Abuse+Committed+by+Gerald+A.+Sandusky&btnG=

French, J. R. P., and Raven, B. (1968). The bases of social power. In Cartwright, D., and Zander, A. (eds), *Group dynamics* (3rd edition, pp. 259–269). New York: Harper & Row.

Gagliardi, J. S., Esponosa, L. L., Turk, J. M., and Taylor, M. (2017). *American college president study 2017*. Washington, DC: American Council on Education.

Gardner, W. L., and Martinko, M. J. (1988). Impression management in organizations. *Journal of Management*, 14, 321–338.

Genshaft, J. (2014). It's not the crime, it's the cover-up (and the follow-up). In Bataille, G. M., and Cordova, D. I. (eds), *Managing the unthinkable: Crisis preparation and response for campus leaders* (pp. 7–17). Sterling, VA: Stylus Publishing, LLC.

Genshaft, J., and Wheat, J. (2004). Leading a university during controversy: Challenges faced by a new president. In McLaughlin, J. B. (ed), *Leadership amid controversy: Presidential perspectives* (pp. 47–60). New Directions for Higher Education, 128. San Francisco, CA: Jossey-Bass, Inc.

Gilley, J. W. (2006). *The manager as politician*. Westport, CT: Praeger Publishers.

Guttenplan, D. D. (2012). Critics worry about influence of Chinese institutes on U.S. campuses. *New York Times*, Mar. 4. Retrieved from: www.nytimes.com/2012/03/05/us/critics-worry-about-influence-of-chinese-institutes-on-us-campuses.html

Harvey, J. B. (1988). *The Abilene paradox and other meditations on management*. San Francisco, CA: Jossey-Bass Publishers.

Herdlein, R., Kretovics, M., Rossiter, C., and Sobczak, J. (2011). A survey of Senior Student Affairs Officer perceptions of the role of politics in student affairs administration. *CSPA-NYS Journal of Student Affairs*, 11(1), 37–61.

Hersey, P., and Blanchard, K. H. (1982). *Management of organizational behavior: Utilizing human resources*. Englewood Cliffs, NJ: Prentice-Hall.

REFERENCES

Hersey, P., Blanchard, K. H., and Natemeyer, W. E. (1979). Situational leadership, perception, and the impact of power. *Group and Organization Studies*, 4, 418–428.

Hill, L. A., and Lineback, K. (2011). Are you a good boss – or a great one? *Harvard Business Review* (Jan.–Feb.), 125–131.

Hill, N. (1978). Democratic and other principles of empowerment on campus. In Robertson, D. B. (ed), *Power and empowerment in higher education* (pp. 21–40). Lexington, KY: University of Kentucky Press.

Hoffman, K. D., and Kretovics, M. A. (2004). Students as partial employees: A metaphor for the student–institution interaction. *Innovative Higher Education*, 29(2), 103–120.

Hofstede Insights (n.d.) *The 6 dimensions of natural culture*. Retrieved from: www.hofstede-insights.com/models/national-culture/

Howell, J. P., Bowen, D. E., Dorfman, P. W., Kerr, S., and Podsakiff. (2007). Substitutes for leadership: Effective alternatives to ineffective leadership. In Vecchio, R. P. (ed.), *Leadership: Understanding the dynamics of power and influence in organizations* (2nd edition, pp. 363–376). South Bend, IN: University of Notre Dame Press.

Jaques, P. (1994). A user's guide to office politics. *Management Services* (Mar.), 16–19.

Jarvis, W. (2019). Florida Universities have turned athletics departments into quasi-private arms. What does that mean for public accountability. *The Chronicle of Higher Education*, June 17. Retrieved from: www.chronicle.com/article/Florida-Universities-Have/246512

Jaschik, S. (2018). 3 more instances of false data in "U.S. News" rankings. *Inside Higher Ed*. Retrieved from: www.insidehighered.com/admissions/article/2018/02/19/false-us-news-rankings-data-discovered-three-more-universities

Jaschik, S. (2019a). Another speaker unable to appear at Middlebury. *Inside Higher Ed*. Retrieved from: http://www.insidehighered.com/news/2019/04/18/middlebury-calls-lecture-conservative-polish-leader-amid-threats-protests

Jaschik, S. (2019b). Oklahoma gave false data for years to "U.S. News," loses ranking. *Inside Higher Ed*. Retrieved from: www.insidehighered.com/admissions/article/2019/05/23/university-oklahoma-stripped-us-news-ranking-supplying-false?utm_source=Inside+Higher+Ed&utm_campaign=52d50b2bd6-DNU_2019_COPY_02&utm_medium=email&utm_term=0_1fcbc04421-52d50b2bd6-197524117&mc_cid=52d50b2bd6&mc_eid=68f27f949b

Julius, D. J. (2009). Developing power and influence as a library manager. In Fritts, J. E. (ed), *Mistakes in academic library management: Grievous errors and how to avoid them* (pp. 71–82). Lanham, MD: Scarecrow Press.

REFERENCES

Kanter, R. M. (2010). Powerlessness corrupts. *Harvard Business Review* (July–Aug.), 39.

Kanter, R. M. (2014). When to resign. *Harvard Business Review* (June), 2.

Kay, K., and Shipman, C. (2014). The confidence gap. *The Atlantic Monthly* (May). Retrieved from: www.theatlantic.com/magazine/archive/2014/05/the-confidence-gap/359815/

Kotter, J. P. (1998). *What leaders really do. Harvard Business Review on Leadership* (pp. 37–60). Boston, MA: Harvard Business School Press.

Kramer, M. W. (1999). Motivation to reduce uncertainty: A reconceptulization of Uncertainty Reduction Theory. *Management Communicatin Quarterly*, 13, 305–316.

Kramer, R. (2009). Rethinking Trust. *Harvard Business Review*, 87 (June), 68–77.

Kretovics, M. A. (2011). *Business practices in higher education: A guide for today's administrators.* New York: Routledge Taylor & Francis Group.

Kruse, S. D., and Prettyman, S. S. (2008). Women, leadership, and power revisiting the Wicked Witch of the West. *Gender and Education*, 20(5), 451–464.

Lane, J. E. (2012). Agency theory in higher education organizations. In Lane, J. E., and Bastedo, M. N. (eds), *The organization of higher education: Managing colleges for a new era* (pp. 278–303). Baltimore, MD: Johns Hopkins University Press.

Leary, M. R., and Kowalski, R. M. (1990). Impression management: A literature review and two-component model. *Psychological Bulletin*, 107(1), 34–47.

Loehr, J., and Schwartz, T. (2001). The making of a corporate athlete. *Harvard Business Review*, 79 (Jan.), 120–128.

Lombardi, J. V. (2013). *How universities work.* Baltimore, MD: Johns Hopkins University Press.

Lorenzen, M. (2009). Change management and risk taking. In Fritts, J. E. (ed.), *Mistakes in academic library management: Grievous errors and how to avoid them* (pp. 83–94). Lanham, MD: Scarecrow Press.

Lovric, D., and Chamorro-Premuzic, T. (2018). Why great success can bring out the worst parts of our personalities. *Harvard Business Review* (Aug. 9). Retrieved from: https://hbr.org/2018/08/why-great-success-can-bring-out-the-worst-parts-of-our-personalities

Machiavelli, N. (1513). *The Prince.* Trans. W. K. Marriott. A Penn State Electronic Classics Series Publication. Hazleton, PA: Penn State University.

Mangan, K., and DeSantis, N. (2016). A president's plan to steer out at-risk freshmen incites a campus backlash. *Chronicle of Higher Education* (Jan. 20). Retrieved from: www.chronicle.com/article/A-Presidents-Plan-to-Steer/234992

REFERENCES

March, J. G., and Cohen, M. D. (1974). *Leadership and ambiguity: The American college president.* New York: McGraw-Hill.

Mattern, K., and Wyatt, J. N. (2009). Student choice of college: How far do students go for an education. *Journal of College Admission* (Spring).

Maxwell, J. C. (2013). *How successful people lead: Taking your influence to the next level.* New York: Center Street.

McClelland, D. C. (1976). Power is the great motivation. *Harvard Business Review,* 54, 100–110.

McLemore, C. W. (2014). *Inspiring trust: Strategies for effective leadership.* Santa Barbara, CA: Praeger.

Menon, T., and Pfeffer, J. (2003). Valuing internal vs external knowledge: Explaining the preference for outsiders. *Management Science,* 49, 497–513.

Merelman, R. M. (1986). Domination, self-justification, and self-doubt: Some social-psychological considerations. *Journal of Politics,* 48, 276–300.

Miller-Idriss, C., and Friedman, J. (2018) When hate speech and free speech collide. *Diverse issues in Higher Education,* Dec. 5. Retrieved from: https://diverseeducation.com/article/133611/

Mitchell, B. C., and King, J. W. (2018). *How to run a college.* Baltimore, MD: Johns Hopkins University Press.

Nickels, W. G., McHugh, J. M., and McHugh, S. M. (2008). *Understanding business.* Boston, MA: McGraw-Hill Irwin.

O'Leary, J. O. (2016). Do managers and leaders really do different things. *Harvard Business Review* (June). Retrieved from https://hbr.org/2016/06/do-managers-and-leaders-really-do-different-things.

O'Reilly, III, C. A., Doerr, B., Caldwell, D. F., and Chatman, J. A. (2013). Narcissistic CEOs and executive compensation. *Leadership Quarterly,* 25, 218–231.

Ouchi, W. G. (1980). Markets, bureaucracies, and clans. *Administrative Science Quarterly,* 25, 129–141. www.jstor.org/stable/2392231

Peter, L. J. (1969). *The Peter principle.* Cutchogue, NY: Buccaneer Books.

Pettit, E. (2018). Southern Illinois U. says it won't tolerate activism by athletes in uniform, then backs off. *Chronicle of Higher Education,* Aug. 30. Retrieved from: www.chronicle.com/article/Southern-Illinois-U-Says-It/244404

Pfeffer, J. (1992). *Managing with power: Politics and influence in organizations.* Boston, MA: Harvard Business School Press.

Pfeffer, J. (2010a). *Power: Why some people have it – and others don't.* New York: HarperCollins Publishers.

Pfeffer, J. (2010b). Power play. *Harvard Business Review* (July–Aug.), 84–92.

REFERENCES

Pfeffer, J. (2013). Power, capriciousness, and consequences. *Harvard Business Review* (April), 2.

Pfeffer, J. (2015). *Leadership BS: Fixing workplaces and careers one truth at a time.* New York: HarperCollins Publishers.

Pusser, B., and Marginson, S. (2012). Power, politics, and global rankings. In Bastedo, M. N. (ed.), *The organization of higher education: Managing colleges for a new era* (pp. 86–117). Baltimore, MD: Johns Hopkins University Press.

Salancik, G. R., and Pfeffer, J. (1974). The bases and use of power in organizational decision making: The case of a university. *Administrative Science Quarterly*, 19, 453–473.

Schmidt, P. (2016) How one college quelled controversy over a Koch-financed center. *Chronicle of Higher Education*. Retrieved from www.chronicle.com/article/How-One-College-Quelled/ 237984.

Selingo, J. J., and Clark, C. (2017). *Pathways to the university presidency: The future of higher education leadership.* Atlanta, GA: Deloitte's Center for Higher Education Excellence, Deloitte University Press.

Skinner, Q. (1981). *Machiavelli: A very short introduction.* New York: Oxford University Press.

Sousa, M., and van Dierenfonck, D. (2017). Servant leadership and the effect of the interaction between humility, action and hierarchical power on follower engagement. *Journal of Business Ethics*, 141, 13–25.

Spencer, C. (2018). Secondhand smoke from college presidents: Lessons learned from proximity to power. *Chronicle of Higher Education*. Retrieved from: www.chronicle.com/interactives/the-awakening?cid=at&utm_source=at&utm_medium=en&elqTrackId=d732816dff4047d6af888f7d621a83ae&elq=753d0008ffc14c5cbc0160f2bef7ddf9&elqaid=21027&elqat=1&elqCampaignId=9970

Stripling, J. (2018a) Inside Auburn's secret effort to advance an athlete-friendly curriculum. Retrieved from: www.chronicle.com/article/Inside-Auburn-s-Secret/242569

Stripling, J. (2018b). Regent's resignation signals turning tide in U. of Maryland crisis, as presidents exerts his power. *Chronicle of Higher Education*. Retrieved from: www.chronicle.com/article/Regent-s-Resignation-Signals/244992

Teal, T. (1998). The human side of management. *Harvard Business Review on Leadership* (pp. 147–170). Boston, MA: Harvard Business School Press.

Thomas, A. (2019) Here's what Trump's executive order on free speech says. *Chronicle of Higher Education*, Mar. 21. Retrieved from: www.chronicle.com/article/Here-s-What-Trump-s/245943

REFERENCES

Tiedens, L. Z., and Fragale, A. R. (2003). Power moves: Complementarity in dominant and submissive nonverbal behavior. *Journal of Personality and Social Psychology*, 84(1), 558–568.

Toma, D. (2012). Institutional strategy: Positioning for prestige. In Toma, D., and Bastedo, M. N. (eds), *The organization of higher education: Managing colleges for a new era* (pp. 118–159). Baltimore, MD: Johns Hopkins University Press.

Tost, L. P., Gino, F., and Larrick, R. P. (2013). When power makes others speechless: The negative impact of leader power on team performance. *Academy of Management Journal*, 56, 1465–1486.

Townley, B. (1993). Foucault, power/knowledge, and its relevance for human resource management. *Academy of Management Review*, 18, 518–545.

Tversky, A., and Kahneman, D. (1981). The framing of decisions and the psychology of choice. *Science*, 211, 453–458.

Van den Steen, E. (2010). On the origin of shared beliefs (and corporate culture). *RAND Journal of Economics*, 41(4), 617–648.

Vecchio, R. P. (2007). *Leadership: Understanding the dynamics of power and influence in organizations* (2nd edition). South Bend, IN: University of Notre Dame Press.

Vigoda, E. (2000). Organizational politics, job attitudes and work outcomes: Exploration and implications for the public sector. *Journal of Vocational Behavior*, 57, 326–347.

Volkwein, J. F., and Grunig, S. D. (2005). Achieving accountability in higher education: Balancing public, academic, and market demands. In Burke, J. (ed.), *Achieving accountability in higher education* (pp. 246–274). San Francisco, CA: Jossey-Bass.

Wolfe, R. J., and McGinn, K. L. (2005). Perceived relative power and its influence on negotiations. *Group Decision and Negotiations*, 14, 3–20.

Yukl, G. (1989). Managerial leadership: A review of theory and research. *Journal of Management*, 15, 251–289.

Yukl, G., and Falbe, C. M. (1990). Influence tactics and objectives in upward, downward, and lateral influence attempts. *Journal of Applied Psychology*, 75, 132–140.

Yukl, G., and Falbe, C. M. (1991). Importance of different power sources in downward and lateral relations. *Journal of Applied Psychology*, 76, 416–423.

Yukl, G., and Tracey, J. B. (1992). Consequences of influence tactics used with subordinates, peers, and the boss. *Journal of Applied Psychology*, 77, 525–535.

Zaleznik, A. (1998) Managers and leaders. *Harvard Business Review on Leadership* (pp. 61–88) . Boston, MA: Harvard Business School Press.

REFERENCES

Zamudio-Suaréz, F. (2018). U. of Wisconsin-Whitewater chancellor resigns after inquiry into husband's alleged harassment. *Chronicle of Higher Education*, Dec. 17. Retrieved from: www.chronicle.com/article/U-of-Wisconsin-Whitewater/245344

Zemsky, R. M. (2005). The dog that doesn't bark: Why markets neither limit prices nor promote educational quality. In Burke, J. (ed.), *Achieving accountability in higher education* (pp. 275–295). San Francisco, CA: Jossey-Bass.

Zusman, A. (2005). Challenges facing higher education in the twenty-first century. In P. G. Altbach, P. G., Berdhal, R. O., and Gumport, P. J. (eds), *American higher education in the twenty-first century* (2nd edition, pp. 115–160). Baltimore, MD: Johns Hopkins University Press.

Index

Abilene Paradox 81, 137–139
Adjunct faculty *see* non-tenure faculty
Administrative assistants 24
Administrative ego 80–82, 117, 202
Advancement 34, 41–42; *see also* fundraising
Agreement Management 137–9
Allen, Elizabeth 25, 94, 110
Alternative facts 110
Ambiguity 88, 148
Amendment First *see* First Amendment
Assessment data: versus comparable data 135
Associate's colleges 31, 35; *see also* community colleges
Association of Governing Boards (AGB) 31–2
Athlete as an administrative personality 51–2
Athletics 34, 42; as auxiliary services 45; influence of 115, 130–2, 166–9, 171–2, 203–4
Auburn University 131–2
Authority: formal 16–17, 26, 139
Auxiliary services 34, 45–6, 178

Baccalaureate colleges 31, 34–5, 37; *see also* liberal arts colleges
Baylor University 168–70
Benchmarking 101, 124
Best practices 117, 124; myth 108–9
Bosses 49, 55–6
Budget process 40, 111
Bureaucracy 11, 29–31, 34, 72, 185; and new technologies 207; navigation of 24
Bureaucrat as an administrative personality 52–3

Cartwright, Carol 78, 194
Charles Koch Foundation 137
Chronicle of Higher Education 8, 23, 93, 118–20, 131–2, 136, 160, 170
Coercive power 5, 15–17, 20–1, 26, 72; culture of fear and 145, 211; Machiavelli and 157
Collaborate 6, 83, *147*, 185, 208, 213; collaboration and 113, 145, 182–6
Collaborator as an administrative personality 53, 214
Commitment 17, 19, 28, 78, 92, 99–100, *147*, 215, 217; and committee membership 62; establishing goals 87; financial *126*, 202; Machiavelli and 155; organizational 10, 146
Communication 32, 37, *63*, 80, *93*, 138, 145, *161*, 172, 182–5, 212;

229

INDEX

communicate and 32, 76–7, 90, 129, 162–4, 212; Marketing and 42; networks 66–9; power and 18, 182; shared governance and 32; social media and 120
Communicator as an administrative personality 76–7, 147–9
Community colleges 35–6, 202, 208
Competitor as an administrative personality 55
Confidence 22, 27, 52, 77–8, 111–12, 148, 155, 186–7, 201; transparency and 90–1
Confidential 147; searches 125–8
Conflict 137, 139, 145, 148: and conflicting goals 7; of interest 126; tolerance of 89; using power to resolve 98; see also agreement management
Confucius Institute 136
Connectional power 15–17, 24–27, 61, 66, 72
Consultants: as mercenaries 156, 176; use of 100–1, 103, 115–18, 124–9
Contrast in decision-making 100–2
Corporations 46–7; influence of 208
Counter balancer as an administrative personality 54, 139
Culture of fear 8, 145, 211

Data: analyst as boss type 56; from institutional research 41; gathering by presidents 188–9; informed decisions 176; need for good 41; technology and 206; use by administrators 16, 22; use of comparable rather than assessment 135
Decepticon as an administrative personality 53
Decision-making 2, 8, 10, 28, 45, 80, 90, 102, 105, 128–9, 132, 141–96, 201, 211–12; and decentralization 73, 111; empowering subordinates and 91, 94–5; garbage-can 117; Machiavelli and 154–6; open-ended questions and 77; presidents and 191–3; shared governance and 204–5; student success and 176; transparency and 67, 90, 102
Deeb, Bassam 49, 76, 80, 94–5, 178, 180–3, 189, 192, 194–5
Delaying as a tactic 102, 104–6
Demographic shifts 81, 200–1
Development see Advancement
Direct support organization 203
Distance education 206–7
Diverse Issues in Higher Education 118
Division of labor 7, 48, 98
Donors 136
Dysfunctional 214; see also Abilene Paradox

Eeyore as an administrative personality 53
Empowerment 91, 94–5, 110–12, 212; feminist perspective 25–7; Responsibility Centered Management and 111
Enrollment management 7, 23, 43, 43; decline in government funding 176; economic downturns and 70
Executive Order "Improving Free Inquiry, Transparency, and Accountability at Colleges and Universities" 119
Expert power 23

Faculty 7, 19–20, 39–42, 70–3, 87–8, 188–92, 204–9; as communicators 76–7; becoming administrators 209; expert power and 23; hiring new 121–2, 213; and paths to the presidency 176–8; shared governance and 32, 156, 204–5

First Amendment 119–20
Flexibility 79–80
Floater as an administrative personality 54, 85, 139
Formal authority 16–17, 26; *see also* coercive power, legitimate power, and reward power
Foundations 136–7, 208
Four-year colleges 1, 30, 34–5, 82, 202; *see also* baccalaureate
Framing tactics 98–9
Free speech 45, 118–20, 199–200
Freeh report 167–8
Fundamental attribution error 75
Fundraising: senior administrators and 37, 40, 79, 176; *see also* Advancement

Gatekeeper 66–7
Gaudino, James 79, 178, 180–1, 183–4, 186–8, 190, 192–4
Gee, Gordon 78, 130
Genshaft, Judy 166, 172–3, 177, 183–5, 189–90, 192
Georgia 208
Goal oriented 183
Green, Albert 18–19, 41, 49, 65

Hate speech 118, 120
Hierarchical structure 8, 11, 16, 26, 29–31, *33*, 34, 37, 48, 99, 212, 215; *see also* organizational structure
Higher education in the United States 1, 29–30; *see also* postsecondary
Hiring decisions 18, 40, 72, 121–6, *125–126*, 130, 213
Humility 80–3, 184, 186

Influence 3–4, 8, 23–5, 26, 39–40, 60, 63–7, 86, 90, 93–4, 112–13, 134, 139, 155, 182, 201, 209, 213–15; athletics and its 130–2;

auxiliary services and 45–46; in decision-making 10, 73, 80, 102, 121, 191; of donors 136–7; of rankings 134–5; tactics 15–16, 18, 23, 25, 27, 146; technology and its 206–7; *see also* athletics
Influencers 63, 67, 115–39, 207–9; post-tenure review and 206
Informal communication channels/networks 37, 149, *see also* connectional power
Informational power 24
Inside higher education 8, 107, 118
Institutional culture 139, 149, 156, 209, 215; consultants' lack of understanding about 115; *see also* organizational culture
Integrity 68, *93*, *147*, 149, 165, 172; and transparency 90–1
Intercollegiate athletics 115, 130–2, 203–4; as auxiliary services 45; *see also* athletics
Interdependent systems 6–7, 10–11, 83; and social powers 16–17
ITT Education Services 162

Johnson, Alex 177–8, 183–5
Junior colleges *see* community colleges

Knight Commission on Intercollegiate Athletics 132
Knowledge power 15, 24, 27

Language 106, 110; and the myth of best practices 108; and word choice 107–8, 126
Lap dog as an administrative personality 52, 65, 72, 85, 89, 92, 139, 214
Legacy 80–1, 83, 156, 163, 168, 216
Legitimate power 17–18, 25–26, 61, 97, 133, 191; within organizational context 29–48

INDEX

Liberal arts college *34–5*, 38, 82, *see also* four-year colleges
Librarian: reference as boss type 56
Listening 76, 89, 146–7, 182, 185, 190, 212
Lying 92

Machiavelli, Niccolo 21, 68, 72, 85, 95, 112, 153–8, 214
Mahony, Dan 49, 86, 121, 178, 183, 185–6, 188, 191–3
Management 2–5, *5*, 11, 32, 61, 75, 146, 172, 176; impression 62, 112; *see also* agreement management
Manipulation 5, 84
Marketing 42, 46, *47*, 117, 206; rankings as 134–6
Me too movement 21, 204
Michigan State University 170–2
Mission creep 35, 82, 134, 199, 202, 208

Narcissism 10, 83–5
Nassar, Larry 170–2
National Center for Educational Statistics (NCES) 1, 46
National Collegiate Association of Athletes (NCAA) 130–2, 203
Navigator: political 143, 146–7, 151
Negotiation 144; ambiguity and 88; negotiator and 88, 147–8; scarcity and 101; search process and 125; with a new hire 70
No confidence vote 108, 162
Non-tenure faculty 204–5

Online 206–7
Open-ended questions 77, *146*, *151*
Organizational culture 89, 171, 215; *see also* institutional culture
Organizational politics 6, 10, 18, 85; as positive influences 143–4

Organizations, inherent features of 7, 11
Orientations: for new board members 31–2; human resources and 40; student 44, 79

Paterno, Joe 167
Perceptions 10, 61, 71, 78, 98, 102, 106, 127, 163–4, 169, 188, 194; Machiavelli and 95, 112–13, 155; of power 5; of scarcity 101; of self 214
Persona 157
Personality 17–18, 21–4, 28, 65, 75, 181: administrative 51–6, 211, 215–16; and authority *16*; do not focus on 148; Machiavelli and 154
Personnel 42, 72, *93*, 129–30; administrative assistants as key 24; decisions as most important decision 130, 192–3, 213
Persuasive power 21–3, 27, 185
Policies 48, 52–3, 99, 133–4, 149, 205–6, 209; best practice 108; enforcement 133–4
Political savvy 143–4, *147*, 149, *150*
Postsecondary education 30, 201; distance students travel for 134; in a downturn 201; *see also* higher education
Power as a decision-making tool 3, 7–8, 15–28, 97–114, 211
Power players *49*, 59, 121; search consultants as 124
Power tactics 97–8
Power modalities: over 26–7; with 26, 28; to 27, 94, 110; *see also* influence tactics
Powerlessness 102, 111
Prestige 70; in pursuit of 18, 82, 134–5, *176*; and mission creep 202
Professional development 214; as a reward 19

Program reviews 110; and the myth of best practices 108–9
Pundit as an administrative personality 52, 214

Question 91, 99, 113, *146*, *150*, *151*, 173, 217; decisions 93, 134, 139, 165, 217; during search process 123, 125–7

Rankings: institutional research and 41, *176*; power of 134–6; unintended consequences of 135–6
Reciprocity rule 65, 85, 145
Referent power 15–17, 21–2, *26*, 28, 112; and competence 72
Research oriented universities 31–2, *33*; and tenure 205
Resource allocation 70, 199, 201–2
Responsibility Centered Management (RCM) and empowerment 111, 201
Retention myth 109
Reward power 5, 18–9
Risk 92–3, 98, 108, 113; Machiavelli and 155, 157; and making changes 116–17; and the road to Abilene *138*; and transparency 90; using coercive power 21, *26*

Salaita, Steven 165
Sam Huston State University 135
Sandusky, Jerry 166–8
Scarborough, Scott 160–3
Scarcity in decision-making 101–2
Search process 121–30
Secret searches 128–30, *128*
Self awareness 214
Self confidence *see* confidence
Senior academic positions 30, 34, 37–9, 60
Senior administrators: bias of 69; no training of 209; positions 34, 38, 60, 62, 66, 72, 99

Servant leadership 28, 80
Sexual: abuse 21, 166–72; assault 204
Shared governance 19, 21, 129, 182, 192; definition of 32; faculty and 204–5; Machiavelli and 155–6; managing ego and 83
Simon, Lou Anna K. 170–2
Singer as an administrative personality 54
Social media 120–1, 207; and communications and marketing 42
Social powers 15–28
Source as an administrative personality 55
Spanier, Graham 166–8
Sports 130–2, 203–4; *see also* athletics
Staff *see* subordinates
Stakeholders 1–2, 7, 10–11, 41, 45, 63, 93–4, 99, 121, 149, 182–3, 185–7, 199; as audience 77, 94; budgeting and institutional 40; donors as 136; search process and 125–129; setting goals and 87, 155–6; and transparency 32, 90–1
Starr, Kenneth 168–70
Strategic planning 10, 81, 87; consultants and 115
Student affairs 3, 7, 67, 69–70, 98; advancement in 86, 178; and auxiliary services 45; in organizational context 34, 39, 42–5, *44*
Student athlete 132, 203–4; *see also* athletics and intercollegiate athletics
Subordinates 11, 17–28, 59, 71, 80, 102, 104, 129, 204; academic affairs and 39; delegate to 88, 94, 110–12; and establishing a reputation 67, 90–1, 212; and their career goals 129

233

INDEX

Supervisor's role *16*–17, 20, 87, 89–90, 105, 133, 172; and position title 59–60; in support of staff 19, 99–100, 110, 129, 180

Technology 100, 103, 206–7; organizational structure and 48
Tenure 177, 204–5; post-tenure review 206; presidential decline in length of 176; as reward power 19–20
Timing: in decision-making 102; when making a change on campus 103–4
Title IX violations 169–71
Tolerance 65; for ambiguity 88; of conflict 89
Transparency 32, 90–1, 187; in decision-making 90
Tressel, Jim 41, 76, 87, 179, 182–3, 186–7, 189–91
Trump, Donald *see* Executive Order
Trust 64, 77, 90–2, 95, 110–11, 214; building 67–8, *93*, 148, *150*, 212; Machiavelli, new leaders and 155; policies lacking 133; and transparency 90, 102, 187; market 90; organizations 144
Tuition bearing units 107

Uncertainty reduction theory 145
University of Akron: and administrative ego 81, 160–3, 179
University of Florida 135, 159, 203
University of North Carolina 132
University of Oklahoma 135
University of South Florida 135
U.S. News & World Reports and rankings 136

Walker, H. Fred 93
Warren, Beverly 79, 82, 177–8, 180–1, 183, 185, 187, 190–1, 193
Western Carolina University 137
Wise, Phyllis 164–5
Wolfe, Timothy 131, 163–4, 216
Word choice: impact of 107–8, 126; *see also* language

234